ORDINARY PEOPLE, EXTRAORDINARY LIVES

A Path to Reconciliation in Our Divided Times

GREGORY J. LEESON

Ordinary People, Extraordinary Lives:
A Path to Reconciliation in Our Divided Times

ISBN: 978-1-970157-46-8

Story Merchant Books
400 S. Burnside Avenue #11B
Los Angeles, CA 90036
www.storymerchantbooks.com

Book Interior and E-book Design by Amit Dey (amitdey2528@gmail.com)

TABLE OF CONTENTS

FOREWORD

"What everyone needs is a good listening to."

Mary Lou Casey

Gregory Leeson calls himself *The Life Chronicler*, and in this fascinating, heartfelt volume, *Ordinary People, Extraordinary Lives*, he exemplifies that moniker in a significant way. On his 65th birthday, he embarked upon the very sort of Out-There, "I've-always-wanted-to-but-never-got-around-to-it" adventure that many of us may *dream* of undertaking but, except for a Studs Turkel here or a William Trogdon there, never—as Captain Picard of *Star Trek* fame would say—"make it so."

Entirely at his own expense, he crisscrossed the United States and Canada—east, west, north, south—for the sole purpose of talking in depth with as many people from as many walks of life as he could manage to meet in just over thirteen months. Some of these individuals he had lined up in advance, some he reached out to at the suggestion of someone else whom he ran into *en route* ("Oh, you've got to talk to my cousin Odell in Sioux Falls!") and some were total strangers he fell into chats with, in a grocery store or laundromat, all of whom shared the ups and downs of their—more often than not, *extraordinary* lives.

Using an interview protocol devised by narrative psychologist Dan McAdams of Northwestern University, Leeson, himself an extraordinary listener (we need more of his ilk in today's fractured world!), pulled out the high points, low points, and turning points and the broad, recurring themes in his tellers' stories, stories that, on more than one occasion, elicited tears in both their eyes and his own as they prefaced what they shared with those magical words, "I've never told this to anyone before, but..."

And then, as you will see, he pulled off the impossible. He captured the gist of their narratives in under 600 words each, a strategy which, while it inevitably shortcuts the countless subplots and subtleties that make up any person's story, affords the reader— me, for one—a soulful feel for each individual's unique life journey. As important, it also gives us a sense of the common ground that, despite obvious differences in backgrounds, opportunities, and the vicissitudes of fate, we all share as human beings trying to make the best and the most sense of the life we've been given to live.

This accessibly worded, carefully crafted quilt of travelogue, biography, and auto-biography (i.e. it was his own car that, between breakdowns, ferried him from A to B!) is rendered particularly timely in that Leeson includes the responses of his American "chroniclees"— assuming that's a word!—to a question which, he writes, "went something like this":

> Some historians will tell you that the United States is as divided
> as it has been since the 1840s and 1850s. How divided do you
> think we are? Why? What does our future look like?

As someone convinced of the healing power of having our stories listened to respectfully by others—a process I call "narrative care"—I believe that by asking such delicate questions and by listening without judgment to the stories of those who answered them, Gregory Leeson has set off a ripple effect of positivity the impact of which he will never fully know. He has contributed, I trust, to a tide of understanding that simultaneously honours the differences of opinion that there will always be among us and yet the commonalities of experience—losses, learnings, and loves—that ultimately unite us as a human family.

Bill Randall, A.B., M.Div., Th.M., Ed.D.
Visiting Fellow, Emmanuel College,
  Cambridge University, Cambridge, England
Professor Emeritus, Saint Thomas University, Fredericton, Canada
Author, *Fairy Tale Wisdom*, Nautilus 2023 Gold Award Winner
January, 2024

PREFACE

"Be the change that you wish to see in the world."

Mahatma Gandhi

Well, that was surreal. An unfathomable idea I had in 2015 just became reality with the release of this book. That was definitely NOT on my life's radar. Based on some early successes in my life and feedback from individuals during that time, I knew my destiny by age 25. I never really talked about it because, at age 27, that future went up in smoke when I figuratively blew myself up with a spectacular failure. As our culture defines it, I went from being near the top (investment banker) to rock bottom (minimum wage work). Interestingly, I never saw it that way. That's not what "the books" taught me. More on those books from my youth later. For me, it was just a sidebar in the bigger story. It took four and a half years before I got my second chance.

With one dream ostensibly gone, I fulfilled my other two dreams when I became a father by adopting a baby girl from China in 2002 at 44, and between 2009 and 2017 when I showed her the world (22 countries). I thought that was it. That would be my societal contribution, and it would cascade through my daughter. But, and I'm sure this will surprise everyone, life sometimes does not work out as we plan. Rather than carve out a career in philanthropy, in performing the research for this book, I gave not my money but my time by listening to the stories of the lives of others. As life unfolded for me, this project fulfilled that lost dream—giving back. My hope is that it cascades.

In taking this journey, I cannot help but recall Lynnette Grey Bull. Her pilgrimage took her from being an insecure, homeless teenage high school dropout to a nationally known figure through the non-profit organization she founded, *Not Our Native Daughters*. Her metamorphosis was such that I titled her story, *A Homeless Teen's Transmogrification into a National Advocate and Politician*. She first ran as the Democratic Party's nominee for the US Congress in 2020 against Liz Cheney in Wyoming. While my story is less dramatic, I feel connected with her because of our second-chance experiences. After reading this book, I hope readers feel better connected with others despite our trying times.

In section one of this book, I elucidate on the project in which I embarked on four distinct road trips spanning one year, one month, one week, and one day to meet and interview random people. These journeys covered 26,403 miles and included multiple-night visits to 53 destination cities in 39 American states and eight Canadian provinces. Additionally, this section offers readers a summary view of our contemporary era, which some American historians argue is the most divisive since the 1840s and 1850s, a period with historical consequences that are well-remembered. If those historians' assumptions are accurate, and you will learn more from the opinions I gathered on the subject, how do we avoid the cataclysm that afflicted the 1860s? Is there a thematic connectedness we all share, and if so, how best can we plug into it? Could knowing others better be a mitigating factor? If so, how would we achieve that? I asked myself these types of questions as I planned this project. A collective understanding of who we are must play a role in avoiding a replay of that earlier period. This book aims to engender that thinking and make it a reality for those who wish to engage. I will provide a tool and explain how that can happen in Appendix A.

The second section features the opinions of 52 anonymous Americans from all age groups, races, political persuasions, and geographic areas on a question about the state and future of our country.

The third section showcases 66 *mini-biographies* of the 71 courageous individuals who responded to my request to learn their life stories. Five declined to have their story published, including the only two people who attempted to take their own life. As you immerse yourself in these narratives, I hope you connect with some subjects personally. Not all stories will resonate equally, as relatability largely depends on one's life experiences. Here are some of the people you will meet.

- *the former model whose husband declined a sheik's generous offer of two camels for her*
- *the man who walked away from his pending wealth*
- *the teacher from a fishing village who received national and international recognition*
- *the scientist who escaped the tentacles of the KGB*
- *the Harvard dropout who lived with Moroccan Berbers and befriended the Dalai Lama*
- *the death row Freedom Rider[1] released after a phone call from JFK to the Mississippi Governor*
- *the kid-klutz who became a surgeon and an Olympian*
- *the gay runaway at 15 who became a well-known minister in a major city*

---

[1] https://en.wikipedia.org/wiki/Freedom_Riders

- *the adopted write-off who obtained a university scholarship and is a classical pianist*
- *the superstar athlete who had to hit rock bottom before he could start a new life*
- *the mother who voluntarily gave up custody of her children to an abusive husband*
- *the woman who engineered her escape from Morocco's repressive culture*
- *the non-Muslim man who, at significant risk, clandestinely snuck into Mecca in disguise*
- *triumphs over trauma (cancer, abuse, poverty)*

The fourth section reflects on the four journeys. Unlike other road trip adventures that resulted in Jack Kerouac's *On the Road*, John Steinbeck's *Travels with Charley*, or William Trogdon's *Blue Highways*, written under the pen name William Least Half-Moon, this was neither a reflective nor a self-discovery undertaking. I have provided a concise account of my travels—with some occasional humor.

In the Afterword, I succinctly wrap up my thoughts and pose a question to the reader.

Appendix A contains the life interview protocol. For some, this might be the most significant part of the book. Please make use of it! It also contains feedback from one interviewee.

Appendix B contains my life story in a format that emulates the "chapters" proposition in the interview protocol. I encourage readers to use this format when writing their own stories.

Appendix C contains the four journey maps.

THE PROJECT

"The farther backward you can look, the farther forward you are likely to see."

Winston Churchill

INSPIRATION, METHODOLOGY, AND OBJECTIVE

In August 2015, I assumed the role of the Master of Ceremonies at my 40th high school reunion in Halifax, Nova Scotia. While being an emcee wasn't new to me, the experience triggered a profound thought. Despite the fleeting nature of my many conversations that night, I picked up on some riveting stories. Having moved from Canada to the United States after university, my knowledge of my classmates' lives was limited, making each story they told uniquely compelling. However, some common threads ran through their diverse stories. Those individuals had embarked on various adventures, and a small handful of my classmates even achieved positions in the public eye. This experience made me ponder: "Has anyone ever contemplated writing a book about predominantly anonymous individuals?" As it turned out, some distinguished authors had already embarked on this path.

Studs Terkel's 1974 bestseller, *Working*, was based on audio recordings of conversations he conducted with ordinary individuals about their daily work routines. He aimed to faithfully transcribe their narratives without embellishment. Terkel was celebrated as a champion of the ordinary person and crafted a compelling portrayal of people and their diverse vocations.

After drawing inspiration from personal experiences, Bruce Feiler interviewed approximately 225 people from all 50 states over two years for his 2020 self-help book, *Life Is in the Transitions*. His research probed into how individuals navigate life's many transitions, forming the cornerstone of his insights. While reading Feiler's book, I remember being in awe that he traveled to all 50 states to talk with people. The thought had never crossed my mind—until it did. I credit Bruce for the inspiration to plan the four journeys. I launched the first on May 1, 2022, which, not coincidentally, was my 65th birthday, and returned to the home I had rented out for 13 months on June 8, 2023.

In his book, Feiler referenced the work of Dr. Dan McAdams from Northwestern University, who developed an interview protocol to understand individuals' life narratives. During my interviews, which ranged from 65 minutes to just over six hours, I posed 24 questions in ten sections. While two questions were of my creation, the remaining 22 were drawn from McAdams' book, *the stories we live by*. McAdams, a personality psychologist, elucidates how we construct a unique life story, a process that begins in adolescence and infuses life with meaning and purpose. My goal was to unearth those narratives. I have more to say about McAdams and *narrative psychology* in Appendix A.

Following the interviews, I transcribed the audio recordings into Microsoft Word documents, yielding between 35 and 85 pages, depending on the duration of the conversation. From these transcripts,

I distilled the narrative of each person's life into concise thematic passages averaging about 550 words. While most interviewees, including a few public figures, are referred to by their first names, some opted for full names, while a handful used pseudonyms.

The uplifting Human Library Project[2], which started in Copenhagen, is an excellent example of an inspired project with a noble objective. Like the purpose of that project, I envision being a voice bridging our society's widening schism. My project needed to start at a grassroots level to achieve anything close to that objective. That meant meeting people where they lived and speaking in public forums wherever there were open hearts and willing ears. During my travels, I interviewed 71 people and gave 19 speeches.

In sharing the stories of ordinary people, I aspire for readers to recognize that our shared experiences greatly outweigh our differences. Prejudices we hold about race, politics, gender, class, and even geography are nullified when we cultivate empathy for the lives of others. I aim to have you, the reader, discover reflections of yourself within these stories. Is this aspiration excessively optimistic? Indeed, that is a possibility. However, the overwhelmingly positive feedback from many of the thousand-plus individuals with whom I have discussed this project instills a sense of hope. While cynics will undoubtedly exist, the triumph of this project will pivot on its ability to reach the right audience: those capable of nurturing its impact. Only time will unveil the outcome.

My project's high point during these journeys came when Bill Lohmann interviewed me and wrote an article published on the front page of the Richmond Times-Dispatch in Richmond, Virginia, on February 17, 2023. The final paragraph reads like this:

> He's been mockingly asked if he thinks he can change the world. "The answer is actually, 'Yes!'" he said. "We all can."

---

[2] https://humanlibrary.org/

CYCLE THEORY OF HISTORY

Having cultivated a deep understanding of economics and history during my university years, I am well acquainted with the notion of cycles and long cycles, such as the *Kondratiev Wave*, which particularly appealed to me. Most recently, I've read several authors who creatively delved into history to understand our turbulent times better. Dr. Peter Turchin's book *End Times* introduces the *cliodynamics* theory of human behavior, in which he discerns how societies experience a crisis when the gap between the elites and the have-nots reaches untenable levels. He asserts this inflection point will soon be nigh. Another contributor to cycle theory is George Friedman, who writes in his book *The Storm Before the Calm* about two cycles, institutional and socio-economic, each with different durations scheduled to converge within the decade leading to a crisis. A third commentator is Ray Dalio, who filters history in his book *The Changing World Order* primarily through an economic prism to understand past empires and how they projected a world order. The current American world order is facing its first bona fide threat from the emerging power of China. The unifying theme from these thinkers is that the near term will be fraught with existential events.

Finally, there is the lucid, relatable contribution of Neil Howe. In his 2023 book *The Fourth Turning Is Here*, Howe presents a compelling theory of a reoccurring societal cycle that mirrors the stages of a human lifecycle known as a *saeculum*. This cycle is economical, political, social, psychological, and philosophical. The confluence of these factors produces not only the eras or *Turnings,* as Howe calls them, but the generations we know so well by name that align harmoniously with each Turning and drive events. Historically, a saeculum lasted about 80 to 100 years, during which four distinct Turnings occur. In his extensive research, Howe illuminates how various scholars have discerned four-phase cyclical patterns in the human experience. He highlights erudite thinkers, including Ibn Khaldun, Arnold Toynbee,

Carl Jung, George Modelski, and Hippocrates. Furthermore, Howe contends that civilizations have adhered to a four-phase construct of the human experience, as exemplified in the Hindu ashrama concept. Elementarily, our prism for the stages of life encompasses youth, adulthood, midlife, and elderhood.

Let's briefly delve into these Turnings and the corresponding generational archetypes as Howe describes them. Note that while the Turning Name and the Years assigned by Howe are clear, my research revealed that hard coding specific years to specific generations is a more subjective exercise. There is often an overlap between the archetype and generation. The Gen Z assignments in the first table below illustrate this, although Howe views the Gen Z cohort as Artists.

Turning	Name	Years	Archetype (born) / Examples	Key Events
4	Crisis	1929-1946	Artist / Silent	Great Depression, WWII
1	High	1946-1964	Prophet / Boomer	McCarthyism, Affluent Society
2	Awakening	1964-1984	Nomad / Gen X	Civil Rights Act, Woodstock, Watergate
3	Unraveling	1984-2008	Hero / Millennial/Gen Z	Culture Wars, 9/11
4	Crisis	2008-20??	Artist / Gen Z/Gen Alpha	Great Recession, New Cold War (China)

Archetype	Description
Prophet	Grows up indulged. Comes of age as defiant crusaders. Principled and moralistic as mature adults. Provides visionary advice as elders during the Crisis.
Nomad	Grows up unprotected. Comes of age feeling alienated. Pragmatic leaders during the Crisis as mature adults. Become increasingly hardened as elders.
Hero	Grows up increasingly protected. Comes of age as team-oriented achievers during the Crisis. Confident with hubristic tendencies as mature adults. Exerts power as actively engaged elders.
Artist	Grows up overprotected during the Crisis. Comes of age as sensitive young adults. Indecisive leaders as mature adults. Exhibits empathy as elders.

The current Crisis Turning was set in motion in 2008 with the collapse of the real estate and equity markets, giving rise to what we now refer to as The Great Recession. Extrapolating from previous Crisis Turnings, a wearied populace will eventually turn away from isolation, animus, and despondency symptomatic of such eras and yield to a new beginning. At that time, we will enter the High Turning, a phase characterized by collaboration, community spirit, and, finally, the establishment of novel institutions and conventions. The middle-aged Nomads, represented by the Gen Xers, will supervise this era with the coming-of-age Heroes, represented by the Millennials and some early Gen Zs, wielding an influence that will intensify over time. The Millennials are analogous to the Greatest Generation (the G.I.s), and we are all familiar with their achievements. Subsequently, the Prophets, who come of age during the Awakening Turning, will scrutinize and question the values and conventions propagated by the Gen Xers and Millennials much akin to the way the Boomers did during the 60s and 70s. This Awakening Turning will inevitably give way to the Unraveling Turning when societal divisions escalate. Ultimately, this fragmentation paves the path for a fresh Crisis Turning, invariably initiated by some momentous incident. As noted above, in the current saeculum, that event was the 2008 financial meltdown.

While this brief discourse does not do justice to the comprehensive analysis of Howe, Turchin, Friedman, and Dalio, I wholeheartedly agree with their conclusions suggesting that a critical challenge awaits the United States in the not-too-distant future. If history, as outlined by Howe, is a reliable blueprint, the ongoing tumult will eventually resolve through a decisive internal or external conflict.

The 1840s–1860s vs. 2008–20??

You may have read or heard historians in recent years comparing our current era with the era preceding the Civil War. According to Howe, the saeculum that began in the late 1700s and ended in 1865 is an anomaly because its third and fourth Turnings, typically lasting 40-50 years, ran their course in just over 20 years. Nonetheless, let's take a deeper look at this period. Are we living in a replay of the mid-1800s?

What are some hallmarks of an unfolding Crisis Turning before the *ekpyrosis*? In this context, ekpyrosis is the event spawned internally or externally during the Crisis Turning, from which there is no return, and society is either gradually reborn or destroyed. Fortunately, in the prior saecula of the Anglo-American context, each experienced a regenerative rebirth and emerged looking different from the preceding period. Four hallmarks today are:

- Loss of civic trust, pessimism
- Extreme partisanship
- Anger, resentment
- Threat of authoritarianism

Loss of civic trust, pessimism

From a September 19, 2023, article[3] published by the Pew Research Center, it's easy to discern Americans have very little faith in government. Despite occasional intervals where trust rose (typically by those affiliated with the party controlling the presidency), the long-term trend following the end of WWII has been down. In 1958, with a Republican President in office, Republicans' faith in the government doing the right thing was just below 80%. For Democrats in 1958, that number was a shade over 70%. In 2020, just before the election of Joe Biden to the Presidency, Democrats polled at approximately 15%. After Biden's election, Republicans' faith in government touched on the lows of the Obama administration, at about 10%.

Furthermore, extrapolating that this trend applies to other institutions does not take a rocket scientist's IQ. Consider the media. Can you say fake news? Consider big business. Does it care a whit about its employees or the environment unless it is profitable to do so? Consider science. Vaccine mistrust is on the rise. Consider financial institutions. Many got bailed out following the 2008 economic collapse. Did you? Consider religious institutions. How many scandals does it take? Consider schools. What happened to the three "R's?" Now, they teach lockdown drills and ban what were once mainstream books.

Extreme partisanship

This one is easy. Does the date January 6, 2021, ring a bell? How about April 15, 2024? The first pertains to the breach of The Capitol, while the latter was the day a criminal trial of a former president began. President Trump faced two impeachments, and the Republicans have launched an inquiry into an impeachment of President Biden. Today, older commentators lament the demise

---

[3] https://www.pewresearch.org/politics/2023/09/19/public-trust-in-government-1958-2023/

of days when politicians argued with one another and then had informal, personal discussions to bridge disagreements. Some more illuminating occasions occurred between two Irishmen, Republican Ronald Reagan and Democrat Tip O'Neill (Speaker of the House). How often do you think that happens now?

As for the populace, it's likely that seven states where in 2020 less than 5% separated the two major parties, Arizona, Georgia, Michigan, Nevada, North Carolina, Pennsylvania, and Wisconsin, will decide the next presidential election in 2024; the rest are decided, in many cases dramatically so. This continues a trend that has been underway for quite some time. Do you remember Ronald Reagan winning 49 states against Walter Mondale in 1984? Today, that united alignment of the voters seems like ancient history in some bizarre twilight zone.

Anger, resentment

On May 25, 2020, George Floyd, a Black man, was killed by cops in Minneapolis. Some bystanders caught it on videotape. That was not the first egregious misuse of power on Black citizens, but it marked a seminal turning point in the Black Lives Matter movement. Riots ensued, and corporations and academia hastily launched DEI (diversity, equity, and inclusion) initiatives to appease employees, students, and, dare I suggest, society.

More recently, a war in the Middle East with existential implications between the state of Israel and Hamas, the United Nations ascribed terrorist organization that governs Gaza, rages. The outcome will be definitive if this war follows the pattern of other wars during a Crisis Turning. In the United States, Islamophobia and Antisemitism, which had already been on the rise, are threatening students and others to a degree, in the case of Antisemitism, not seen since WWII.

Professors are excoriated for their words and actions, merited or not. Some tenured academics have given up on the pedagogical framework they aspired to as young students, considering it an outdated artifact of another era. People are choosing sides—hard!

Threat of authoritarianism

In recent years, books portending the rise of authoritarianism have percolated on the literary intellectual landscape. It is not only an American concern but a worldwide phenomenon. Some factors playing into the hands of those wishing to impose authoritarian rule are:

- Economic Instability. According to the World Bank[4], of the top economies from North America, Europe, and Oceania in 2019, the United States ranked fifth worst in economic disparity as measured by the *Gini coefficient*. It ranked only behind the small economies of Panama, Honduras, Costa Rica, and the Dominican Republic.

- Political Polarization. This has already been discussed.

- National Security. On December 5, 2023, FBI director Christopher Wray testified before the US Congress and stated he had never seen so many "blinking lights" going off at the same time regarding terror threats.

- Erosion of Democratic Institutions. As noted earlier, the stunning decline in the people's faith in government creates a vacuum for authoritarian politicians to exploit.

- Ethnic or Religious Strife. As also noted earlier, Islamophobia and Antisemitism are on the rise, as is aggressiveness towards East Asians (COVID-19-related) and Hispanics (immigration-related).

- Populism. The wealthy Western world has experienced a striking surge in populism. In recent years, we have seen the following:

  ➤ In the United Kingdom, the former mayor of London, Boris Johnson, successfully helped engineer the 2016 Brexit "Yes" vote.

---

[4] https://databank.worldbank.org/reports.aspx?source=2&series=SI.POV.GINI

➤ In Italy, populist movements such as the Lega Nord, led by Matteo Salvini, and the Five Star Movement, led by Guiseppe Conte, have gained significant support by opposing traditional political elites, advocating for stricter immigration policies, and challenging the European Union. The recently elected Prime Minister, Giorgia Meloni, caters to the hard right crowd.

➤ In Hungary, Viktor Orbán of the Fidesz Party has taken a strong stance against immigration, emphasized national sovereignty, and faced criticism for actions that some viewed as undermining democratic institutions.

➤ In Poland, the Law and Justice Party, led by Jaroslaw Kaczynski, has pursued nationalist and conservative policies. The government's stance on migration and its push for judicial reforms align with populist sentiments.

➤ In France, Marine Le Pen, leader of the National Rally Party (formerly National Front), has been a key figure in French politics associated with right-wing populism. The party gained support by opposing immigration and advocating for nationalist policies. In the 2022 presidential election, she won over 41% of the vote, up from just under 34% in 2017. Is a victory next in 2027?

➤ In Spain, the right-wing populist Vox Party led by Santiago Abascal saw increased support, particularly in recent elections. The party emphasizes anti-immigration policies, nationalism, and opposition to regional autonomy movements.

➤ In Germany, the Alternative for Germany (AfD) Party led by Tino Chrupalla and Alice Weidel has gained traction by opposing immigration and criticizing the European Union. While not as dominant as some populist movements in other countries, the AfD has become a significant force in German politics.

➤ In Ireland, the Violence or Hatred and Hate Offences Bill 2022 states, according to Pauline O'Reilly of the Green Party, "We are restricting freedom, but we are doing it for the common good…"[5]

➤ In Canada, if you were one of the peaceful protesters in the infamous 2022 truckers' march on Ottawa, you may have been temporarily *debanked* for expressing unacceptable viewpoints as part of Justin Trudeau's Liberal Party's enforcement of the Emergencies Act. And the Act's provisions allow for other draconian actions against its citizens.

➤ In the United States, we've witnessed anti-establishment candidates like Donald Trump gain traction in elections. Policy initiatives such as the 2017 *Buy American, Hire American* executive order speak to economic nationalism. Like in Europe, a significant anti-immigration tone emanates from the body politic. Regarding international institutions and agreements, in 2017, the United States withdrew from the Paris Agreement on climate change, and politicians have increasingly questioned the merits of the United Nations and its agencies. It has since rejoined the Paris Agreement, but while out, it joined only three non-ratifying nations: Iran, Turkey, and Eritrea. Given the war in Ukraine, a non-NATO member seeking membership, is withdrawing from NATO next to preclude an unwanted entanglement "over there?"

➤ If you believe only governments can impose authoritarianism, you would be wrong. In homage to China's well-established *social credit system* that rewards "trustworthy" behavior as adjudicated by the Chinese Communist Party, private companies are beginning to enforce their interpretation of

---

[5] https://www.reddit.com/r/Libertarian/comments/1852ty1/irelands_green_party_sen
_pauline_oreilly_we_are/

justifiable Big Brother behavior. In one example, ubiquitous PayPal will now shut down your ability to do business on its platform should you engage in commerce, once acceptable but now deemed inappropriate per their updated policy.

➢ Finally, there is the body politic. The *cancel culture* pervading societies arising from wokeness manifests a complicit populace unwittingly bending to the will of authoritarianism. Just look at what is happening on campuses to the free speech of professors and outside speakers. This may be the most dangerous development of all. When Benjamin Franklin left Independence Hall following the 1787 Constitutional Convention, a woman allegedly asked, "Well, doctor, what have we got, a republic or a monarchy?" Franklin reportedly replied, "A republic, if you can keep it."

Everyone reading this book is familiar with the tumultuous events of the 1860s that transformed American life. So, there is no reason to elaborate on them here. But what happened during the preceding years leading to the ekpyrosis that sparked the American Civil War?

The 1840s and 1850s saw a growing abolitionist movement advocating for the immediate and complete abolition of slavery. This movement faced strong opposition in the South, contributing to societal tensions. Economic realities created socio-economic disparities as the industrial North and the agrarian South developed distinct economic structures. The North's burgeoning industry contrasted sharply with the South's reliance on slave labor in agriculture, deepening the economic divide between the regions. Party realignment and the disintegration of traditional party structures characterized the political landscape in the 1850s. The collapse of the Whig Party and the temporary rise of the secretive American Party (anti-immigration, anti-Catholic) reflected the uncertainty and lack of consensus on critical national issues. This political instability contributed to a sense of pessimism regarding the ability of the political system to navigate the nation through its challenges. Some specific events during those years that highlighted the growing social gulf included:

- In 1845, the annexation of Texas as a slave state fueled tensions between the North and the South. The debates over whether Texas should enter the Union as a state of enslavement or a free state highlighted the deepening national divide.

- In 1846, the Wilmot Proviso was a proposal to ban slavery in the newly acquired territories from the Mexican-American War. The debate over this proviso highlighted the deepening divide between Northern and Southern states about the expansion of slavery.

- The debate over the status of newly acquired territories from the Mexican-American War led to the Compromise of 1850. It included provisions like the Fugitive Slave Act, which intensified the divide between abolitionist and pro-slavery states.

- In 1857, the Supreme Court's decision in the Dred Scott v. Sandford case declared that enslaved people were property and could not sue for their freedom, further polarizing opinions on slavery.

- Finally, in 1860, the escalating strife of the preceding two decades culminated in Abraham Lincoln's election as a Republican President without winning any Southern states. This prompted several Southern states to secede from the Union, forming the Confederate States of America led by Jefferson Davis.

Although the day's issues in the 1800s differed from today, parallels between the two eras are irrefutable. Although a rise in authoritarianism was not a hallmark of the mid-1800s, unmistakable pessimism, partisanship, and anger indeed were.

Conclusion

This is not a history book. However, understanding our society's divisiveness is essential to understand better my motivations for undertaking this project: providing a voice that bridges those gaps. As demonstrated in the books I have recited, the division you likely sense is not in your imagination. It is tangible, and our society will need to address it. This is unavoidable. We cannot just sweep it under the rug and hope it goes away.

So, how can an individual mitigate feelings of alienation from "them?" As suggested earlier, reach out to others to learn about their lives. I recognize this is not an easy task, but when you're the first to reach out, you might be surprised to find how willing others will be to reach back. That was my experience. As you read the stories herein, reflect on how your life mirrors part of the storyteller's life because those will be the people you will find in your quest to bridge gaps. Yes, I know, I am Pollyannish. But if you had to choose between being a Pollyanna or a curmudgeon, which choice would you make?

THE QUESTION

*"The most important of all revolutions; a revolution
in sentiments, manners, and moral opinions."*

Edmund Burke

THE FUTURE OF THE UNITED STATES—52 OPINIONS

In addition to interviewing individuals in-depth about their lives, which you will read in the next section, I talked anonymously to countless others with a different aim. I stressed the anonymity of the exercise so I could best assure candid input. I covered the ages, sexes, races, political affiliations, and geography.

My question went something like this:

> *Some historians will tell you that the United States is as divided as it has been since the 1840s and 1850s. How divided do you think we are? Why? What does our future look like?*

Here is a sampling of their responses. Be forewarned, some of these thoughts are raw. Some, you may find familiar. Some, you may not. And some you may find downright disturbing. But most importantly, they are honest. Their responses fell into the following categories:

- Political (18: Female-7, Male-11)
- Generational (4: Female-3, Male-1)
- Societal (13: Female-4, Male-9)
- Racial (4: Female-3, Male-1)
- Media (9: Female-3, Male-6)
- Morehouse College vs. Wichita State University (4: Female-1, Male-3)

There is some overlapping commentary, particularly in the Political/Societal realms.

Political

Female, 50s

They've done it more than 150 times throughout history. Our history has questioned the results of elections. It's part of our right to make the system correct to fix problems. Why are the Democrats so opposed to simple corrections of voting rights? Instead of throwing everything out with the bathwater, and just saying that certain things would be beneficial to us, like showing your ID, that would lessen the chance of causing voter fraud.

You know, it's become so that we're not one people: like it's them against us. You know, it's like we have to come to some common ground and logical, sensible things. We used to be more moderate. It's just sad because Joe Biden was supposed to come in and be the healer. In the end, he did the exact opposite.

I think part of the problem is that we watch Fox News, and then you watch CNN slanted the whole other way. I agree with a lot of the Democrats' positions, and I agree with a lot of the Republican positions. I do. But it's these goddamn lunatics. I don't know if the United States is going to implode on itself. I think it's one of those other crazy bastards that's gonna cause trouble for the world.

I think ten years down the road, they're gonna look back, and this is going to be history. I personally think we're gonna get more intelligent, and they're going to turn the country around.

I think Trump has to disappear into the history books, but the Republican Party is going to nominate him again.

⚜

Male, 30s

I see several probabilities. The secession of certain states into fragments is a high possibility. Like Miami, maybe the Texas region, they become one over there, and then more liberal states, they become one. That's a fairly high possibility. Another would be maybe just no secession, but just more authoritarianism and just more control over the individual. I think those are two great possibilities.

I like to think I'm an optimist. Human nature is to grow and succeed, to figure it out.

⚜

Male, 50s

I think we're going to start to see more extremism and more violence. You know, we're seeing lawmakers literally trying to restrict the vote in supposedly the most democratic country on earth. You know, there's no way America's the preeminent democracy; we struggle with running elections. A lot of the voting laws of late are being changed to make it harder for minority people to vote. It should be easy to vote. We should be encouraging people, not restricting them. And any time you start to limit people's ability to vote, you're headed down a very, very slippery slope.

I'm probably in the middle but leaning pessimist. Since I've been in Los Angeles, there have been seven mass shootings in this area. I was part of one. I was teaching at a university at the time, and we lost a student. But the level of denial of gun violence and what impact it's having on society is just astounding to me. We've created that society, leveraging the so-called Second Amendment, where there are so many guns in circulation that people probably should have them. And isn't that a sad statement? I've been in education my entire life. When we're talking about arming teachers in schools, what the hell are we doing? Yet there's this constant denial that while we can't fix the problem totally, let's just do nothing.

⚜

Female, 60s

I am very worried. At this point, I think we are potentially headed in a very dangerous direction. I think we're gonna lose our touch with democracy. I think we're getting into this non-reality with people who don't believe in reality anymore. You know, Trump started with his alternative facts. And people seem to have grasped onto that as a philosophy or something because they're believing these things that are patently not true. And the thing is, it's all about threats; they are afraid. They are operating on fear, which is what frightens me. When people operate on fear, their frontal lobe is not working, the rational part of their brain, the part that considers consequences, planning, decision-making, and judgment; that's not operating. Their limbic system is operating, that's the emotional part of their brain, which is reactive to fight or flight or freeze. And so that's what terrifies me.

You know, it's interesting, they did a study comparing the brains of conservatives and liberals and they found some interesting differences. I don't know the validity of that, it was just interesting, because they did seem to find that more conservative people respond to ambiguous stimuli as if it were a threat more often than liberals. And they see more threats in their lives. So, they're scared.

✺

Male, 40s

We won't be a superpower as a country anymore. China is, for the most part, taking our lunch and eating it right in front of us. Poor leadership.

There's an establishment, and there's us. So, what percentage of the people is us, 95%? Maybe even more than that? Voting used to mean something. It doesn't really mean anything anymore. I think they want this globalist superpower, in a sense, where they want one government to rule the world. We want to talk about universal government income, you know, being able to not own anything and be happy about it. Everyone's kind of surviving off the system versus the American way, where we build and make money.

Davos and then, you know, I think the whole climate control thing is just one big Ponzi scheme. Do I believe there's probably something happening? Maybe. But it's being sold to us as a way to get us to give up our rights and our money.

I honestly see us becoming more socialist. And that's just sad to see. I'm very pessimistic about everything right now. In the 90s, I was more optimistic. Very divided. I'd say possibly a Civil War.

✺

Male, 70s

I am almost 74 years old. In my entire life, I am more concerned about this country than I ever have been. The late 60s were nothing compared to this. It's more rural people that are supporting Trump. It's more urban people that are supporting the Democrats. I think we will have direct domestic terrorism for the foreseeable future. And if certain parties continue to talk about the elections being rigged, that sets the stage for a violent revolution, which started before January 6, but the first battle was that day.

There is hope. But I'm not optimistic. I looked seriously at moving to Canada in 2017 because of Trump. And if he'd been reelected, I would have been gone.

I'm glad I'm old. I've said that to a lot of people in the last few years. In the year 1955, we went under our desks for fear that the Soviets were going to be sending nuclear weapons. But I didn't worry about my fellow Americans coming in and shooting at me. The leading cause of death of children in this country now, between the ages of two and nineteen, is gunshot wounds. A country that cannot protect its young is fucking doomed. I have hope, but there needs to be a miracle. I'm prepared for the worst.

⚜

Female, 20s

With Trump running, people will elect him again because they feel, regardless of how racist or sexist he is, that's who they want.

People who sit on top of the government, on top of health care, the Big Pharma industry, the big food industry, you know, are rich for a reason. I wouldn't say they're selfish, but we live in different worlds. If you have money, if you have a stash, we have your back; if you're not a person of color, the world might be good for you. Joe Biden isn't a good president, and Trump is worse. So, who do we pick to run the country? You feel helpless a lot. It's like drowning.

⚜

Male, 60s

I don't really see there being a civil war because when there was a civil war, it was very geographic. In some states, such as Texas and California, whites are not in the majority anymore. The majority of the people in Georgia are not right-wing. You know, it's turning far more purple than anything else. No state is going to try to secede from the Union. In the Civil War, Mississippi was the most prosperous state in the Union. If you take states like Alabama and Georgia, they can't cut themselves off from the rest of the nation and survive economically.

The infrastructure that protects democracy must remain in place. Is a legislature gonna turn around and overrule the votes of their own citizens? Is it possible? Yes, but it seems unlikely. And it seems unlikely it will survive a court challenge.

The country has been very split on things before. Sure. One thing I have noticed is that the number of people voting has been going up and up. The last presidential election was as high as it's gonna get. All these claims of election fraud are virtually nonexistent.

I'm optimistic as long as the institutions hold. But I am concerned about the Supreme Court. I mean, people like Samuel Alito and Clarence Thomas should be in jail. They seem to have an agenda.

⚜

Male, 70s

Our division is 10 out of 10. And the reason I say that is just looking at the national government now, nobody is willing to talk to, listen to, or think of each other. I just went through a major battle with Lincoln County, which is the county we live in, over a dairy. The county commissioners absolutely will not listen to anything. They're only interested in the dollar sign and the revenue they would get by adding a dairy condensing plant and not taking into consideration the township whatever. They couldn't care less.

So, until we start listening to each other and thinking away from me, myself, and I to us, we're going to be in a hell of a mess. I'm not optimistic at all. Because I don't see any movement. It just keeps expanding more negatively every year.

How might this play out? I could see a revolt happening because we're seeing it already. The Proud Boys is a good example of that. And I hope it doesn't happen, but I am fearful. I think most people recognize we've got a problem in this country.

⚜

Female, 50s

I think about what's going on in the US Congress. It drives me crazy because the shit they argue about is irrelevant. I don't want it anymore. Irrelevant. What the hell are they talking about? Do I give a crap about who drives what kind of car? Do I care if it's electric or not? I don't care. I mean, I think what is important is that children get to grow up and feel safe.

By the way, let me just say I grew up a tomboy. I wanted to play for the LA Rams. If I was five now and how I acted, they'd give me puberty blockers. Yeah, right. And then all of a sudden, I got boobs, and they'd take my boobs off.

⚜

Male, 20s

I think the division is pretty high. At the same time, I hope we're not close to the Civil War, but the closest example I can think of is the insurrection. I saw that as literally as a coup to overturn democracy. But then some people saw that as a coup to save them.

I think a Civil War is not going to happen, but I don't think it's out of the question, given how a lot of conservative people talk in the media. They will say we have to hoard weapons; we have to hoard food like the government's gonna come for you. But then, on the other hand, liberals are saying, what are you talking about?

I feel pretty patriotic. I love the idea of America. I think we could be a great country. The things that we stand for are good ideals. I just think we have a lot of room to grow. I believe in our institutions. I'm optimistic.

⚜

Male, 20s

I don't think that the separation we have is detrimental. I don't think it would cause a civil war. I think it's about time in the history books for there to be another Martin Luther King or somebody. If we could just start having some people pop up that think a little bit more collectively, they could tap into that collective consciousness and give us ideas. So that's why I think maybe the person to come along that would be able to help would be someone who studies human behavior.

So, it's going to take an inspirational person, obviously. I think that the main thing is that we have people, plenty of people that have these big ideas and plenty of people that have the ability to start approaching these issues, but there are not enough people to listen to them with an open mind. I think that it boils down to education.

I think it will take a tipping point to get rid of the division between states that would really help us think more like a country. Even if you have a democracy, you don't always get what you vote for. So, I guess in times like this, I would be more of a pessimist.

⚜

Female, 40s

There's a part of me that does think we're going to Red Dawn or that movie might be happening but within our own country. But I don't know if I believe all of this fearmongering that's happening on both sides. So, I think that all this anger is going to die out. Even if hypothetically this red MAGA anger wins, I'm in Palm Springs, OK, I'm pretty safe here. It will suck for the rest of society. [**Author's note:** MAGA = Make America Great Again, a Donald Trump campaign slogan.]

⁂

Male, 60s

We will see social strife, by all means. We've seen that with the January 6 thing. But I see it more as a vocal minority. I think there are more decent people than not.

How do we get through it? The only way we can get through it is with love. That's the only way we can really do it. See, that's a hard one. Because if you're on one side or the other, you're conditioned and trained. You hate them. How can you love them when you hate them? We must find a common ground; we have to take a breath. I mean, we really need something outside of us that we can focus on. That's very true in history. It's really the only way we can get through the division.

You're red or you're blue and we hate each other. So, everything's about division. I'm enough of a fringe person where I can think outside a little bit because I live in nature and I'm an escapist. I've escaped it all my life, so I can look at it from the outside more than being inside the snarl. I'm an optimist for myself and my little world but a pessimist about the bigger picture.

⁂

Female, 30s

I'd say we're divided. We're definitely not divided by civil war yet. I think there are enough moderates in the country to keep us from that. But the polar sides have a bigger voice than they used to.

Normally, I am an optimist. But lately, I've been getting so annoyed with the division in this country. I still think we can fix it. I think we can pull it back. I think we can get to know each other and fix it. So, I guess I am still an optimist. I'm just a sad optimist right now.

◦◦◦

Male, 20s

I think I'm a little bit more optimistic. There's a very big difference between how much we perceive we're divided versus how divided we actually are. I think we are definitely divided. I don't think that's the question. But we perceive the divisions are worse than they are.

I come from a very international background myself, so I keep an eye more on world issues than domestic. I grew up all over via foreign service. I think that we have growing tensions with other countries, specifically China. We're going to have a pretty big conflict with them within the next 15-20 years, probably less. I think that's going to turn our attention away from a lot of the internal divisions that we're focusing on now, although there will still be a divide.

◦◦◦

Female, 70s

We definitely have to change on both sides, Democrats, Republicans. I mean, we both realize that we can't go on like this. I have hope that it's gonna change, that this nonsense is going to stop. Plan for the worst, hope for the best and take what comes.

I hate to say I don't think this current president (Joe Biden) has done much. I'm very sad about that. As much as I think Trump did, he had a big handle on what our economy was, etc. Still, he was a big part of what happened to separate us. His approach was too much Billy Badass and too independent. We absolutely need new blood. And not just in the presidency, but the Democratic Party, the Republican Party, the US Congress, the US Senate, we need new blood. I hope and pray for people who are willing to sit in meetings and be on committees and take action and serve that are honest, caring, and want to serve in a good way for the whole United States.

Male, 50s

I don't think there's a quick resolution to any of this. This country is so divided. You got half on the left and half on the right. I don't think that there's a silver lining to any of this, at least in the next ten years. You go back to 2008 when Barack Obama got elected, and then all hell broke loose on both sides of the aisle. I hate to say it, but you know, there probably has to be some sort of national catastrophe that happens to bring everybody back to the center.

Generational

Female, 50s

Whether you say we're older and maybe set in our ways, I think most of us are. I think part of the problem we're having is the way they're taking over how I raise my children. But part of what we're finding is that people are just getting tired of being slammed in the face. They're reading books now to our children who are five years old about whether it's okay to masturbate. It's okay to do this. How do we protect them from people who could take advantage if we're away? We're saying everything's okay. I'm okay with a child who's 12, 13, 14 starting to talk about different things because they're starting to grow. But for a five-year-old, they don't care about sex. But now they're trying to introduce that. And that scares me.

❧❦❧

Male, 20s

The generational question is a good question. From my own experience, I see the aging population still holding onto how society was when they were growing up. And we're all seeing a different society that's been changed through the generations. I think a lot of young people are coming to this idea that at one point, we were more unified than we are now, so how can we get there? And the aging population's thinking this worked for me in the past. It's gonna keep working for me. I think young people are kind of pushing back in a sense, but at what cost?

❧❦❧

Female, 50s

If I look at my daughters and the age they are, they don't have this divide. They don't even think about the divide the way we do. My daughter is a friend to all different people; she's friends with all different races, gays, lesbians, all trans, whatever, she doesn't care. We, as an older generation, have grown up in a set way. I went to Catholic school; we did a bigger number of things than the younger generation. Like they're not even listening. They don't care who Nancy Pelosi is or what's going on in the frickin' government. They're more worried about how they get along and how they feel. If you say there's a 20-year gap between us, I feel they're going to make it go away.

❧❦❧

Female, 20s

I think the whole idea of political parties divides people a lot more than needs be. And we're kind of forced to choose one side, even if you aren't necessarily completely in love with all those ideals. So, I would say we're still very divided. But I'm optimistic about our generation.

Societal

Male, 60s

While it may look like it, and there's been chatter and discussion about a threat to our democracy, I don't see that as really being the problem. I think what we're looking at, or what we're seeing, as it relates to the threat to our democracy, is a symptom. I think it's a symptom of, obviously, something that is deeper but probably more subtle. I think the issue is a buzzword: relativism.

There's less tolerance for one person to say what is right. And so, you have like-minded individuals forming groups. For example, in the Democratic Party, you have the traditional Democrats. And then you have a progressive movement. Sometimes, you hear the proponents of the progressive movement disagree with each other. So, there's some variation even within the progressive movement, but they still sort of come together and join forces to move society in a particular direction. To some degree, you have the same thing in the Republican Party. You have the old guard, and then you have the MAGA movement. I don't think that the issue is a threat to our democracy.

As we begin to erode from the inside, parents no longer have a say over what their children say or do, what's being taught in schools, and so on. This type of social deterioration is going to spread like a pandemic. A lot of people will say that you can actually see how we're deteriorating – our morals, our values. You know, there's no absolute truth. So, if you don't have that, how can you continue to be strong?

If we continue to morally decay, you'll begin to see other symptoms. As I said at the beginning, this discussion about a threat to our democracy is just a symptom. *There's something deeper, you know, there's a cancer, in my view, in our society. If you're of the religious persuasion, which I am, this is what I see.*

I think from a political perspective if it came to it, our country would come together if there was an enemy. But again, if the cancer is at the root, at the core, that's more difficult to deal with. I think of what's happening to our children, in terms of something as basic as their gender. Now, a lot of young individuals who've had the surgery want to have it reversed. It's another symptom of something being wrong at the core. And when that generation of people grows, what is our society going to look like if they're confused about who they are?

In terms of American hegemony, if our leaders continually, even in the midst of inflation, tremendous deficits, and such, say we're going to give billions of dollars to other nations to help them with their climate control, that is most definitely one of the dynamics that will bring down a hegemony. Wealth is one of the most important components of power. Another country will rise.

The Bible says that things are gonna get progressively worse. Nation will rise against nation. Son will rise against father; daughter will rise against mother. This is after the disciples asked Jesus, you know, when will the end be? And he said look for the signs. Well, we can see those signs.

I appreciate the opportunity to speak with you as I think what you're doing is valuable. I think it can help improve the quality of people's lives. I think, even as I've laid out how I see us moving or evolving in time, that something like this and the interaction that you're having with people can bring joy into their lives. And I think that's important. I think it can also wake people up to think about some of the questions that you're asking, about what's happening in society.

Male, 30s

When you look at the world and how divided it is, a good example of this is Saudi Arabia, where they treat their women very differently than the United States. Right? Of course, we're a little too woke, if you will let me use that word. And then, on the other side, they're a dictatorship. It's just totally wrong. What is the result? I think we are looking at World War III. If you read about Falun Gong in China, that religion used to be almost 1/3 of China. [**Author's note:** The movement peaked at about 70-100 million people in China.] *Now, they're the most suppressed. I shouldn't call it a religion; I should just call it a practice, right? But they do have some guiding books, just like any religion does. Ukraine, we're fighting a proxy war here with Russia. Hong Kong, they're replacing good leaders to meet their objectives. And this is going to continue to happen on a massive scale. I think it's just the beginning of World War III.*

I think we have some big challenges with population collapse. The powers are getting more money but less support from the people. I think it's going to collapse. And that's a good thing.

Female, 70s

I do not think civil war or loss of democracy is gonna happen. But I don't think there are enough people that see the hate that I see. California just ought to become a separate country. Let them go. They're so far beyond liberal. I wish California would secede from us. [**Author's note:** The commentator lives in West Virginia.]

It's unfortunate the racial tensions are still with us. I just don't understand that. I have no concept of how you can hate a person because of their color. Or judge them because of their color. I was not raised that way. And I truly just don't understand it. But they're brought up that way. I would like to see more people like Martin Luther King, Jr. Black people, especially in underserved areas, need to learn to respect for each other and not to turn to violence. I think that would go a long way.

Drugs that are coming from China and Mexico; fentanyl, is killing us.

❧

Male, 20s

I don't think we're gonna crumble and fall or anything like that. Divisions are natural within a country. It's unrealistic to get rid of them. But to try and treat those, I think it's something we need to focus on maybe a little bit more.

I'm a history guy. In recent history, for the past eighty years, we've had the fortune of economic prosperity brought by WWII and the recovery from that. In looking at numbers and whatnot, that sort of trend is running out and that there will be some really serious economic and environmental issues in the coming ten to twenty years. There is no magic wand for resolving this social issue that can change people. You can't really help this stuff. I think it's going to be intensifying for all these issues. That's going to cause some things that we don't have an answer for. So, I'm more pessimistic because of that.

❧

Male, 60s

I do think we are a very divided country right now. There has always been some division. But in some ways, we are more divided today than we have been in the past. A lot of that division follows very much along the political lines that people have, and people bring their political platforms to other areas of life. And I think that gets to be pretty obvious, whether we are in community gatherings, churches, or even with families, about how strong some of those opinions are at this moment.

Just looking at, before the 2022 elections, the tone of the campaign advertisements that were on TV. It makes you aware of just how strongly people are divided. People have always had opinions. But right now, there seems to be a very militant view of opinions that people have. I think that will change at some point. Whether it's going to change with something major happening or just with people realizing that we need to have a different way to move forward together, I do not know.

Things won't be able to continue the way that they are right now. I come from the perspective of faith. I would hope that faith could come in and help people to refocus on what it means to be human, to be respectful, to share a common heritage, and just to have basic decency in the way that we treat other people.

I expect that growing secularism will continue for a while. What does that mean for the future of the United States? Will there come a time when it is possible to get to a place where a future generation will rebel against the secular aspect? That's a possibility. For me and the way that I look at life, my worldview, my perspective of faith is what gives me the greatest hope.

Female, 60s

I'm not sure if we're going to have a full-fledged civil war, but I think we're going to have continuous small to medium explosions. Protests? Those things will get worse, I believe. Nobody seems to be cooling down. I'm not, I can tell you that. Do I think there will be a full-fledged civil war? I honestly don't believe that most American values are that strong that they would be willing to put themselves out there like that to protect those values. Now, in terms of when whites become in the minority, perhaps they (whites) will be more likely to lash out. I don't know.

I don't feel that safe. You know, it affects my going out, even sometimes to go on the street and take a walk. So much freedom has been impinged upon.

I'm worried about my son having kids. I feel sad when I think about my son in the world today. Because my childhood, it was so amazing. And largely positive. I used to wander all over the neighborhood. I used to walk almost 25 minutes to get to the bus on my own when I was nine, and it was totally safe. The bus driver watched out for me. That's how life was.

⚜

Male, 60s

Russia doesn't have any noise, right? But you kick down their door, and the whole place will collapse. Our democracy seems brutal from the outside, but it's strong from within. We're much stronger than you think. Because we allow people to have their own opinions come to the surface, and no one's going to pull them down. So, it appears bad. But it really isn't. Other places appear strong, but they are weak. So, I don't believe we're divided.

⚜

Female, 40s

I can't imagine having children and sending them to school these days. I'm terrified. I would homeschool my children, and they'd be weird little kids eating paste in the corner. Fine. I don't care. I couldn't send them to school. There's just no way I can do that these days. It's terrifying. Do you remember the Boomtown Rats in the 80s? They did a song in '82 or '83 called "I Don't Like Mondays." It was a true story based on this girl who shot out of the classroom. And the whole reason they interviewed her was, why did you do that? She's like, I don't like Monday. And they made a song about it because it was so unique at the time. Nobody did stuff; now it's every fucking day. It's everywhere.

35

It shouldn't matter if you're born rich or if you are living in foster care; you should have the same opportunities as a human being. And I really hope that that's where our country is going.

❧

Male, 50s

I believe we are divided. There are clearly factions in this country that are dividing us. And they want to divide us, but we have a lot more in common than not.

I don't like it when people have no tolerance for anything different than their own opinion. And this is what our country has been made of, is having different opinions on every subject. That's how we learn. Diversity really is part of our history. What we need to get there is, I hope it's not a national disaster, or war or something like that, it is a true leader that really brings us back to the center. And we need to give free airtime back to our politicians, rather than having only six companies owning all those stations. It was never meant to be that way.

❧

Male, 60s

Well, that's an important, big, complex question. Clearly, the demographic shifts are happening and it's going to be more and more diverse. The more people get integrated, the fewer people are the "other." You see more intermarriage; we're seeing more multiracial, multicultural families. And you're seeing that also with young people as it relates to issues around sexuality and so much more.

There is also the dynamics with males; males are falling behind in terms of participation in higher education. They don't have the same career prospects.

That facilitates these other dynamics happening, which leaves them susceptible to demagoguery. And there will be political leaders who will want to take advantage of that, whether they believe it themselves or not. People feel vulnerable, they feel like rights are being taken away, and that leads to issues. To the degree that that gets manipulated, that's a problem. So, I am concerned when thinking of long-term trends. One wants to have some hope here, right?

⁓◦◊◦⁓

Female, 20s

I feel like our country is really divided right now. Race, religion, sexuality, class, disability, crime rates. Even if we could be the same race, if you're part of the LGBTQ, or you have a disability, or if you're of a lower income, there it is again. There's so much going on right now with school shootings, politically, the economy, and housing, and it just doesn't seem like it's a good place right now. I feel like no one really wants to have a baby.

I don't know if there's a way of fixing it because there are so many issues. Just trying to be alive, the high prices on medication; they shouldn't feel like they have to wait until they are dying because they don't want to go into debt. And it's sad because people shouldn't have to live like that. Children can't go to school without being worried about dying. It doesn't seem like you can hide from it, the world we live in. LGBTQ people are afraid for their rights. I have two moms, and they got married, but it's scary to think about our future sometimes. I wish I had been blissfully unaware.

I'm a nursing major and there's just so many people hurting right now, like women, everywhere. It's domestic violence, sexual violence. I just did a paper on the 'Me Too' movement and how it's affecting society and how society should change. People that are wealthy, Black or white, if they're on top and really benefit from people that are working, will they actually distribute their wealth because they want to help people? And I don't know if it's realistic.

Maybe it'll become a country that's worth living for. Because being American is just not something to be proud of right now.

Male, 70s

I think it's important to know that we, despite what the news media and social media would have you believe, people haven't really changed that much. Kids have always revolted, and kids have always set the pace for the next change coming up. So that's always going to happen. Politics are always going to change, but what will stay pretty much the same is he who has, will keep, and he who does not, have struggled in our particular society. I'm totally convinced, after experience in other economies and societies, that ours is the fairest for the largest number of people.

At 70 years old, I can look back to so many periods of time when we had political turmoil. I've seen it come around, I've seen our system keep it together so that we could fight out our differences and come up with compromises. And compromising is what it's all about. We can't let a dictator dictate.

I see a real major upheaval in the United States in the works. I think our economy is solid, our capabilities internationally and nationally, are solid. We're competitive people, survivors, hard workers. The younger generation right now, after three years of COVID-19, I think they want to go out and return to a society where they can excel. So, I am upbeat about where we're going. Our education system could be better, and we have drug problems and other issues. But overall, we've got as good as you're ever going to find, and that's as even-handed as any society I can imagine.

We just need to stick to our guns and fight all this stuff. I mean, we're allowed to fight. If we don't like what one side is doing, we can vote them out. And when we vote them out, that means the other side's gonna get voted out four years later because everybody's gonna hate the guy that's got all the power. It doesn't get any better than that. You can't do that in a dictatorial society.

I think our economy has to stay like it is; a commercially driven economy. I don't think we want central planning. That has proven to be a lousy way to do it. I mean, look at all those states that are really centralized. That's not right. That doesn't give the initiative to keep moving and growing. In Germany, you become like a machine walking through the streets. I worked with the Germans, and it was depressing to see how devoted they were to being normal. That willingness to accept authority was just ingrained. I didn't like it one bit.

We have this structure that allows for fighting. We're going to come to an event tired and noses bloodied, and we're gonna go to some room and come up with something. The media's a misleading kind of thing. But we have to be smart enough. We have to teach our kids to be smart enough to say, okay, that guy's bullshit, you know, and I realized that he's not God. So, we must keep that balance that we have, but we can't lose the freedom we've got to fight amongst ourselves, or we become like everybody else. I'm really devoted to that process, you know, the thought process.

Male, 60s

I think the major problem is there's no longer an agreement about what is or is not true. There's a dispute about how you define the truth. If truth is relative, then there's nothing in common anymore. And there's nothing that binds a nation. There's no ordinary narrative. We're all seeking our own truth. And if your truth conflicts with my truth, you will go your way and I'll go mine and there are no reconciling alternative versions of the truth. So, I think that's the great danger. There's no longer a belief that there is a common truth.

Events reflected in the collapse of Christianity in this country are in church attendance, which is declining like crazy, the young people are more and more secular, they're defining their own reality. And if you tell them their reality conflicts with genuine truth, they simply call you a hate monger, and it shuts down the possibility of dialogue. If there's no more common understanding of who we are as a nation, I don't see any hope that it will get better unless there's some perceived national threat that'll somehow bring us all back together. But I don't know what that might be.

The next twenty years could be a great revival. We've had those in the past. The Charismatic Renewal was percolating in all the denominations. And it made some headway. But secularism is also a powerful force. It might be the prevailing force.

I like to believe life has value for its own sake. That we will cherish each other for our own sake. But read the news and see what's happening. People are just too dang greedy. They want something that isn't theirs. That's been how human nature has been since the get-go.

Racial

Female, 20s

Racism is taught and so many people learn it and there will always be people with that hatred and there's no way to eliminate them. I live in Texas. It's terrible. I'm Black, and it's not safe to be there. And then, Florida. It's going crazy right now, and despite all the gun violence, he (Governor DeSantis) loosens gun laws even more.

But you know, me and my family have our passports and have been debating moving to somewhere else that would really be a better life. The United States is mean; it's built on racism. It's built on putting other people down, especially people of color, and I don't know if there's an actual way to change it. It's the government; the government doesn't even tell us everything that's going on.

Male, 20s

I think there's some racial divide, but that's only due to how it's portrayed in the news. If you put me in front of someone of a different race, I'm not just going to look differently or look down upon them. And I don't think they would do the same. That's just portrayed in the media. The media is part of the problem. And that includes social media.

⚜

Female, 20s

*I'm a Black individual at a predominantly white institution. [***Author's note:*** University of North Carolina.] We aren't necessarily at civil war times, I don't believe, but it definitely isn't easy navigating life in America because it's very divided and very racial. And I can't step away from that because I can't take my skin color off.*

How we get past this is a very difficult question. I don't necessarily know. I think, rather than fixing corrupt systems, we just need to destroy them altogether and start over. OK. We have so many loopholes that keep people of color from political roles and other positions of power. And maybe if we destroyed the system and found new ways to build it up, that would be better.

⚜

Female, 50s

You know, in the 1970s, when I was growing up, my husband took the test for the fire department and scored like 100. It got thrown out because they were saying that the Black people didn't have a fair chance, and they dumbed down the test. This is where I find the problem. This is why the Supreme Court should throw this out, because going to college and getting a job should go to the person who is best qualified for the job. Back in the day,

I believed it was necessary. Honestly, I do. Even my husband who didn't get the job feels the same way that Blacks didn't have a fair shot at getting it back then. But now the playing field is totally level. So, I feel that if it gets through the Supreme Court, [**Author's note:** The commentator is talking about the then-pending SFFA v. Harvard University and SFFA v. the University of North Carolina cases that would effectively eliminate the use of affirmative action in college admissions. It was subsequently struck down.] *it'll be the end of the Supreme Court. I think it will really cause such dissension in this country.*

Media

Male, 50s

The media has an agenda and always has an agenda. But a divided country cannot have a dictator because nobody can ever take control. So, the division is a good thing. But the media would have you believe the division is a nine out of ten. Because that sells. Even our politicians want us to be at nine because they need things to raise money.

Female, 50s

We have a lot in common. And then social media is evil because it can be an echo chamber. But also, social media connects people more than before. So, when we strip out all the ideology, we have a very strong foundation. Social media is supposed to connect us in that way. If you realize that, I think our kids are much smarter than us because they know how social media works. And they use social media better than us. I really hope so. They are better at differentiating what is more harmful. I think our generation has the biggest hurdle if we don't realize that the echo chamber is really a prison for our generation.

I'm a scientist. Now, with any noise, you cannot differentiate the real signal from the noise. For kids, they grew up with all the noise, so I think the next generation is smarter than us at differentiating the drama of all the noise and then they look for the real signal.

Male, 30s

Divisiveness, I think, is cumulative. Because of social media and access to information, you have the ability to compare yourself to others. And that puts people in a state of running the rat race. In the past, maybe you were content with your own little corner of the world. Now we have so much access to everything else, that you see everything, that you see how much you are missing. And that drives, I guess, the gap between the rich and the poor. That's a big gap, too.

I think people's ability to think independently has really been eroded. And maybe people are, in this day and age, scared to say a lot of things they want to say. So, you can't; you don't have freedom, especially if you don't have the luxury of financial stability.

Female, 20s

I think social media probably plays more of a positive role, because I am able to connect with people that are different than me. And empathy comes from that because you're understanding people and understanding cultures through social media. I can definitely see a negative role as well. But I do see more of a positive role, especially because I'm a college student.

Male, 60s

Divisiveness, I think a lot of it, is more perception than actuality. Because when you poll people, there isn't that much difference between Democrats and Republicans on what their core values are. This perception of divisiveness is pandering to outrage because that's what our media does. Critical race theory has been around for 30 years, which is nothing more than the study of the effect of race on American society. And it's been turned into a weapon to make people think that White kids are being taught to feel guilty about things. You've got perceptions of Democrats as all being pedophiles. I would think that if you turned off the cable news today, half of this would disappear.

I certainly would like to see places being held responsible for their content, whether it's Facebook or Twitter or whatever. You watch the cable news, and you hear about the divisiveness in this country and everything else; you will think there are wars in the streets. But there has never been incidents of Republicans or Democrats attacking each other in the streets. Can it become reality? I mean, a spark can set something off. But if you look at the polls, the people who say they think there will be civil war, they also are the same ones who said that they themselves would not participate in it.

Male, 20s

The media is where smaller people can start to have a voice. But the problem is, they've been pushed down so much, a lot of the people that are starting to get that voice that didn't have it before have grown bitter and hateful. They've closed their minds and their hearts to just suffer the division.

For some of those people, there's the whole neo-Nazi movement. And there are just so many bad things that come out of it. Getting rid of social media might be the better solution. I'm not saying getting rid of social media altogether would be a big help because I'm sure it would make it worse. But what I think would be the smart move would be to, and I hate to say this, do what China is doing with their media where they're really on top of it. You can't say this, or you can't say that. But it needs to be used in a much more appropriate way.

⚜

Female, 30s

This is actually a question I've been wrestling with; of how can we move past this? Firstly, we just need to talk to each other. Social media is so divisive. You find your group that agrees with your echo chamber. We just need to get the divided groups to sit down together and talk to each other. I had a roommate who had very strong, polar opposite opinions to mine about Trump. She was a huge supporter. One day, I asked her to explain to me what she liked about him so much. And we just sat down, and we talked. It didn't change my opinion about Trump, but it did bring us closer together because we understood each other better. Well, at least I understood her better. I don't think she really listened to me. But that's okay. I understood her better, and it made our relationship better. And just doing that is what this country needs.

⚜

Male, 50s

Sadly, I think we're heading for even more political division. I think that there isn't a willingness to listen and to educate ourselves on major issues. But there's a lot of the electorate, I think, that simply aren't informed, are not educated on issues, they're not open to learning those kinds of things. And that's dangerous; ignorance is very, very dangerous, especially when it's willful ignorance, you know, denial of facts, not using evidence. I don't know what it's going to take to change that because of the way people now get their news, and I hesitate to even use the word 'news' because it's not. A lot of the sources where people get their news are not news vendors, and the mainstream media is kind of middle of the road, and that's where we should be.

To me, news should never be entertainment. It's become that. But when we start questioning, without evidence, the mainstream media, we're in a lot of trouble. And there's a lot of history in that. That's one of the things that Donald Trump has been successful at, is getting people to question. Fox is certainly not a news company, that's for damn sure. It's a propaganda company.

⚜

Male, 70s

We have what's called social media. Although I still read two newspapers every day, newspapers aren't being read at all. Now, people are basically getting news from whatever source they choose, and they tend to stay with that source. They don't sample others very much. And right now, we have a lot of division here.

The strength of this country is our diversity. But there is, let's say, a party that is using diversity and differences to divide us. And it's because of the media. The social media outlets are not constrained in any regard to telling the truth. I see no end to this; I see it only increasing.

Morehouse College vs. Wichita State University

Two institutions of higher learning. Four participating students: one Black man, one Black woman, and two white men. Morehouse College is a private school in Georgia and one of about 104 Historically Black Colleges and Universities (HBCU) in the United States. Wichita State University is a public school in Kansas.

I decided to separate the commentary of these four students to illustrate how we intuitively speak most passionately about the issues closest to our own experiences despite being asked the same question. I met the two Morehouse College students on the campus while sitting outside on a warm day in February. Both grew up in California but sought the welcoming bosom of an HBCU to further their studies. I met the two Wichita State University students on the campus inside an expansive student facility. They graciously agreed to talk with me after I interrupted their two-man bible discussion and explained my quest.

For Morehouse College, the gentleman was significantly more loquacious than the woman. Please do not read into the brevity of commentary afforded the woman with any editorial bias.

Morehouse College

Gentleman

I think it is very important that we acknowledge that some people have these very detrimental ideas and are still in positions of power to manifest those in our current world. Until those people die off, those ideas will continue to manifest or until we're able to get them out of positions of power. They have to acknowledge that their ideas are actually what's curating all the violence or all the negativity that's going on within certain communities. It's a complicated system, which is nearly impossible. So let Mother Time do the job.

But hate is taught. So, unfortunately, these people who have had this influence and have these hateful ideas, I think they have already made that impact upon their kin and future generations. So, it might not be that time can, you know, heal the wounds completely because their kids are taught the same thing. Racism isn't, you know, innate; it's like we're not born racist. Race is a social construct. Race is something that was made up by a white man trying to classify people. So, I just think that it is going to continue, unfortunately.

I feel like, eventually, and this might be an "out there" statement, to think there's going to be a race war. And I feel like there's already one in place. But it's gonna be more prominent, it's gonna be more above the surface, because right now, it's kind of below the surface.

That's why retaliation isn't so much in our (Black people's) *bones, we just see that as a method of progression and our country's history. And the more American you get, the more violent you have to be. Do you want to continue to be oppressed, and utilize love and all these other kinds of ideas to fight back against violence? Where's that getting you? Or do you adopt the same war mechanisms that have been used against us for centuries that flip the script? We were taught we're supposed to be bred to work for somebody else. You have to ask the question, why it is that if this is a society which is supposed to be able to be successful, is the American dream a falsified idea?*

Once you start seeing things for what they really are, we get educated on what things are, and how we can work towards ideas like democracy, entrepreneurial wealth, or generational wealth. We can instill those lessons amongst ourselves. And this is for anybody, doesn't matter what race you are.

The problem really is white fragility. They don't want to take accountability. And it hurts them. They don't want to look at their past and see what they did wrong. Because they don't feel like it was really them. But it was them. It was their family. It was their grandparents; it was their great-grandparents.

When you understand your past, it helps you understand the present and how your present influences the future. And that is scary for people in positions of power. They control the narrative of history like any great conqueror. I feel like it's the reason why as oppressed people, militant people, will never see great positions of power in this country. In this society, it is because we are too good people innately to adopt the principles that the country was built upon. So, it's either we rise up and have a revolution, or we let time do what it does. It's really one or the other, and we keep trying to operate in the middle, and we don't get anything done.

That's the reason why Roe v. Wade was overturned because they wanted more white bodies, they wanted more white babies. Our background, Black people's background, is not rooted in hate. It's rooted in love. It's rooted in spirituality and social relationships with each other. I mean, that just emphasizes my point, that people just don't understand the origin. And what happens if you don't understand? If you don't have a good grasp on your history, your present is going to be a little bit blurry.

It's definitely white privilege to live in bliss; it's definitely white privilege to be able to say, oh well, this doesn't happen. And this doesn't happen. It's because you haven't experienced it. I'm sure your daughter [**Author's note:** The white author's only child was adopted from China.] *has probably talked to you about that. And you know, you've never experienced it, but you can empathize with her. That's where it starts. Empathy is the* *most important thing that humans have. It's our ability to feel other people's feelings. It's our ability to sympathize and really get an understanding of where they're coming from.*

I'm an engineer. Every engineer understands that you cannot rebuild a great thing on a bad foundation. Right? I understand this country is built on bullshit, let's destroy it. Whether it's us trying to rebuild the ship, I don't really care as an individual in terms of, like, the world. My personal life will never be affected. I just need to finesse the system. All I want is for the people who come after me who look like me and who don't look like me is to live in a certain type of harmony.

We have to take a look at ourselves. We don't do that as a country. There's no unification. It's kind of blame, blame, blame, blame, blame. America is a golden place or whatever, come here, and your dreams come true. Like it's fucking Disneyland. That's not the case. So, what I truly wholeheartedly believe is that America is gonna go to shit. There's going to be an educational revolution when it comes to AI, there's going to be a government revolution when it comes to biotechnology, it's going to be a bio war. I think that COVID-19 was a test of a bio war just to see how America reacted.

Every time, and this is gonna sound messed up, every time somebody gets killed in the streets, there's a glimpse of positivity for me. I hope it sparks one individual to say, "This is enough." That's all we need. Somebody in the right position to say that this is enough and there needs to be some destroying of the system.

Woman

Everyone around me looks like me. When I go ten minutes that way, people still look just like me. I rarely see white people, and I hate to say, but I love it. I love being here. And when I go back home, and I'm in the airport, I'm like, damn, there are really white people. Here, it's like a utopia because my whole life, I've experienced microaggression; my whole life, I've experienced racism. People have told me the most obscene and absurd and most hateful and racist things. But the point is, for me to be here, I love it. And it's going to be sad for me because this is going to be the only experience I'll ever have because the real world is going to be coming for me and I'm going to leave here and I'm gonna go into more white spaces and I'm gonna have to deal with it. I have to cold switch; I'm gonna have to hide how I feel. And that's the problem because I can fully and authentically be myself in this place. HBCUs are wonderful. A utopia, at the end of the day, is a utopia. Always, you know, at the end of utopia is a dystopia. Genuinely, that's what happens.

I'm smart for somebody who looks like me, or I'm pretty for a Black girl. I've never heard that here. Or if I see another person who looks like me in a white space, I'm gonna gravitate to that person immediately. And sometimes, Black people in those spaces are put off by that. But that's just a natural thing that I do. Because I don't want to be by myself. I don't want to feel ostracized; I don't want to feel marginalized.

Wichita State University

Gentleman 1

I don't believe all of America is divided. However, I think that two of the major factors that are dividing people today are religion and politics. I believe the news media would like to portray that America is divided as a way to demoralize people and to become even more divided. However, I think there are more unified people than we give America credit for. And I do believe we're coming to a moment or coming to a period of time, or coming to a climax, where America will actually become more unified than we've ever been before.

Now, what might precipitate that? As a person that has all the faith in God, I believe there's going to come a day when every knee will bow, and every tongue will confess that Jesus Christ is the Lord. I believe it's the will of God for all humanity to be saved by the grace of God. And what I mean by that is, I believe a day will come when the Lord will actually turn our hearts towards him, and we will be unified as one. I believe wholeheartedly the reason why America is so divided now is because every force that is against God is at work, trying to either tear down our faith or tear down what we believe as a country. I still believe America is a Christian nation. I still believe in the Pledge of Allegiance. I would say, as of now, we are greatly divided, but there's a day to come when we will be more unified.

People would like to think that America is becoming a secular nation. The only way that that will ever happen is if we change the foundation of America that was built on, The Constitution. The men that wrote The Constitution believed that this country was founded because of God. They believed that we were indivisible. They believed that as long as we were under God, that we would be protected and be safe. Every person, on the inside, believes in a moral code. I would say that secularism does worry me when it comes to an educational standpoint. Even in a small, rural, conservative county college there are still secular teachers, who teach secular principles and refuse to even believe or acknowledge the existence of God. Secular teaching and principles were taught to me in junior college, and then I came to Wichita State University, and it's even worse. And so, the secular world has begun to seep into the educational world. It's almost scary the number of kids that have never, ever expressed a belief in God, or in their Christian faith, or if they were once Christian when they lived with their parents, but now they started college and their lifestyle changes, because they weren't forced to go to church, they weren't forced to pray, so forth and so on. It's so worrisome, especially because now, in our generation, they live emotion, their hearts are on their sleeves.

People are so easily offended that you can't have a proper conversation. The art of conversation has been lost within our generation. People hide behind a telephone screen. They text in short words. They don't know how to hold an adult conversation. Kids are more socially awkward, and their generation is more apt to suicide, more apt to depression, more apt to anxiety, more apt to prescription pills to help ease their nervousness when they walk into a classroom.

What I would say is that there is actual, believe it or not, hope for our generation. And it's not as bad as it looks on the surface. But there is a generation rising up that is going to have beliefs that are going to be more unified, that are going to know how to tackle social issues together as a collective. [**Author's note:** Just as Neil Howe's theory predicts!] *And* *so, what I would say is to be careful of reading into headlines and dive into the story and see what the details are.*

∾❖∿

Gentleman 2

If you read the headlines and you just look at what the media tries to force down your throat, you will very clearly see that there's a lot of division. But if you really look deeper into it, I think that you'll find that there are a lot of veins of different groups of people. And they are all unified in their own sense amongst their own beliefs. So, while we are divided, if you just look at the headlines, I think if you dive in, there are collective groups of people trying to solve problems together. What it comes down to is the biblical principle that a man can't serve two masters. To overcome division, you really have to be careful which master you choose to serve because you can either choose to serve God or you can choose to serve this world. A lot of people don't really consider that as they're making their decisions, and they do whatever feels right to them at the moment. And that creates a lot of tension that we're not designed to experience in this world.

We never trusted the news media because we know that a lot of the companies are owned by the same small group of people. And they all say the same exact words to tell the story. It's all a forced agenda. We have to be really careful to read and not trust anything because people are so quick to listen to the New York Times when they come out with a big headline that so and so did this. It's like, oh, no, we gotta go crazy and cause a riot in the middle of our big cities. You have to really consider, like is this true, and then you have to break it down and think about it logically. And then you have to think, how am I going to react, and your reaction is very critical to the division of our country. Because if you choose to react in a harsh, dramatic, radical way that's not out of a place of love or a place of just wanting to make the world a better place, then you're going to get a lot of violence or tension.

I think of social media echo chambers. The more technology advances and the less we're able to communicate with each other on a personal and adult level, it's going to become increasingly difficult for people to unify. And so, people within their groups are going to get more unified and the different groups will get more divided. That's what's going to happen as we use technology.

I'd be curious, in your studies and travels, to see the difference race and culture have to do with the way they answer your questions. Because every race, whether we want to believe it or not, or maybe every different culture, has their own perspective on what America is like, or what this world is like. People who have experienced true racism, for instance, would obviously have a much different perspective than someone that hasn't. [**Author's note:** The insights in this paragraph are illuminating.]

Conclusion

When I interviewed the two students at Morehouse College, I recognized the privilege of having two young Black students attending a Southern HBCU letting me into their world. It was an engaging conversation, and I knew it would somehow make it into my book. I did not envision how that would look at the time.

After interviewing the two Christian white gentlemen at Wichita State in America's Heartland, I reflected on that earlier conversation in Atlanta. I had my epiphany. The contrasting approach to the same question could not have been starker. While all four participants recognized division in the country, they viewed its impact and solution through entirely different prisms. It made me wonder, as we prepare in 2024 for perhaps the most divisive presidential election since 1860 if we are even talking the same language when discussing the issues of our day.

What would a conversation between those four students look like? There might be fireworks, but the important takeaway would be that they were talking. We all need to do this with the intent of finding common ground. As I write this in the spring of 2024, the temperature on college campuses has reached a level not seen since the 1960s. The difference is that, back then, the invectives were aimed almost exclusively at the government and "the man." While governments will always be targets, today, students are increasingly pitted against students. To where does it lead?

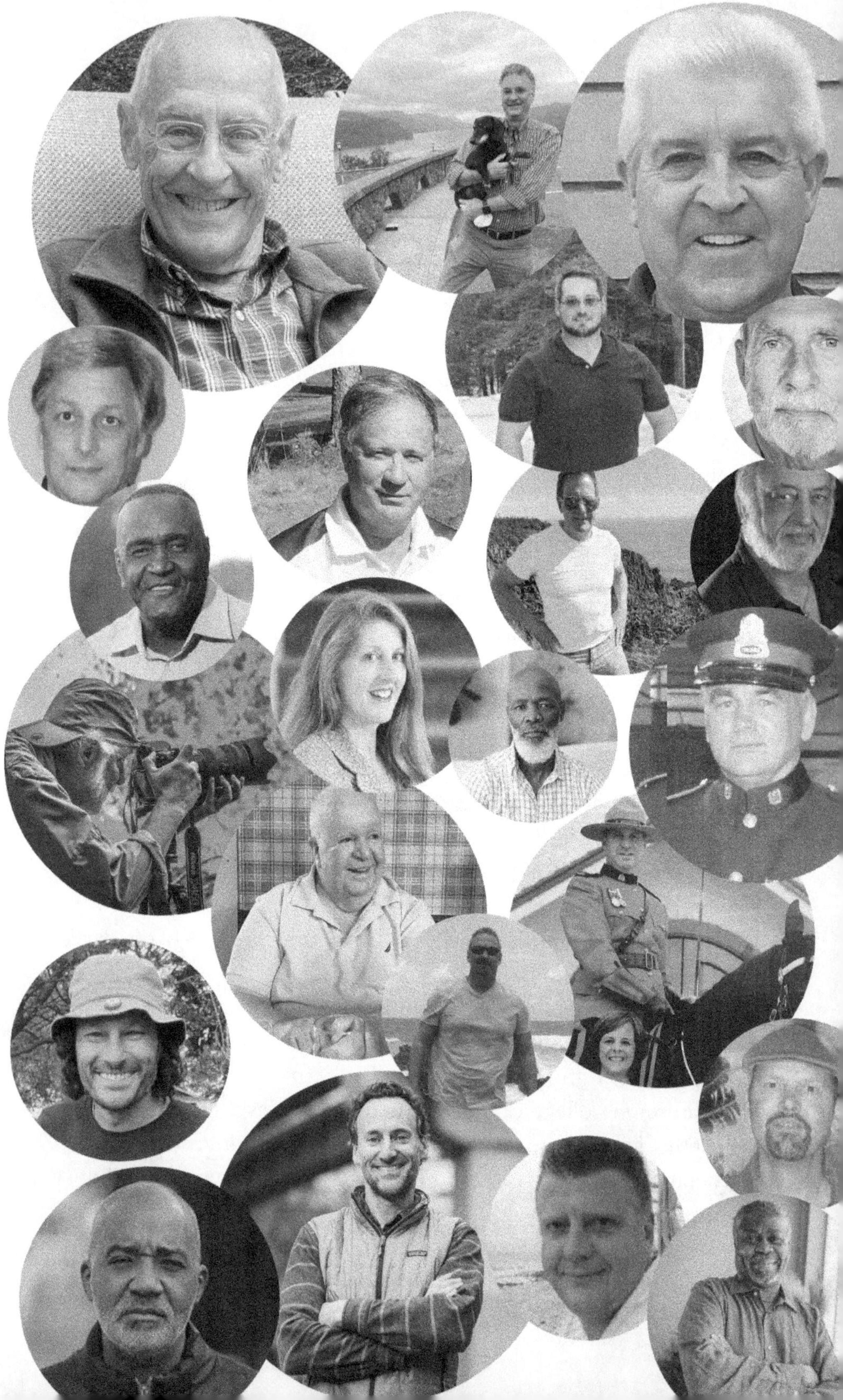

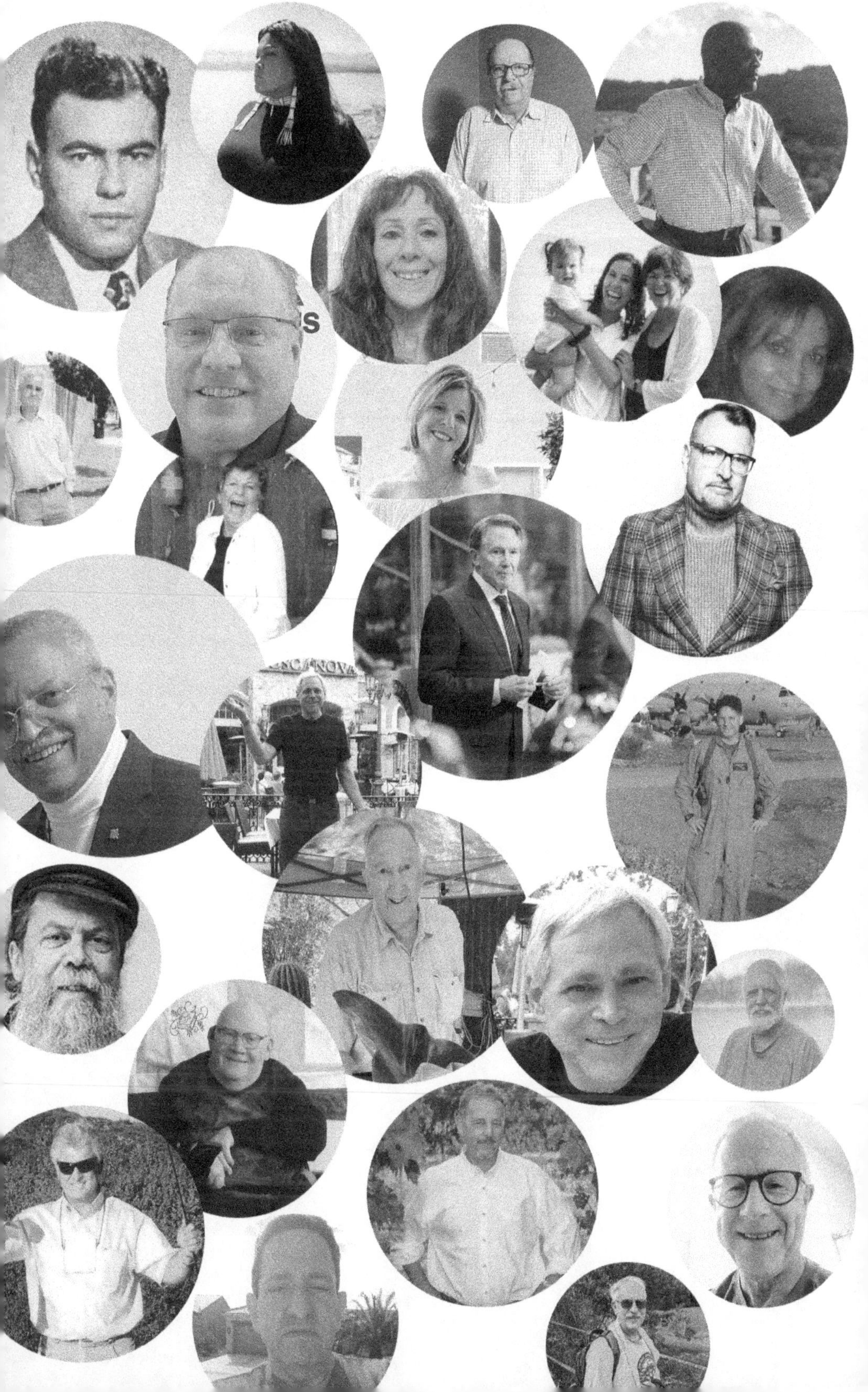

SECTION 3

THE PEOPLE

"In everyone's life, at some time, our inner fire goes out.
It is then burst into flame by an encounter with another
human being. We should all be thankful for those people
who rekindle the inner spirit."

Albert Schweitzer

In the following pages, you will discover 66 concise mini-biographies about individuals who participated in the project. These narratives are designed for quick and engaging reading. As you delve into these brief life stories, take a moment to contemplate your journey, considering the individual about whom you are learning. What commonalities do you perceive? Do these shared experiences make the person's story more relatable to you?

Now, let's dive into the data. Here is a revealing table about the 66 individuals and the unique journeys on which I had the privilege to interview them. Of the five interviewees who did not agree to have their stories included in the book, three were women and two were men.

	East	West	South	Plains	Totals
Male	19	15	8	8	50
Female	4	7	2	3	16
20s / 30s	2	2	0	2	6
40s	1	2	1	1	5
50s	3	3	3	1	10
60s	9	8	3	5	25
70s	6	2	3	2	13
80s / 90s	2	5	0	0	7

This table shows where they are from. Growing up in Nova Scotia and living my adult life in Illinois explains those outlying numbers. California? Well, it's California. Isn't it always an outlier?

UNITED STATES				CANADA	
Alabama	2	Montana	1	Alberta	3
Arizona	1	Nevada	1	British Columbia	1
California	7	New Hampshire	3	New Brunswick	1
Colorado	1	New York	1	Nova Scotia	6
Connecticut	1	North Carolina	1	Ontario	3
Florida	3	Oregon	2	Quebec	1
Georgia	1	South Dakota	1	Saskatchewan	3
Idaho	1	Texas	1		
Illinois	8	Utah	1	**OTHER**	
Kentucky	1	Washington	1	New Delhi, India	1
Louisiana	1	West Virginia	2	Shanghai, China	1
Mississippi	2	Wyoming	2		

And now, it's time to meet the real stars: the storytellers. Each has a unique tale and I'm excited to share their stories.

TEACHER, COACH, SERVANT, AND THE MAGIC OF SMALL

A story from Nova Scotia

I lead with a story about the most amazing person I have ever met.

I met Kent in 1975 as an 18-year-old freshman at Acadia University. He was a 26-year-old teacher returning to school to raise his credentials. While I was forging my path, Kent already knew his. He grew up in a tiny Nova Scotian fishing village and ultimately applied his considerable talent to impact the lives of the small community he loved. During his teaching career, he developed a measurable performance-improving math program, received a rare Canadian Prime Minister's Award, was honored by Furman University in the United States, and received an offer from the United Arab Emirates. Upon retiring from Lockeport Regional High School (LRHS), the latter hired him as a Cluster Manager at the Abu Dhabi Education Council in 2007. He was one of the few teachers from across the world selected to help that country modernize its educational system.

Kent also entered the Nova Scotian Basketball Hall of Fame in 2017. During his tenure at LRHS, Kent coached more provincial basketball champions than any other coach in the province's history. While classified at the "B" level, his team often competed on an equal footing with "A" teams. John Wooden, the renowned UCLA coach Kent met on two occasions, influenced his coaching and philosophy, most notably via Wooden's famous *Pyramid of Success*. Kent imbued that philosophy deep into his students' and athletes' hearts and minds.

Although I didn't know it when we met, Kent is of Middle Eastern descent. As such, he had darker skin in his youth, and this led to painful, discriminatory experiences growing up. However, Kent was blessed with highly supportive parents, whom he identified as the most influential people in his life. He described his family ethos as supportive, generous, adventurous, and unique. This environment inspired him to achieve and to think creatively. Kent is the father of two accomplished sons, Shea and Josh, but in 1991, he experienced his life's most painful event. He said that it took 8-9 years to overcome the trauma of a divorce. That time frame aligns with Bruce Feiler's conclusion, as noted in his book *Life is in the Transitions*. Today, Kent serves on the town council.

Kent, a two-time cancer survivor, like any great teacher, lives a philosophical life with the primary goal of serving others. While in the United Arab Emirates, his studies into the etymological meaning of his last name yielded "to serve and expect nothing in return." How fitting!

The most notable aspect of Kent's life is his decision to stay in a small village despite his immense talent. My New York City-born and educated sociology professor at Acadia University could not stress enough how much he loved the unpretentious people in the fishing villages of Nova Scotia. I think Kent was attuned to this thinking and recognized all he had right where he was born. Not many ambitious people would have made the same decision. How many people can achieve local, national, and international recognition? Kent earned all those accolades from his hometown of tiny Lockeport, Nova Scotia.

THE ACCOMPLISHED TRAVELER FACES A LIFE CHALLENGE AT 70

A story from California

Jim was born into a chaotic and demanding family in Long Island, New York, that expected achievement. While still at university, he was hired by a major manufacturer to work in aerospace engineering.

Industrious from an early age, Jim eventually broadened his horizons and built his financial net worth in real estate as a reasonably young man. Today, he is semi-retired, living in one of the most affluent suburbs of Los Angeles, where many Hollywood stars dwell.

Despite professional success, Jim was socially awkward and never saw himself as father material. That thinking changed following an enlightening experience in India, one of about 87 countries to which he has traveled. That worldwide travel was punctuated by the clandestine entry into Mecca, the closed-to-non-Muslims holy city in Saudi Arabia for which he dressed the part. Domestic travel for work took him to Texas and California, where he finally married at 40. Following that short-term marriage, Jim remarried a few years later to a woman with children, only to see her develop the scourge known as cancer, to which she tragically succumbed.

Jim had a near-death experience as a teenager, and in its aftermath, he came to know his parents loved him even if they had difficulty displaying it. He had gotten intoxicated at a party and was coaxed to drag race. While speeding about 90 miles per hour, he encountered an 18-wheeler that should not have been there. Unable to avoid the collision, Jim's car abruptly stopped while his body assumed the force of the impact. He recalls darkness and a light behind him, all ostensibly outside his body. A voice told him that it was not his time, and soon, after he "watched" the paramedics extricate a figure from the car, he was reunited with his body in the ambulance. According to the doctors, given the energy of the impact, there is no logical reason for his survival.

Jim recognizes his social challenges, likely connected to brain trauma from the accident, that will lead him to say something that comes across as inappropriate, such that people will sometimes feel hurt by what he said. That did not happen when he met his second love. They were the last two in a hot tub one evening, in birthday suits, when warm tantric energy engulfed them. For Jim, this resulted in a spiritual bond that transcended other relationships.

Some things in life turn one's emotions inside out. After dealing with the loss of his soulmate, Jim has recently had to deal with the sexual identity of his daughter. She realized her sexual identity as being different from her cisgender beginnings. It began with homosexual experiences early in college life and progressed to recent testosterone therapy to begin the transformation. For Jim, the self-described dinosaur, this is an experience he cannot yet process. He does not support his daughter's path and has even updated his will to reflect that stance.

The loss of his wife to cancer left Jim pondering his future. His intellectual and emotional struggle with his daughter's decision will undoubtedly be essential to the next chapter in his life. Perhaps, in time, there will be room in his heart for a cathartic rapprochement.

A PRODIGY'S LIFE: POVERTY, ABUSE, SUCCESS, BLISS, TRAGEDY

A story from Alabama

At age two, Kate could recite the alphabet forward and backward and play the piano. Following aptitude testing at a local institution at age 7, she was encouraged to enroll at Duke University after turning eight. But...

Kate, her mother, stepfather, and younger brother lived in abject poverty. Not surprisingly, the talented girl resolved never to be poor and was always looking for ways to make money. Her father, whom she learned at age 35 was her stepfather, sexually abused her from the time she was a toddler. He was naturally pleased that his wife, oblivious to the abuse, declined to send Kate to Duke. Shortly after that, she told her mother about the abuse, and when confronted, he admitted to pedophilia. Although he never physically abused her again, the damage had been done, as young Kate lived in constant fear of a stepfather who went unpunished. Fearing oppressive financial repercussions, her mother did not report it nor separate from him. The journey of those in great need can sometimes seem incomprehensible.

At 14, Kate had a spiritual awakening and found forgiveness as she supplanted her stepfather with the Heavenly Father. At 17, she enrolled at Louisiana State University in her hometown of Baton Rouge, Louisiana, and moved out of her parents' place. Kate had taken control of her life. At age 19, while getting into her car, a thug shoved a gun in her face, got into the car, and proceeded to abduct and rape her. After that horrific event, she was diagnosed with post-traumatic stress disorder, and her college career tragically came to an end. Pressing on, she started two businesses to restart her life.

In her early twenties, Kate faced a career decision between a terrific corporate offer or going full-time at a smaller business. She accepted the small business's offer and eventually, under societal duress, married the owner. They had a son, but the relationship became increasingly toxic, as is the pattern with a controlling, narcissistic partner. Despite the tumult, she worked hard, and the family lived a charmed financial life. In February 2014, it ended. The last straw was a bitter fight involving their son and her husband being jailed. Kate filed for divorce. Unfortunately, none of the multimillion-dollar business value was to accrue to her as it was all in his name. Kate decided not to fight for anything except her son and soon started all over at age 44.

Kate had another spiritual experience that helped her navigate the destruction of a lifestyle. Her presentation skills led her to a new career as a life coach and motivational speaker. She had a wealth of experience, including overcoming an autoimmune disease, on which she could draw. She co-authored a best-selling book, but more importantly, she met her soulmate.

During COVID-19, Kate's health had gotten to the point that she and her new husband had psychologically been preparing for her death. But death would not claim her. Both contracted COVID-19 in 2021 following a rare night out. She got sick first and is unsure whether he contracted the virus from her that ultimately took his life. With minimal insurance proceeds and debts to pay, Kate is again rebuilding.

THE LINGUIST/MUSICIAN/AUTHOR COPES WITH DEPRESSION

A story from Oregon

David B. did not meet his biological father until the age of 30. His mother had gotten pregnant as a young single woman and severed relations with his father. She eventually married another man to whom David applied the moniker "Ivan the Terrible." While growing up with his younger siblings, he had always suspected something was askew but did not learn the truth until age 18. David's mother is now deceased, but he does maintain a relationship with his biological father.

Despite Ivan being a successful engineer, he would occasionally beat David. Oddly, David has no memory of this except for the recounting from his siblings. On one occasion, at only seven or eight, he encountered Ivan dragging his mother up the stairs by her hair. Although life at home could be chaotic, the saving grace for David was a supportive mother who adored her son. Despite the chaos, he did well in school and graduated from Portland State University with a Bachelor of Arts degree. One of the requirements at PSU was at least one course in a foreign language. For the musically talented David, that language was French. A love affair had begun.

1981/82 provided the most incredible time of his life as an exchange student in France at the University of Poitiers. Poitiers, a town about halfway between Paris and Bordeaux, is nestled in a region where French is spoken in such a way analogous to the King's English in England. This perfectly suited the enthusiastic young student who assiduously applied himself to mastering the intellectual dialect. For David, it was much more than a student exchange and pursuing his Master's degree; it was the turning point in his life as he was metaphorically reincarnated as a child.

David was married for 17 years and had one stepdaughter. He's struggled with depression throughout the years and eventually wrote a book titled *Suicide Prevention: Step Back from the Abyss, A Self-Help Memoir,* under the pseudonym David Sherwood. Although he had a healthy relationship with his mother as a child, there was an incident at the age of ten that seemed to leave an indelible scar of abandonment. She, overwhelmed by an argument with Ivan on a road trip, exited the car in the middle of nowhere in South Dakota and disappeared into the night. David, fearing he was losing his mother, got out to find her but never got over the incident. When his financially successful wife left and filed for divorce, that same sense of abandonment manifested itself anew. David sought counseling from several therapists without substantive results until ten years ago. Today, although depressive thoughts continue to linger in the ether, he is coping better as he engages with the world. His creative intellectual abilities have led to writing other books, including one about the Hoyt Arboretum in Portland.

David, the linguist, musician, and author, like many of his generation who are divorced, lives alone with his dachshund, Buddy. However, he is also an Airbnb host, filling as many as three guest rooms at a time. His musical gigs, Airbnb hosting, and productive therapy help David cope with his background depressive thoughts. There is a lesson to be learned from his experience that he has articulated in his book about suicide prevention.

GAY RUNAWAY AT 15 GIVES A LIFETIME OF COMFORT TO OTHERS

A story from Quebec

Arlen John Bonnar is a loquacious storyteller; fitting, because he is known as Reverend Bonnar at Saint James United Church in Montreal, but it did not come easily. A runaway at 15 from a loathsome, abusive, drunken father, Arlen jumped on a train in Nova Scotia destined for Montreal with nothing but $21 given to him by a relative. In a moment that one may interpret as divine intervention given Arlen's yet-to-be-realized journey, he narrowly escaped the Quebec provincial police who boarded the train in Quebec City in search of him. Arlen's life had begun.

Born into a poor working-class family, Arlen was raised mainly by his maternal grandparents, who openly gave love and support. Nearby, on the same property, was his parents' house. That juxtaposed dichotomy was not lost on him, as he paradoxically described his upbringing as affectionate and harsh. During one of the many beatings his father inflicted on his mother, Arlen ran upstairs, grabbed a knife, and brandished it with intent. As usual, his mother intervened, and a crisis was avoided. That ended at 15 when, following a paternal beating, Arlen had had enough. Despite his love for his grandparents, it was time to leave and board that train.

As if his predicament in Montreal wasn't complex enough, with just $3 in his pocket upon arrival, Arlen began to comprehend his homosexuality in an era when that proclivity was not well accepted. After passing himself off as 19, he moved in with the much older friends of a fellow Maritimer he had met on the train. One of the men helped him get his first job. His schooling was finished, for now. At age 16, Arlen had his first boyfriend, and life in the gay community of Montreal suited him. Arlen found his first long-term partner at 19, a clergyman who introduced him to the United Church of Canada shortly after that.

As Arlen progressed economically, he found time to volunteer at an institution for the mentally challenged despite some trepidation. Unknowingly, he was beginning to hear his calling, as that volunteering soon became a vocation. Before long, he was part of an enlightened movement to change the archaic practices in such institutions *sans* credentials. At 25, he was accepted as a mature student at Bishops University. Mortified by the challenge, he froze on his first test and handed in a blank paper. The benevolent department head, who saw Arlen's potential, took him under his wing. Another intervention.

Arlen continued his education in theology at McGill University. At 30, he and his partner of 11 years separated in part so that he could escape his elder's shadow. Arlen's first internship was at a highly progressive Winnipeg church. His second was in South Africa, where he witnessed the atrocities of apartheid. His first ministerial assignment was near Ottawa in 1984. In 1989, he became the executive director of a United Church outreach mission. In 2000, he assumed the ministry at Saint James.

He relates that the high point in his life was being appointed chaplain at Montreal General Hospital. That experience in palliative care during a time of great uncertainty about the burgeoning AIDS epidemic opened doors for him, and he stated that he gained insights into "social justice, spiritual faith, and other invaluable aspects of the human journey."

Arlen knows about being different. In his calling, he seeks to bridge differences by working with Jewish, Muslim, and other religious leaders and finds no dissonance in this mission.

AUSTRALIAN ADVENTURER FINDS SUCCESS AND FAITH IN AMERICA

A story from Montana

Sean B. grew up poor in Sydney, Australia, in a family that was always on the move. His father was a gambling addict who physically abused his wife. Despite those challenging years, including one incident in which Sean told his father that he would kill him unless he ceased brutalizing the family, he was an enterprising lad who started selling newspapers at age eight. Raised Catholic, although his family did not actively practice, Sean never forgot the inherent value of faith. Entrepreneurship and faith resonate in his life to this day.

Despite his father's failings, he imbued Sean with the value of hard work, and by his mid-teens, Sean had started voraciously devouring the wisdom of self-help books. He began working as a mechanic's apprentice after leaving school at 16 and, by the age of 20, had migrated to the furniture business, where he earned serious money leading a team selling products to protect couches and chairs. Flush with cash, he began to travel, first to Asia and then America for several weeks.

Sean developed an interest in real estate investing, but before he began building his empire in Sydney, he embarked on a worldwide adventure. He purchased a one-way ticket to London but stopped to visit the United States on the way. During that fateful stopover, Sean met a beautiful older woman with four children in California and began renovating her home. A love affair blossomed, and after marrying in Sydney, Australia, Sean's American chapter started in earnest.

At 29, Sean and his family moved to Seattle, where he started to buy homes as investments. However, Sean had something else in mind besides being a real estate mogul. At 24, he had written down precepts for a long-term business model he wanted to run. His introduction to Nu Skin of Provo, Utah, a company with a platform aligned with his writings, triggered an epiphany that inspired a business empire. Although there were lean times initially, Sean's business acumen, much of it gleaned from readings and seminars, won the day as his incessant globetrotting paid off with business income streams from about 40 countries. He has built a significant reputation for himself and delivered speeches supporting the expansion of the Nu Skin business.

His introduction to Nu Skin occurred when he considered moving back to Australia, as he had been separated from his wife. A tall, blonde woman named Sherry sat beside him at a meeting, and a friendship blossomed. Following a trip back to Australia to visit his ailing mother, Sean spoke with Sherry, who asked him to return to her in Billings, Montana. Sean agreed but with one condition. They were married about eight months later. Together, they have faithfully partnered to build the business across the world.

Sean's journey to success in America came with great effort. There were long separations from his wife and a familial sacrifice for leaving his home country. Once a heavy drinker, he now forsakes the practice to appease Sherry, a Mormon. He is a devout man of the Mormon faith, fulfilling a promise he once made to himself as he envisioned family life.

ECLECTIC LIFE COMES FULL CIRCLE, BUILDING BRIDGES AT HOME

A story from Louisiana

Kevin always knew he was a bridge builder with a destiny. That is to say, the Caucasian social worker/therapist, talk show host, author, and finally, professor eventually returned to his New Orleans roots to navigate the oft-perilous quagmire between his minority inner city constituency and the greater community.

Born into a family with three younger siblings, Kevin's father, after being "kicked out of Canada" as a young man, settled in New Orleans where he built a hugely successful ministry. As Kevin grew up in this sometimes-chaotic environment with a preoccupied father, he knew his future needed to start elsewhere. Instead of choosing a local university, he enrolled at a prestigious Christian school, Wheaton College in Illinois.

Kevin became his own man in his adopted state of Illinois. He completed his Bachelor's degree in Psychology, started a band that got showcased on MTV, and completed a Master's degree in Social Work at the University of Illinois at Chicago. His next planned academic move was to undertake a Master's in Divinity Studies at Princeton Theological Seminary. But there was one small problem. The woman he had met on his journey issued him a proposal. Me or Princeton. She was not onboard for being the wife of a preacher-man. Kevin has been happily married for 35 years and is the father of three wonderful children.

Kevin's big work break came from a Christian counseling organization called Minirth Meier Clinic. That led to various exciting developments, not the least of which was a talk show for youth therapy. He wrote three books, all while continuing music gigs. That latter pastime was eventually driven into the abyss one morning when he realized it impaired his ability to be a devoted father. Sometimes, he ponders the wisdom of walking away from a passion but, ultimately, affirms the self-actualization of fatherhood.

One fateful day, he bumped into Bill Bright, who ran Campus Crusade for Christ and attended seminary with Kevin's father. Bill invited Kevin to an event where they encountered several luminaries. He felt in over his head, yet there he was, and his life was about to change. After losing his wife to brain cancer, Kevin's aging father was a grieving, withered ghost of himself in the New Orleans community. In an inspired moment at the event, Kevin decided to leave Illinois and become his father's replacement in The Big Easy. Life had come full circle.

Academic posts have been the primary means by which Kevin carried out his mission to further the plight of inner-city youth. He taught at multiple schools and completed his Master's and then a Ph.D. degree at the University of New Orleans. Can't complete both degrees in one year. Drop the year completely. When Katrina devastated the city in 2005, Kevin was an instrumental force of service, and honors came from the President of the United States, the US Attorney General, and the US Marshal Service.

All sons seek their father's approval. With his father's sanction, Kevin left for an out-of-state Christian school on the journey of self-discovery. Some 20 years later, he picked up the mantle of his now-deceased father's work to serve.

EMMY AWARD WINNER, HALL OF FAMER, MANCHESTER INFLUENCER

A story from New Hampshire

John Clayton is one of the most prominent and influential personalities in New Hampshire. An Emmy Award winner as host of the PBS show *New Hampshire Crossroads*, he also wrote a column titled, *In the City*, for 20 years while a reporter at The Union Leader newspaper in Manchester. His writing was so powerful that it appeared on the front page of that conservative newspaper even though John does not consider himself so politically aligned. He had taken the job on the condition that there were no conditions. That rendered him carte blanche for his column writing and later his authorship of seven books.

Born third into a blue-collar family of six children, John was a peacekeeper and, as it turned out, the scholar of the family. Although his family was highly supportive, a university career seemed out of reach financially, so he never really applied himself academically. That was until a benevolent guidance counselor, privy to some astonishing aptitude test results, figuratively delivered a slap to wake him up. A scholarship to study journalism at Northeastern University in Boston ensued.

John experienced a couple of sobering moments in his youth. At age six, he was given last rights even though he was not Catholic. On his 20th birthday, he found himself a cub reporter writing about a Boston plane crash from which all perished. It had taken off from his hometown of Manchester. That day, the destiny he had envisioned for his life changed. Life in Manchester, in some capacity, was to be his future.

Upon graduating, unable to find a suitable job in journalism, John eventually found himself working in public relations for New Hampshire College in Manchester. That school paid for his Master's degree at Boston University, during which time he completed an academic exchange in Cardiff, Wales, on a Rotary International fellowship. While there, the *Yank* was a starting point guard on the Cardiff University basketball team. Although John enjoyed his foray into academia, where he was an associate dean at age 31, he still yearned for a career in journalism. When The Union Leader newspaper came calling, the die was cast.

As John's reputation grew, other opportunities emerged, including a PBS offer that resulted in his winning two Emmys. In 2001, he was a member of the first group inducted into his high school's Hall of Fame. He proudly relates the time his father handed in his police badge because he had been asked to look the other way. John gets emotional, recalling the time his tiny daughter hugged a physically disfigured man whom John had helped free from unjustified imprisonment.

With a few exceptions, such as the pain of a divorce from his first wife, John has lived a mostly wonderful life. His dedication to his hometown is eminently admirable. Before his 20th birthday epiphany, he was likely on his way to making his dream of writing for Sports Illustrated come true. Reversing the course from such a budding big-time career to administer his talents back home shows a depth of character the fortunate ones possess. As the Executive Director of the Manchester Historic Association, his hometown's legacy/future is being well shepherded. [**Author's Note:** John recently retired from his Executive Director post at the Manchester Historic Association.]

FORMER BRAZILIAN PROFESSOR MAKES A NEW LIFE IN CANADA

A story from Saskatchewan

Caroline's family upbringing was the opposite of her husband's (another story here). Born into a close-knit extended family with many cousins, leaving Brazil to make a new life in Canada came with considerable emotional duress. What was not painful was exiting the stifling professional gutter into which she had stumbled for several years.

After her parents divorced when she was 6, Caroline and her older brother lived with their mother. Her emotionally distant father remained so but continued to see Caroline, who never felt he was the father figure upon which she could rely. Her relationship with her mother flourished, from whence the little girl drew her strength. At the tender age of 15, she traveled to Finland to study for one year. While there, young Caroline became convinced her future was in political studies. After returning to Brazil, she completed high school and enrolled in university at age 17 to study International Relations.

Caroline was fortunate to meet an encouraging mentor while working on her undergraduate degree. Pursuing a Master's or a Ph.D. would likely never have been in the cards if it weren't for his belief in her. Acquiring her doctorate was not easy; it took eight years due to her need to work contemporaneously. In her work, she encountered outright discouragement and criticism that, like in her husband's case, led to a critical inflection point. The environment had become so toxic that she sought counseling. That intervention facilitated Caroline's preparation for saying goodbye to her mother, cousins, and country.

Until recently, one unpleasant constant throughout Caroline's life was obesity. To address this, she had bariatric surgery the same year she defended her Ph.D. thesis. Although the surgery was a turning point in her life psychologically, it took more than a year for her to fully embrace her new body as the weight began to fall off. It was not only physically that Caroline morphed. Born into a devout Catholic family, her faith in organized religion diminished as her secular educational experiences continued and her intellectual curiosity grew. Today, she views religion as an "opiate of the masses," borrowing a phrase from Karl Marx.

Caroline is socially conscientious and has given her time and money to various causes. She firmly believed in social democracy and was appalled at what happened in Brazil under President Bolsonaro, a slavish Trump acolyte. Philosophically, Caroline believes that humility is humanity's preeminent value and freely expresses gratitude for all she has.

Leaving one's country after realizing it holds no future for you can be traumatizing. Caroline felt compelled to do so despite the pain of leaving her mother and other beloved family members behind. In Canada, she envisions expressing herself intellectually and building a meaningful and happy future with her husband, from whom she draws strength because of his disconnected family life. In his story of enduring oppression, she realized the humanity of being an individual with value.

FORMER CHEMICAL COMPANY LOBBYIST SAVES RIVERS IN WEST VIRGINIA

A story from West Virginia

Bill Currey has always been an ambitious doer. Born the oldest in a family of five, Bill's father ran the only Schwinn bicycle dealership in the entire State of West Virginia. While that venture was ultimately successful, as it became the largest Schwinn dealership in the country, its nature ensured that the family was constantly moving around the state. Eventually, the family settled in the western part of Charleston, the State Capitol. With his father's business as a template, Bill learned invaluable entrepreneurship lessons.

Reality found Bill in his first year of university. Unprepared for the rigor of intense academic demands, he flunked out of school. Undeterred, after some travel, he re-enrolled at a recently desegregated Black school despite his Caucasian ethnicity. An athletic kid, he played sports as he had in high school, and after attaining specific academic goals, he transferred to Marshall University. Bill had benefited from one of America's gifts: a second chance.

Bill studied business but developed expanded horizons in art and mechanical drawing, skills he used as a stone sculptor in retirement. Following his junior year, he landed in Germany for a 14-week work/study program, although he was linguistically unqualified. Married in his senior year, Bill launched his career in Public Relations as a lobbyist for a large utility company, and following the requisite job changes typical of those intent on ascending, he landed a big job as FMC's national Public Relations Director. As environmental pressures closed in, Bill left FMC and went into business for himself, where he combined his lobbying skills with a new-found acumen for completing real estate deals until he retired. Along the way, Bill fathered three children.

As successful as Bill was in his corporate career, he may have eclipsed that summit in retirement. The rivers of West Virginia are as expansive as they are ecologically, commercially, and recreationally vital. However, as long-time dumping grounds, their vitality had been severely compromised, and they were once deemed the dirtiest in the nation. An avid paddler, Bill started The Coal River Group with a few others about twenty years ago. As its leader, Bill has helped transform the Coal River watershed into an award-winning entity. In January 2023, Forbes magazine listed the top 50 travel destinations worldwide. Tiny Saint Albans, one of the towns along the Coal River, was included on that prestigious list.[6] That

---

[6] https://www.forbes.com/advisor/credit-cards/travel-rewards/best-places-to-travel-2023/

accomplishment is in no small way attributable to the revival Bill and his team engineered.

Bill's life has been blessed with essential mentors who have played vital roles in the story. However, like all people, he has experienced setbacks. His parents divorced when he was a young man, and he has been divorced twice. Furthermore, his grandson was born with a rare disease, *von Hippel-Lindau syndrome*, for which there is palliative treatment but no cure.

Bill has lived a life of accomplishment. Despite his early academic setback, he ultimately made the most of his gifts and transitioned from chemical company executive to an award-winning environmentalist.

A MOTHER INSPIRES HER DAUGHTER'S EMIGRATION TO THE USA

A story from North Carolina

Saadia grew up in Morocco in a stable family with several siblings. When her mother died when Saadia was only 17, stepsiblings joined the family. Her mother, the bedrock of the family, was especially encouraging, as she, unlike Moroccan women in her day, encouraged education and independent achievement for her children. Saadia had a special relationship with her mother. When she was about eight, Saadia clandestinely learned of her mother's illiteracy and vouchsafed never to disclose the secret to her siblings.

When Saadia was 16, her mother started to feel sick and was eventually admitted to a local hospital. After concluding that nothing more could be done, her mother returned home and died three days later. Saadia's religious father, who worked at a company owned by the King's family, quickly remarried, and home life was never the same.

Following high school, although she had been accepted to a university in France, she stayed home to study agronomy for financial reasons. Following college, she hastily married despite having misgivings about her beau, as Moroccan women had restrictions imposed upon them that limited their freedom unless they were married. While working at an institute, Saadia started to plan her eventual escape from the repressive Moroccan society. In 1994, after securing appropriate authorization from her husband, she boarded a plane headed to the United States under the guise of attending a brief academic conference. Upon landing in Washington, DC, Saadia was free with one dollar in her pocket! That ruse led to her studies at North Carolina State University and a divorce from her husband.

After finishing her Master's and Ph.D. degrees at NC State in 1996 and 2001, respectively, things got dicey for the student immigrant. In 1997, she married a naturalized American. However, he developed psychological disorders and, for technical reasons surrounding her visa status following 9/11, she faced an uncertain future in the United States. In 2004, Saadia found herself back in Morocco and understandably depressed. She found a job, though the pay for a person with a Ph.D. was insulting. But what choice did she have? After about a year, she found a better job, but it was still in Morocco, where she continued to endure its patriarchal ways. In 2007, at a conference in Rabat, a well-connected woman mistook Saadia for someone else while in the lady's room. A conversation ensued in which Saadia informed the woman of her US educational qualifications. As luck would have it, the woman had connections, which ultimately led to a position for Saadia with the US Pharmacopeia organization. She returned to the United States the following year with an H1B visa and has lived there ever since.

A life-changing bundle of joy entered her life when she adopted a Moroccan girl in 2019. However, another immigration heartache, this one related to her daughter's status, prevented Saadia from traveling to Morocco to visit her ailing father.

Saadia's quest for intellectual and personal freedom was beset with myriad challenges. She counts her mother and Ph.D. advisor as the key people in her life who helped her aspire and achieve. Success is never a solo journey. Today, with the love of a beautiful daughter, Saadia remains upbeat about what the future might hold for them.

THE GOLDEN BOY GIVES BACK

A story from Ontario

Charles has lived a very fortunate life and is the first to recognize that. Growing up near Montreal, Charles was the only child of enlightened parents who never spoiled him. They were proactively involved in his life and ensured a solid foundation was built. His friends and sports, especially skiing, were mainstays in his life: a typical day growing up involved seeking out his friends and disappearing for the day. There was never a lack of things to do. Because of his father's work, they moved twice within the greater Montreal area. After the first move, Charles quickly made new friends and was reunited with old friends after the second. Vacationing with his parents was another staple from which he had wondrous experiences.

An average student, Charles was not exactly keen on books. However, he knew his parents expected him to attend university somewhere. Unlike most Quebecers, he avoided CEGEP after completing 11th grade to pursue 12th grade at a private school. CEGEP is a program unique to Quebec in North America. Since he did not attend CEGEP, Charles had to consider schools outside of Quebec and chose the University of Western Ontario in London to study economics. After graduation, he moved back in with his parents. He had no intentions of immediately looking for a serious job, but with the support of his parents, he landed a job at one of the large, multinational Canadian banks. A lifetime career had serendipitously found him.

Charles' career first took him to Calgary in the early 80s. He returned to school for an MBA and, in 1986, landed at another bank in Toronto. Before starting, he requested and was granted a three-month delay in his start date so he could gallivant around Europe skiing. Quintessential Charles! He married soon after beginning work in Toronto, but his wife, sadly, could not conceive. In 1999, they traveled to Russia and adopted a girl from Yakutsk, the world's coldest major city.[7] A few years later, following a restructuring at the bank that afforded Charles a generous severance package, he landed a final gig at a third major bank. About a dozen years later, he was once again a restructuring target. This time, he received an even more generous severance package that allowed him to retire at age 56. Charles was The Golden Boy.

Despite this success, Charles never takes his fortune for granted. He lost his father at a reasonably young age and knows that life can be tenuous. With that philosophy, he and his wife compassionately contribute to a home for battered women. Along the way, Charles has lived life to the fullest while always being conscientious about approaching life responsibly. To him, life is not complicated. Protect your reputation through action and always treat others with respect. He says that respect is humanity's preeminent value.

Charles may appear as simply a receiver and, thus, "The Golden Boy" moniker. Not so. In addition to his contributions to battered women, he and his wife support four children in remote lands who are less fortunate. With his daughter's full knowledge and support, he has provided for those children in his will. Sometimes, you must look deep beneath the surface to learn a person's true character.

CANADIAN HOCKEY COACH MAKES AN IMPACT IN LOS ANGELES

A story from California

Mark was the youngest of three boys in the small Maritime province of New Brunswick. His father had alcohol problems and left the

---

[7] https://en.wikipedia.org/wiki/Yakutsk

picture when Mark was ten, at which time he became involved in sports. That decision set in motion the blueprint for the rest of his life.

Hockey (fall, winter) and baseball (spring, summer) were the two sports that appealed the most to Mark. In his second year of hockey, he played for a provincial championship team and duplicated that feat later in baseball. As an athlete, he was fortunate to have mentors who taught him the mechanics of the sport and the great lessons one can learn from competition. Following the completion of a degree in physical education at the University of New Brunswick, Mark headed to Vancouver and landed his first real job with the British Columbia Lions of the Canadian Football League. His coaching career in baseball started in British Columbia. However, when the Lions began having financial problems, Mark found himself out of a job and decided to head back to his hometown of Fredericton.

Mark enrolled at UNB again to obtain a degree in education, intending to become a high school teacher. He found substitute teaching opportunities while also coaching hockey. In his first year, he led Fredericton High School to its first provincial title in 17 years. Unable to pin down a full-time teaching job, Mark hit the road teaching English in South Korea and Mexico. The first of two international calls had beckoned.

After finishing in Mexico, Mark returned home and secured a full-time teaching job. As for coaching, he moved up to university level as an assistant hockey coach at UNB. In 2004, Mark talked with a former professor who convinced him to pursue an MBA with a concentration in sports and recreation. Growing tired of the Canadian winters (odd for a hockey guy, no?), in 2008, he reached out to a fellow Maritimer, a coach with the Los Angeles Kings of the NHL. He soon began thesis fieldwork for his MBA as a Kings hockey ambassador. Exposure to the big city convinced him it was time for a significant life change. Mark was about to mount a career rocket ship.

In 2010, Mark enrolled in a one-year certificate program at UCLA. With a student visa secured, he started a networking campaign that led to him being named the head coach of the UCLA hockey team. A random call to the UCLA Anderson School of Business about a course led to an offer to teach. In short order, Mark went from a person without status in the United States to an instructor at one of the preeminent business schools in the country. With time, this has led to increasingly influential roles in academia and business where he can achieve his real goal of being an influencer in the world of sport and his community.

Mark's leap of faith had indeed borne professional fruit. However, single, he intimates that he sold himself short some 20 years ago by not marrying his fiancé, who, unlike him, grew up on the "right" side of the tracks. That aside, Mark has lived the Horatio Alger story. Few, if any, could have predicted such a meteoric rise upon his landing in Los Angeles.

A HOMELESS TEEN'S TRANSMOGRIFICATION INTO A NATIONAL ADVOCATE AND POLITICIAN

A story from Wyoming

Lynnette Grey Bull, a.k.a. Morning Water, has roots in the Lakota Nation with the Standing Rock Sioux Tribe in the Dakotas as a descendant of Sitting Bull and with the Northern Arapaho Tribe of the Wind River Reservation in Wyoming. It was this heritage that inspired her life's work. Lynnette runs "Not Our Native Daughters," a non-profit that seeks to address the alarming trafficking, abuse, and disappearance of Native American girls and women. She has also twice run for the US Congress in Wyoming, including one campaign against Liz Cheney. Her early life, however, was quite different and no harbinger of these outstanding achievements.

Lynnette's parents were born on different reservations and, like many native people, experienced extreme poverty and the psychological cruelty of the boarding school system. Both escaped that purgatory at a young age to pursue education and seek a better life. They met in Billings, Montana, and soon moved to Los Angeles to begin a family free of the reservation. Lynnette, the oldest of two girls, was born shortly after arriving in the City of Angels, and life seemed normal for about 12 years.

Trauma, however, wields an ominous truncheon that can punish those who have lived it. Over time, Lynnette's successful parents became alcoholics, which led to a lost job, eviction, and homelessness. Her father's near-fatal car accident continued the downward spiral for the now homeless-sheltered family. The Door of Hope Christian Shelter's sobriety requirement and other charity helped the family regain its footing and imbued Lynnette with a profound faith. After the birth of her much younger sister, the drinking came back, and her parents separated when Lynnette was 15. At 17, one evening, she returned to the hotel where she, her mother, and sister lived, only to learn that her mother had abandoned her. She dropped out of school and entered survival mode.

Lynnette had relationships, including one with an abusive man with serious psychological issues. That relationship ended after he held a gun with two loaded chambers to her head and pulled the trigger. After escaping that horror, Lynnette worked hard to support herself, even if finding a permanent home remained elusive. At 24, she got pregnant via a different and much better relationship. That experience served as a wake-up call. Lynnette returned to church, where she found support and slowly began building the self-esteem she'd lacked. During a church retreat, Lynnette had a supernatural experience with God that shaped her future life mission.

Work life had been a struggle until, with emerging confidence, she applied for an office job with a company contracted to the financial powerhouse Capital One. There, she excelled, and her income and status grew steadily over the next six years. Now married, her family moved from California to Arizona, where she initially worked for the same company before accepting a role at Bank of America, where she ascended to management. Along the way, another son joined the family before she filed for divorce, unknowingly pregnant with her daughter.

While at Bank of America, Lynnette's life changed again. The company encouraged volunteering, and she became active with United Way's homeless project. It seemed natural. That volunteer experience morphed into others that left an indelible impact on her. When the bank announced a massive layoff, Lynnette was affected but planned to return later as the company had made such an offer. But it was not to be. God had commanded her to pursue other things. Lynnette began researching the plight of Native Americans and was appalled at what she learned. What started small with an initial visit to the Pine Ridge Reservation in South Dakota became her life's calling.

Since that fateful visit, Lynnette has founded her non-profit and began giving talks. She skillfully parlayed this new-found ability into becoming a two-time Democratic Party nominee for the US Congress. The once insecure, homeless dropout, mirroring the plodding caterpillar, has transformed into a beautiful butterfly confidently soaring with the wind at her back, spreading her message of hope.

THE ACCOMPLISHED ARCHITECT TRANSITIONS TO VINICULTURE

A story from California

Gustavo is a dreamer adept at finding inspiration. His parents, both doctors, particularly his internationally renowned father and colleague of Dr. Che Guevara, instilled in their son the gift of confidence and adventure. A citizen of Buenos Aires, Argentina, young Gustavo enrolled in university to study medicine. However, a vacation to Rio de Janeiro changed that trajectory. The architecture of Rio inspired him to abandon his medical ambitions and, with the full support of his parents (and following an opportune, inspiring encounter in California on another vacation), Gustavo eventually found himself studying architecture in the United States. His path was set.

Gustavo enjoyed an active childhood, including competitive rugby, to which he attributes a great deal in building his character. Rugby is as much a brotherhood as a sport. To this day, he maintains friendships with his former comrades in cleats. Drafted by the Army after high school, Gustavo served at an intensely dark time in Argentina's history following Juan Perón's last presidential term. People were disappearing, leading to the *Mothers of the Plaza de Mayo* movement. Having a Jewish heritage did not help Gustavo's plight in the Army, as he was the subject of cruel harassment. Upon serving his obligatory 14-month term, Gustavo began his medical studies before sojourning in Brazil, only to experience his life-altering epiphany.

While studying at SCI-Arc in Los Angeles, tragedy struck in 1981 when Gustavo's older brother died in an automobile accident. Even though he was the only child left, his father told him to return to the United States to pursue his dream. At the end of that school year, tragedy struck again as Gustavo's beloved father died of complications from brain surgery. This time, his mother told him to return to California. Not long after returning, he married and had a daughter. Unfortunately, it was a doomed relationship. While his wife looked after their child so Gustavo could finish his last year of school, he was granted full custody of his daughter after graduating. Although still a young man of 26, Gustavo was entirely dedicated to his daughter, and for years, he never dated to avoid engendering potential discord.

Gustavo was fortunate to study under great architects such as Ray Kappe and Thom Mayne. His career flourished, as did his personal life when he married for a second time. They had a daughter some

16 years after the birth of his first. He also sponsored his mother's move to the United States. Over the years, Gustavo has designed many buildings in the Los Angeles area while maintaining an office on the famous Wilshire Boulevard. He had built a comfortable life in Los Angeles.

Gustavo always had a connection to agriculture in Argentina. When he built his second California home, he unfortunately had no choice but to sacrifice an olive tree. Naturally, he decided to harvest and press the olives to make oil. Gustavo was hooked. Some years later, he decided to consider something more sustaining: grapes. Finally, in 2020, Gustavo received a call from an agent telling him to be in Napa Valley the following day. Gustavo had his vineyard. His first vintage, dedicated to his father, is now on the market.

THE FATHER: A JOYOUS GIFT FOLLOWS A HEARTBREAKING LOSS

A story from Colorado

Michael Desantis is one of the few lucky people whose greatest dream was to be a parent. That happened earlier than expected but soon resulted in a breakup with his girlfriend, and two years later, she moved to another state. He has not seen his daughter in six years. The process was emotionally and financially draining.

Michael, the son of a physicist father whom he only met at age 21, remembers yoyoing between public and private schools. He started public kindergarten a year late and moved to a private school (Waldorf/Steiner education) for first grade. Following that year, he spent second grade in a public school but required a reading tutor who, painfully for him, would remove him from class during reading time for instruction. He returned to the Waldorf school again for grades 3-5. The Waldorf experience infused him with a sense of history and morality. In public schools for grades 6-12, he was active in sports and excelled in math, sciences, and music. But perhaps because he was left to his own devices with no paternal guidance, Michael started to delve into drugs and partying.

After graduating high school, he enrolled in a film school in Denver. There, he found himself back in his element, a Waldorf-type environment. Michael has parlayed his education and jack-of-all-trades acumen (in addition to the various disciplines of videography, he learned coding) into a productive career in which he has never had a boss. His skills have taken him to venues nationwide and gigs with some well-known entertainers.

Michael met his long-term future partner during a semester at the University of Colorado. However, during a three-year period in which they were separated, he met with the previously mentioned woman, who got pregnant early in their relationship. He pursued a relationship with his daughter via the legal system only to be met with a lengthy, bitter, and unproductive entanglement. After a rapprochement with his now partner, he was blessed with another daughter two years ago. As is often the case, the universe will not deny a pure heart.

As a result of the unpleasant episode concerning his daughter, Michael founded a Facebook group called *Strong Fathers, Strong Daughters.* [**Author's Note:** As the father of a daughter, I am a member.] He has also gotten involved at the state level with parents' rights initiatives by testifying at Bill hearings and other assorted initiatives.

The critical point in Michael's life occurred when he started a business in college. Inspired by Ayn Rand's *Atlas Shrugged*, he learned about persistence and standing by one's values. A Libertarian at heart, he believes that Americans must participate more actively in resolving local issues. He asserts that if we all did that, the most significant problems would take care of themselves.

Despite the painful experience of having his first daughter taken away by a vindictive ex, Michael remains a positive individual who advocates for change and hosts a social network where men can extol the virtues of fatherhood to daughters. His professional success is a testimony to his faith in a positive attitude and hard work.

THE WOMAN WHO SPIRITUALLY EMBRACES CANCER

A story from Idaho

Edna was one of four children born in Montreal to educated and sophisticated immigrant parents from Vienna, who arrived at Halifax's Pier 21 in 1953. She was raised in an ethnically diverse community of Europeans and French Canadians, did well in school, and showed an interest in medicine at a very early age. Edna's peaceful life ended at 14 when, at her mother's behest, her parents divorced, an event she blames on the women's liberation movement.

Unable to see her father for years, life was tumultuous, but Edna applied herself in school and excelled at sports. With finances an issue, medical school at McGill University was out of the question, but she studied respiratory therapy and education and spent her 20s teaching. In her late 20s, she met her future husband from New York. Edna, however, had no intent of moving to the United States. After a couple of years of dating and a treacherous night on a boat in Hurricane Charley, 1986, where her then-boyfriend took over from the captain and saved the day, Edna yielded to the karmic attraction and soon found herself living in NYC. Life was getting interesting.

She secured a great job offer in New York due to her professional and academic work in the McGill University medical system, but paperwork issues put her future in peril. Fortuitously for her, the medical profession was so desperately short-staffed that she worked under the radar until her status was legitimate. That occurred a short while before her marriage.

While staying home with children and tending to the house and garden, a former colleague Edna had fired sued her for $7M for wrongful dismissal years after the fact. Although her former employer indemnified her and she won the case, that ordeal extracted an enormous emotional toll. In 2003, now into holistic energy medicine and pursuing doctoral studies, Edna was challenged by an unanticipated divorce. She timidly acquiesced to mediation after being traumatized by the lawsuit and other challenges. It was an unfortunate choice.

Cancer, according to research uncovered by Edna, can often be connected to emotional duress but will typically show up years later. It happened to her father and her brother, who both died young. She also lost five close female relatives to cancer. In 2009, it was her turn with breast cancer. While she had a left-sided lumpectomy done for the first tumor, two more developed within months on the right side, and she was encouraged to go to Brazil for spiritual healing. She practiced energy medicine and, in Brazil, met with the now infamous shaman, John of God. Three months after returning to New York, scientific tests (CAT, MRI, mammograms) showed no signs of cancer.

Post-divorce, Edna continued to co-parent her two children, enjoy relationships, travel, speak, consult, and work in healthcare marketing. The 2008 recession took a toll on real estate investments and finances. Following the breast cancer diagnosis about five years after divorcing, Edna dropped her Ph.D. studies six months short of completion to travel to Brazil. In 2010, Edna moved to Idaho after her children went to college. After ten cancer-free years, during which time she founded a nonprofit called Transcending the Pink, the breast cancer returned. Having lost healthcare coverage in the United States, Edna returned to Canada and McGill University for treatment before returning to Idaho in 2021.

Despite learning that money matters most for holistic, integrative medicine, Edna has continued pursuing integrative medicine protocols for metastatic breast and ovarian cancers. Looking forward, she hopes to continue metabolic-based therapy and wants to move to the East Coast to be closer to her family. In that quest, Edna eagerly anticipates a radical remission. One can only wish this courageous woman well in her next chapter. [**Author's note:** Sadly, Edna died of cancer shortly before publication.]

THE HERO: A POOR JEWISH KID FIGHTS THE NAZIS

A story from Illinois

Art is a WWII war hero who fought in The Battle of the Bulge. That 1944-1945 wintertime battle was part of a major German offensive on the Western Front in an area known as The Ardennes (Belgium, Luxembourg). With over 89,000 casualties and over 19,000 deaths, it was the bloodiest battle for Americans in WWII.

Raised in a poor, working-class neighborhood on the northwest side of Chicago, Art was Jewish but had many friends from various backgrounds. Neither color nor creed meant a whole lot to him while growing up. However, Art noticed Black people in his neighborhood were often deferential and accepted that life would not be easy. Although born poor, Art understood in the 1940s that he had an advantage over some of his friends: white skin.

Shortly after the Americans got involved in the war, Art was in college but knew he had to fight. He'd heard about the Nazi atrocities and had developed a bitter hatred of the Germans. Assigned to Company D, Art learned how to handle heavy weapons. Before the German offensive in which he fought, he decided to befriend a Black soldier who always seemed to be alone. Soon, they were lunch buddies. Despite receiving dirty looks from some, Art's humble upbringing allowed him to traverse boundaries. He remembers an incident in which he came across a dead German soldier. The soldier was about 45 years old and wore a wedding ring. Art wondered about his family. Did he have children? How will his wife find out? At that moment, it was only Art who knew he was dead. He also remembers praying in a foxhole even though he never considered himself religious. It is interesting what can go on in the minds of soldiers under such extreme duress. Even in war, humanity never left him.

Art came very close to being killed one day by incoming mortar fire. Luckily for him, it hit a protruding ice formation so that the destructive energy from the explosion was directed away from where he was standing. It was his closest call to meeting his Maker. On a different day, one of his friends was not so lucky.

One evening, Art found himself in a foxhole with his friend, Jack. Jack was about 30 or so. The next day, as they were marching to meet the enemy, Jack was shot. As death befell his friend, Art suddenly became enraged and lost all sense of his situation. He started to run straight towards the German soldiers, yelling and firing his gun. Luckily for Art, a comrade ran to him and guided him back to safety. But Jack was gone. Art eventually returned home, with his duty to his country served.

After the war, Art worked as an electrical engineer and built a life outside Chicago. In 1953, he was introduced to the love of his life, Janice, a school teacher. They married and had two daughters. He and Janice traveled extensively and visited all but one continent, Antarctica. Sadly, Art's "Puffy" passed away in 2021 from a heart attack after battling Alzheimer's disease. Often, a moment or series of moments defines us. Art can best be described as a true hero. [**Author's note:** Art died late in 2022.]

THE ACCIDENTAL SUCCESS STORY: OR WAS IT, YOU DECIDE

A story from Florida

Terry is an unassuming man whose humble career beginnings resulted in a later payoff which afforded him and his second wife a comfortable lifestyle. He began his long-term career filling empty vending machines, proving that success can be found in many ways.

But one must be ready to seize the day when the opportunity presents itself. Terry was ready.

Terry was raised with three siblings (one is a half-sister) outside of Saint Louis. His father was a commanding man and supportive influence, while his mother was a strict disciplinarian. Although he could have been a more diligent student, he performed well enough to obtain an Associate's degree in business and accounting. He also partook of certain substances during his rebellious youth. Nevertheless, Terry joined the Marine Corps at 18 before leaving at 22. Two years later, because of his training in nuclear, biological, and chemical warfare, they tried to activate him for the first Gulf War. Fortunately, his two-year reserve commitment had expired, and he was spared deployment.

Next for Terry was a series of dead-end, low-pay jobs before he eventually stumbled onto a commission-based job filling vending machines that required a 3 a.m. start. Remarkably, the money was quite good, so he decided to stick with it. As time progressed, although he was not particularly enamored with the work, he was promoted repeatedly and one day found himself running the company. While in that executive role, Terry heard about a company promoting a game-changing product that could transmit real-time data from vending machines. Following a presentation he attended in Michigan, he met with the company's owner and agreed to give the product a trial run. It worked wonderfully, but the owner of his company lacked vision and refused to invest. Discouraged, Terry resigned and began his own home inspection business.

One fateful day, while cleaning out some old stuff, Terry came across the contact information from the technology company. After touching base with the owner, he boarded a plane in 2007 destined for California, and, after a delay, a job offer was made. Over time, he acquired stock in the company, and in 2018, when the company was purchased, Terry cashed in for financial security.

Terry married his high school sweetheart after having been separated for several years following school, during which time she had three children. Despite sensing his marital relationship never seemed whole, he was a good father and raised them as his own. His youngest daughter gave birth to twins born three months prematurely. While both had brain hemorrhaging, one was so severe there was little chance of survival. Not a religious man, Terry nonetheless prayed for the baby. That baby lived while the healthier one died due to a hospital mistake. That cruel irony marked the lowest time of his life, superseding even the death of his parents in 2018 just days apart.

Terry was blessed with material paternal influence, three children, service to his country, and a diligent work ethic that has borne financial security. But his greatest blessing occurred with his 2015 remarriage to a woman as well-grounded as him.

A VIETNAM VETERAN SERVES HIS COUNTRY AND OVERCOMES POVERTY

A story from Illinois

Rick grew up the personification of the face of poverty even though, as a child, he was not fully cognizant of his unfortunate lot in life. After losing his father at age 5, he, his older brother, and his mother were hurled into the elements with a minuscule safety net. The Social Security payments his mother (who could not afford to work full time with two small children to look after) received totaled about $120 per month in the 1950s. An extended family and an understanding landlord helped when possible, but that could not prevent Rick from his teenage destiny in which he painfully learned the reality of his plight. Despite the economic hardships, he credits his mother for providing an affectionate environment and, along with a beloved uncle who taught him responsibility, imbued him with aspirations to escape the pernicious cycle of poverty.

Rick joined the Army after graduating high school and engaging in life for one year as a self-described bum. It was Vietnam time, and Rick was a devoted patriot who wanted to serve his country and defend its values from the communist threat. While many who enlisted or were drafted took an easier route, Rick was willing to put his life on the line in seeking combat. Think what you may about that war; to this day, he is particularly proud of his service as a helicopter gunner. Like all wars, it brought out the best and worst in people. He relates one incident in which his crew discovered a young, solitary figure who was a potential Viet Cong. Rick, from the helicopter's rear, aimed his machine gun, at which point the youth fearfully ran. Rather than kill a questionable combatant, Rick shot over his head until he disappeared into the thick forest.

Upon his return to the United States, Rick found himself in the South and soon married. Following the dissolution of that ill-advised three-year entanglement, he returned to Chicago to make a new start. He remarried, this time to a woman who had two boys. That marriage would stick, and together, they had another son. Life was starting to become normal.

Vocationally, Rick worked at a mediocre job in Chicago that entailed a long commute. After asking for a raise, his boss declined and said, "Take it or leave it." So, he left. His goal of becoming a freelance commercial artist had begun, and his income went from $14k to $50k per year. Rick was achieving escape velocity from a potentially crushing and precarious existence.

Like anyone who has walked this earth for 76 years, Rick has seen it all. His high point was becoming a father to his wife's children and, on equal footing, having a biological child. Family means everything. On the flip side, the death of his uncle, his pseudo-father, hit Rick hard. Finally, and not surprisingly for a former soldier who saw so much death, he says respect for life is humanity's preeminent value.

Although not affluent, Rick escaped poverty, built a life that includes a nearly 50-year marriage, has close relationships with his children and grandchildren, and continues to work independently as a graphical designer and website developer. Rick built the prototype for *The Life Chronicler* website, on which this book project was documented.

REJECTING HIS WEALTH, A TORMENTED SOUL SEEKS A NEW WORLD

A story from Ontario

RJ is a member of a rare club. Born to an overbearing father who had immigrated to Canada and a quiescent mother, he had two sisters and found prosperity in the real estate business his father started. By 30, he had turned his back on the enterprise and his father to live a subsistent life in Toronto. A gifted athlete who could have turned professional in either skateboarding or snowboarding, RJ decided not to work for six years but instead joined the local flourishing sand volleyball community, where he once again excelled. Since then, RJ has been seeking meaning and living in the moment while developing a philosophy based on compassion that he is particularly eager to share.

RJ's relationship with his father was never on solid ground. In his early years, his parents occasionally left him and his sisters to their own devices. Some would call it abandonment. As he grew, he realized this had instilled a sense of freedom. However, like many sons, he wanted desperately to please his father, so he followed him into the real estate business. RJ became the rock in the background essential to a successful enterprise. Before long, he was driving an expensive car, and the family had moved into a beautiful house euphemistically known as "The White House." The mixed-race family had attained success, and he was an integral part of it. Problematic feelings, however, do not always dissipate with financial success. RJ felt compelled to pursue his destiny.

RJ seeks to understand. In his 30s, he flew to the Thai/Burmese border to illegally live in a refugee camp. After a month, the authorities found out and threatened arrest if he did not leave, so he did. RJ seeks to influence. After learning about Warren Buffett's social consciousness, RJ drove to Omaha, slept in his car for 26 days, and left a letter at Berkshire Hathaway's office for Buffett every day. Getting no response except for a conversation with security, he ingeniously learned of Buffett's home address and left a note in the mailbox. The next day, he received a call from security asking him to leave permanently. Upon returning home, RJ sent Buffett a certified check for about $100,000, asking for a few minutes of the mogul's time to talk about critical social issues and how the wealthy can help. It represented about 50% of his net worth, as was noted in the letter. Buffett sent the check back with a personal note intimating that although he admired his conviction, thanks, but no thanks. In 2010, about 5-6 years later, Buffett and Bill Gates announced the creation of The Giving Pledge, urging the world's billionaires to donate at least 50% of their wealth to philanthropic causes. Quoting The Giving Pledge[8] website, "It is inspired by the example set by millions of people at all income levels who give generously." Did RJ, a Berkshire Hathaway shareholder, remarkably plant the seed for this 50% giving movement via his interaction with The Oracle of Omaha?

Sadly, RJ can't see his beloved daughter, "Bow Bows," whom he fathered with a woman from a prominent family before COVID-19. Upon learning of his new relationship, she and her family ceased honoring their informal, non-binding visitation agreement.

While RJ hopes for a renewed relationship with his father, he is pessimistic that humankind will deal with pressing issues such as homelessness, the environment, and hunger. Nonetheless, he has become his own man by proselytizing these causes to whoever will listen and continues to seek support from those with the resources to effect change. [**Author's note:** RJ's father took his own life about six months after this story was written. They never reconciled.]

---

[8] https://givingpledge.org/

THE WANNABE TEACHER WHO BECAME AN NHL HEAD COACH

A story from Oregon

I have known Mike since second grade, and we were roommates in our first year at Acadia University in Nova Scotia. Like me, Mike was athletically inclined and, unlike me, most gifted at hockey. Born into a loving, faithful, and supportive family, he did well in school and had thoughts of being a teacher. It turned out he realized his dream, just in a different manner.

It all started in Australia, as most great hockey careers naturally do. Following his university playing days at Acadia University and then Brandon University in Manitoba, with a dearth of teaching opportunities on his plate, Mike and another childhood buddy drafted by the Toronto Maple Leafs decided to look at playing opportunities in Europe. While at Brandon, Mike played in a few European countries, including Austria. After getting in touch with a contact who had names, she mistakenly gave him contact information for someone in Australia. "No, Austria," Mike exclaimed. Well, he got the European information he needed, but since he had the Australian guy's contact information, he thought, why not write to him also. And like Jed Clampett, the next thing ya know, Mike and Ray are off to Sydney to play.

The opportunity to play came with responsibility. Mike had to coach at all levels to help the Australians build a viable hockey program. Although Mike had no tangible coaching experience, he had the one intangible and unquestionable ultimate qualification. He was Canadian! To his youthful charges in Sydney, this gave him Odin-like abilities.

After two seasons in Australia, Mike returned home, applied for a head coaching position at a junior college in Alberta, and was awarded the job. By his fifth year, he had taken a formerly mediocre team to a fourth-place finish at the national championships. Mike moved up one level from there by assuming the head coaching job at the University of New Brunswick. While at UNB, he took that languishing program to a spot in the national rankings.

Mike's coaching resume grew with stints as Head Coach of Canada's National Team and associate coaching positions in the National Hockey League in Vancouver and Los Angeles. Following Los Angeles, he joined the WHL's (a Junior league) Portland, Oregon franchise as, ultimately, Vice President/General Manager/Head Coach. In 2014, he was offered his dream coaching job as Head Coach of the NHL's Pittsburgh Penguins. Unfortunately, like the fate of most coaches, Mike was fired part way into season two at Pittsburgh and returned to Portland.

Before his Pittsburgh job, Mike experienced a professional low in Portland when the WHL suspended him from coaching for alleged recruiting violations. At that time, a witch hunt reverberated throughout Canadian hockey, and somebody had to be served up. The suspension was lifted at the end of the season. The fact the coveted Pittsburgh offer materialized is a vindication of Mike by the hockey world.

Mike will tell you he is a teacher first and a coach second. He instills values first in his young players and then in hockey instruction. The 80 to 90 goals he carries on paper and revises every three years testify to how he believes people can achieve great things.

THE AIR FORCE CALLS AND THE INNER-CITY KID RESPONDS

A story from Texas

Antonio is a former United States Air Force enlisted airman who, by age 50, had lived half of his life abroad. His demeanor is calm and precise, as expected from any individual with such regimented training and intercultural exposure.

Born in Chicago, Antonio and his family moved to Buffalo around the age of ten as his sometimes-abusive stepfather had found a better job. His deeply religious mother was the rock of the family; she managed the finances and invited her stepson to join Antonio and his younger stepsister. Unmotivated by academics in high school, the foul-mouthed youth joined the Air Force and, at age 18, found himself doing basic training in San Antonio, Texas. Not long after being assigned to Plattsburgh Air Force Base in New York, he enrolled in an educational program at his supervisor's suggestion. Antonio was about to forge an academic legacy.

Antonio finished a two-year Associate's degree, Bachelor's degrees in Management Studies and English, and a Master's in International Relations. He was working on his Ph.D. in Organizational Leadership when his interest dissipated following the death of his program chairperson. Later, while working on a Master's degree in Divinity Studies, Antonio received a cancer diagnosis, forcing him to drop that program.

Divorced in 2001, Antonio has four children with the same woman, who now live in three countries. He left the Air Force in 2002 to join the civil service and remarried in the late 2000s. Unfortunately, for various pragmatic reasons, that union lasted only months. At that time, he was living in Arlington, Virginia, before moving to his present residence in San Antonio. One of the high points in Antonio's life was finding his biological roots via Ancestry.com. Although he learned his father was deceased, he was successful in connecting with four siblings. On the flip side, he had to conquer prostate cancer about the same time as his daughter faced a challenging health crisis. Additionally, Antonio experienced a parent's worst nightmare with the tragic death of a son.

In 1983, Antonio began his walk with Jesus Christ. It started innocently enough when a buddy refused to hit the town with him one evening. He was a Christian seeking to be more faithful. Alone,

Antonio returned to his room and opened a book published by the Watchtower Organization that contained writings germane to the Jehovah's Witness faith. That night, Antonio was overcome by an ethereal euphoria but simultaneously felt an ominous presence that he dealt with by prayer. Something had existentially changed. Today, he attends a large nondenominational church. In 2003, while dealing with conflicting internal strife, he sensed a message from God in his heart that relieved the conflict and served as a lasting memory of God's existence and love. This spiritual healing experience taught him that atonement was not in pursuing vocational ministry but simply by being a good father.

The unscholarly, rough-around-the-edges inner-city kid has an advanced education, has seen the world, and has overcome cancer. He remains devoted to being present for his children and strives to walk daily in faith with Christ.

BIRTH FAMILY CHAOS, FOSTER FAMILY CHAOS, A BOY IS SAVED

A story from New Hampshire

Dan did not have an auspicious debut in life. Born into a drug-addicted family, he had a brother two years his senior and a much older maternal half-brother. Although both parents worked hard, much went to support their addicted lifestyle; his mother, mostly alcohol, and his father, cocaine. Dan's half-brother, also a substance abuser, and his father never got along. Ultimately, tragedy befell the hapless family when Dan's half-brother killed their father during a drug-fueled dispute. With his half-brother out of the picture, his mother tried to keep the small family together, but sadly, family life ended two years later for Dan at the tender age of six.

The foster care system is broken, and the reason will surprise nobody: money. That is Dan's conclusion. His foster family had six other children in the house. There were not even enough beds, let alone other necessities. His foster mother was a wretched human being. In contrast, his foster father, a decent person and nurse, was ultimately overwhelmed by his wife, and his response to the dilemma was to abdicate involvement. Dan increasingly found himself looking for any means to escape. One good experience he had from those years was doing outside chores. It allowed him to escape temporarily and provided a vital lesson about the intrinsic value of work, something he never forgot.

Dan was figuratively reborn at age ten when he and his brother were adopted by a loving couple in their 50s. Who does that?! Rather propitiously, his adoptive mother was an English teacher. At the time of his adoption, Dan was reading at a first-grade level, although enrolled in fourth grade. By the end of the school year, he was reading at a sixth-grade level. However, since working with numbers is his innate strength, he enrolled in a tech school for high school. In addition to academics, Dan started to study carpentry. Dan enrolled in an elite high school after moving from Connecticut to Florida for his junior year. His brilliance in the sciences inspired his chemistry teacher to apply to university on his behalf, leading to a full athletic scholarship. Dan, incidentally, was a soccer star and an accomplished piano player. The life of chaos was in the rear-view mirror, or so it seemed.

Despite obvious potential, having completed high school with a 3.9 GPA, Dan turned down the scholarship and attended school for heavy machinery operations. He wanted to be a family man as soon as possible, so he believed a university career was not for him. Upon moving back to Connecticut, Dan started to plan a wedding with his fiancé. Before he could get married, that relationship dissolved, and Dan found himself, at age 19, getting into trouble with the law. Paradoxically, he moved into the home of his biological mother, abandoning the secure grounding imparted to him by his adoptive parents. It took him almost five years to extricate himself.

With parental encouragement, Dan sold his landscaping business and moved to New Hampshire for construction work. After doing so, his girlfriend joined him, but today, she is merely a best friend. Now stable, Dan recently bought a home and is concentrating on building a secure financial life, something a potential bride would undoubtedly find appealing. One cannot help but cheer for this man whose motto is, "Just do better."

FINDING LOVE AT 15, AN INCURABLE DIAGNOSIS, A REEVALUATION

A story from Nova Scotia

Barbara has found purpose in the face of adversity. After finding a life-long soulmate at the tender age of 15 to "witness" her life, not even her husband's heartbreaking diagnosis of a rare neurological disorder, *corticobasal ganglionic degeneration* (CBGD), in 2011 could prevent her indomitable spirit from being a beacon to all.

Born into a stable and responsible family, Barbara had an older brother, a younger sister, and a half-sister from her mother's previous marriage. Life could occasionally be unpredictable, which was ostensibly the case as she, for some reason, assumed the mantle as the perceived favorite one. Unsurprisingly, this caused resentment from her brother and younger sister that lingers today. In addition to other privileges, Barbara received private dance lessons that she and Paul, her husband, leveraged to become competitive ballroom dancers.

A tall girl from a young age, Barbara often felt awkward and insecure. Nevertheless, she became a fluid reader in her church and was actively involved in Girl Guides. She did very well in school and had aspirations of becoming a teacher. However, following a major *faux pas* from a trusted high school guidance counselor who informed her history was not mandatory for university acceptance, Barbara decided to drop the subject. This led to great disappointment when her application was rejected. Although her unachieved dream of attending university remains a regret, she found a rewarding career in the airline business that enabled a lifetime of travel. Finally, Barbara demonstrated mature, adult-like sagacity when, at age 18, she purchased an island and cottage with money she had saved from her teenage working career. That feat won her the sometimes-elusive paternal approval many inevitably seek.

Barbara's love interest was not well received by her family as he was Catholic and she was Anglican. Things changed for the better following a tête-à-tête he had with her father. Following marriage at 21, life was good as financial security, dancing, and travel found her. Barbara, however, never wanted to have children. That changed after she unexpectedly found herself pregnant with a girl. A few years later, a second girl arrived. After each successful pregnancy, she experienced miscarriages. In between the birth of her girls, at age 32, she lost her mother. As the years went by, and perhaps simply by sharing the experience of parenthood, Barbara began to understand her demanding father better. In so doing, she acknowledges compassion as humanity's preeminent value.

For many, the CBGD diagnosis of a spouse would lead to inevitable self-pity. Thankfully, that limited thinking had no embrace on Barbara. Following a cathartic reassessment of life and its often-entropic journey, Barbara decided it was time for a third "child." This spawned a commitment to leave behind a sizable insurance policy for charitable causes. In doing so, Barbara has ensured that she and her beloved of 49 years will live on after exiting this plane of existence.

THE SELF-PERCEIVED UNDERACHIEVER FINDS HIS WAY REGARDLESS

A story from Connecticut

Eli is an unassuming scientist who finally got married after a false start in the era of COVID-19. He met his wife during the chapter of his life which he titled "Hobbies are for Life Partners." An avid aficionado of ceramics, he met his wife in a class, although he did not initially have romantic thoughts. He cherished the friendship and did not want to impinge upon that. He figured he would be forced to find another class elsewhere if his advance was rebuffed. So, naturally, she asked him out. Eli's eyes were opened, and things ultimately led to a planned wedding ceremony for June 2020. Oops. They married in a small ceremony in July 2020 but had two 2021 backup dates for a large ceremony. Sadly, neither happened.

Eli grew up in a supportive and affectionate family with two wonderful older sisters, one of whom has always inspired him because of a specific physical challenge she endures. As a somewhat overweight kid growing up, Eli had an uncomfortable body image about himself even though he participated in sports. While Eli, like many boys, experienced social insecurities in school, he did well in his studies and was especially inspired by his chemistry and physics teachers. Despite aptitude tests that indicated he would best be served by seeking an artistic career, he went to university to study the sciences, particularly pharmacy.

Eli was ready for the real world after completing his Bachelor's and Ph.D. degrees at the University of Wisconsin. His doctorate program had been a mixed bag in which he was not pushed, nor did he particularly apply himself. So, with minimal academic connections and very few publications to his credit, he concluded a career in the private pharmaceutical business world made the most sense. At 28, he accepted an introductory post at Hospira. That company soon became a part of Pfizer, with which he had envisioned an association long before it materialized. Following a stint in India, Eli returned home and moved through the ranks, ultimately leading to his latest posting in Connecticut, where he recently purchased a home and is considering having children. Life for this easy-going man was unfolding commensurate with his background.

Although Eli has achieved in a notable and predictive manner, given his upbringing and innate talents, it was not without tribulations. In addition to his insecure body image, he has an unsettling feeling that he never really lived up to self-imposed expectations. This was most acute concerning his graduate school activities. After joining Hospira, despite being in a committed relationship, Eli accepted an offer to spend several months in India, perhaps a compensatory move to ameliorate self-doubts about accomplishment. Concerning his body image issue, Eli is in excellent shape and physically active today.

Few individuals have the aptitude to aspire to acquire a Ph.D. degree, and even fewer achieve it. Only the most highly esteemed employees would be asked to spend time in India as part of their corporate training. Whether he realizes it or not, Eli, the unassuming scientist, is unquestionably an elite achiever.

NAVY PILOT FIGHTS THE 9/11 BATTLE, MORPHS AS AN ENTREPRENEUR

A story from Florida

Jim's life changed when he was only in second grade. Following his parents' divorce, he lived with a newly working mother, resulting in a heightened sense of independence. In seventh grade, he and his younger brother moved in with their father while his two sisters stayed behind. His brother moved back a year later, so it was just Jim and his dad. Like his mom, his dad was a hands-off parent, so Jim needed to learn autonomy.

An industrious youth, Jim took a liking to the sky. His father gifted him a flying lesson for his 16th birthday, and the deal was sealed. Jim was destined to be a pilot. The summer before his senior year in high school, he approached the Air Force but was met with an aloof reception. A Navy recruiter at the same mall approached him and convinced him to sign up. Despite receiving average grades in school, he aced multiple Navy aptitude testing regiments and entered the highly selective nuclear reactor training program.

A few years later, not long after the start of the first Gulf War, Jim studied mechanical engineering at the Naval Academy. He needed a degree to be an officer, a prerequisite for pilots. A man with some moxie, he finagled his way into an exclusive ceremony to meet John Glenn of Ohio. Upon hearing that Jim was an aspiring pilot from his home state, Glenn intimated a secret that he was planning on entering space one last time. He did. As matrimonial vows were prohibited for Naval Academy students, Jim and his sweetheart were married following graduation. He delayed enrollment in flight school to live near Alexandria, Virginia, where his wife worked.

Serendipitously, Jim's next adventure started as, after saving a woman great embarrassment, she got him into a Special Operations intern role for the Joint Chiefs of Staff while he was merely an ensign. In real life, that does not happen for ensigns. From there, it was on to Pensacola for flight school to realize his childhood ambition. In addition to preventing terrorism while in Special Operations, Jim saw airborne action on several fronts, including during the Balkans explosion prompted by Yugoslavia's disintegration and also in the Far East cleaning out Al-Qaeda camps in the Philippines. After three years based in Japan, he spent three more years working on covert activities before ending his active duty in 2007. It was time for his reserves chapter.

That reserve era lasted until 2020, when he served as a test pilot for NASA, flew corporate jets, and founded an aviation company. When COVID-19 plagued our society, Jim started his new company, deploying Honda jets to cater to upscale travelers.

In Jim's personal life, his father's estrangement is a source of acquiescence from which he sees no relief. Notwithstanding his paternal dismay, he fathered a daughter and learned from his wife how to be a more complete, empathetic human. As he reflects on his service to his country, Jim believes the work being done in the land of our Middle East adversaries is paying off in the attitudes of their young, who reject the oppression in their countries. Over the long term, this, he asserts, will bode well for humanity.

FRACTALS: GOING WHERE NO MAN/WOMAN HAS GONE BEFORE

A story from Washington (state)

Fractal (def.): a curve or geometric figure, each part of which has the same statistical character as the whole. Geeky math, but nature is replete with fractals. Snowflakes, for example. Rob Leonard's ambitious goal is to create art that is fractal-based. To the best of his knowledge, he is the only one anywhere in the world attempting to master this intricate realm of math via physical art. His art can be found on the *Mathscaper* website[9].

Rob, whose favorite word is undoubtedly "curiosity," has had an eclectic journey. He recalls his early years when he enjoyed incessantly playing outdoors in the Vail area of Colorado. After moving to Seattle aged seven, he was involved in a severe car accident on the long commute to school. His mother subsequently moved with Rob and his sister to be closer to the school, likely precipitating his parents' divorce. He finished high school requirements at a community college where he could concentrate on skiing. It was also at that time that he discovered his affinity for computers. He eventually started a consulting business as a teenager and lost interest in formal schooling, much to his parents' chagrin.

Not long after that, Rob found his way into a tech startup, where he had the good fortune to learn about the business from the ground up. His passion for startup entities was born. After resigning, one of the primary investors offered him another opportunity. With that offer, he started a company he later sold for a handsome profit. However, after working for one year as contractually obligated following the sale, Rob found himself a father to a daughter with a woman he had no intention of marrying and lost himself to drugs and alcohol.

---

[9] www.mathscaper.com

A father, unemployed, addicted, and going broke, Rob's life looked a lot different from prior years. Following a heartfelt talk with his older sister, he was inspired to seek help. With situational help from some friends and a bit of luck, he found a job in the staffing business owned by a former client. In that role, he learned a new skill set: people skills. His human capital was now developing as a double threat.

A few years later, after the staffing business had been sold, Rob started a sales and business development job at Orb Optronix. During his time there, he soaked up knowledge of optical metrology and other cutting-edge engineering. His next gig was at a startup, Next Lighting (innovative LED lighting). At Next, Rob's autodidactic nature served him well, and despite no pedigreed education, he had his name on more than one intellectual property submission. He also made good money, but the business model ultimately failed, so it was time to move on to another lighting company, Echelon, as Regional Director of Sales. After leaving Echelon in 2018, he joined a product development company, Pensar (medical devices, Xbox), as Managing Director. In July 2022, he parted on happy terms.

Rob, now married and with a one-year-old, has recently entered a partnership to pursue his love for technical things (fractal math and physics) and merge them with art. This self-taught man also has ambitions of building an in-residence artist's dorm in a section of his art studio.

EVEN THE FORTUNATE ONES HAVE THEIR BATTLES TO FIGHT

A story from California

Ephemeral (a pseudonym) was born into an environment about which many can only dream. Her parents attended Harvard University, and each earned a Ph.D. (anthropologists). She has visited many countries and attended one of the famed boarding schools in

Switzerland while her parents plied their talents in the Far East. Life was going to be fabulous.

Ephemeral's parents encouraged her and her two brothers to achieve and provided an excellent environment to grow up. When not living in Europe, she lived a stone's throw away from the ocean playground in southern California and loved riding horses. Ephemeral worked hard in school, garnered awards, and chose to attend Brown University in Rhode Island primarily because of its open curriculum approach to education. She majored in psychology with a minor in partying. The latter led to struggles she had to address later in life.

After graduating from Brown University and having to live with "the one that got away," Ephemeral moved back to California to work and have a good time. By the time her late 20s came, she was managing real estate properties in Los Angeles and decided it was time to up the ante and pursue an MBA at UCLA in Marketing. It did not take long for her to realize her misguided thinking, and by the time she was in her mid-30s, she had completed her Master's and Ph.D. psychology degrees. She married in her mid-30s and had a son, only to be divorced before age 40. While Ephemeral's 30s "sweet and sour" decade was tumultuous, she found herself professionally. She eschewed the corporate world and was practicing as a psychologist in her own business. That decade also featured the death of her father and health problems that, at one point, reduced her to being on disability. Her mother moved to Palm Springs a couple of years after the death of her husband, and Ephemeral followed. She set up shop in the desert and has been there since, despite that not being her imagined life blueprint. She was an ocean gal.

A psychologist's job is to help others deal with acute problems. Although Ephemeral cannot recall the exact year she decided to join Alcoholics Anonymous, it was essential to her well-being that she did. The many years of ignoring the obvious needed to end. She found that people from diverse backgrounds were more similar than different during the process. She found catharsis in the melting away of the pain and shame with which one is burdened when having debilitating addictions. In others, she witnessed empathy that has undoubtedly impacted how she listens and empathizes with patients she is commissioned to help.

Medical news for Ephemeral has not been good for quite some time. She suffers from chronic pain, not to mention a handful of other afflictions. Two things help her cope. The first is mindfulness, and one can only suspect that her parents' interest in Eastern philosophies somehow rubbed off. Her other coping mechanism is engagement with others. She is a beacon for the people in her life, and in that way, she helps herself. Nonetheless, very recent medical news will be daunting for her to navigate.

Ephemeral has lived a wonderful and challenging life, and she draws on this experience to help others as a clinician.

THE VOLCANO MAN!

A story from Utah

How does the destiny of those with a destiny beyond the commonplace unfold? Is it determined by a series of purposeful decisions? Or is it determined by a confluence of events, some of which are beyond the individual's control? For G. Brad Lewis, it was unquestionably a combination of the two.

Born last with two older sisters into a maternally led family from which his father left when Brad was young, a working mom offered him the opportunity to discover his sanctuary, the great outdoors, on his terms. Seeking male influences, he gravitated to the Boy Scouts and became the youngest Eagle Scout in the Western United States. A fifth-grade teacher, Mr. Thomas, helped Brad cope with a severe stutter and instilled confidence in the lad. Later in life, Brad would (divinely?) postpone a trip to thank him for the significant influence he imparted, not knowing that just a few days later, his beloved teacher would die.

After he and his mother moved from Salt Lake City to Denver, Brad longed to see his friends and engage with the environment he knew. He moved back to live with his sister, who wrote notes explaining his frequent absences from school. He wasn't sick; he was immersing himself in his sanctuary by either skiing or climbing. Nonetheless, Brad was a straight-A student, and with his strict disciplinarian mother in Denver, for her, nothing was amiss.

Brad attended the University of Utah but dropped out after recognizing neither English nor Psychology was his future. Having had a camera since the age of five and having a childhood steeped in nature, he soon found himself on an epic journey that would set the table for the rest of his life. Brad was Alaska-bound. He arrived with $50 and a rickety Volkswagen bus. On day one, he was offered a jade cutter job in the Brooks Range after walking into a photography store occupied by owners who knew his grandparents. On a drive to Homer on day two, he picked up a hitchhiker who invited him to stay at a cabin with her and her husband. That unexpected event led to a gentleman's agreement for Brad to buy the place someday. During his first two days in Alaska, he had a job and a house lined up. Life was good.

Over the next few years, Brad held down several jobs: cook, field investigator, and archeologist. While doing mineral exploration, he learned to fly a helicopter under the tutelage of a legendary Canadian, Ron Sheardown. One day, he bumped into an old Utah buddy who convinced him to take a trip to Hawaii. There, he found his true calling. A gifted nature photographer, he was gobsmacked by the 1983 eruption of Kilauea and, naturally, took pictures. To make a long story short, G. Brad Lewis is now known as The Volcano Man. His work has been covered by numerous national and international publications and the media. His love of nature, his decision to visit Alaska, and an unexpected meeting with an old buddy had led Brad to his destiny.

Brad married a woman he met in Alaska and had a daughter, but a divorce followed her coming of age. He also suffered the pain of losing his younger half-brother when he cut off all contact for no apparent reason. Despite this, Brad's quest for being present with nature has always grounded him.

A NEGLECTED JEWISH KID MEETS THE CHALLENGE

A story from Nevada

Steve grew up in a family where he was the youngest of three children and was unsure if he was wanted. His father was a fundamentally good man but engaged much more with his older children. His mother suffered from emotional challenges that became more acute with time. When he was nine, his parents divorced. After that, his home environment became increasingly toxic following his mother's remarriage to a man with a gambling problem that Steve deemed mentally ill. That man eventually committed suicide.

Since Steve was not particularly close to his family, he found refuge with good friends, some of whom remain in his life to this day. He had an affinity for aviation and obtained a pilot's license at 17. Immediately following college, he took the Air Force exam but failed due to poor vision. Aside from that post-graduation disappointment, Steve's college years were liberating. He discovered he had a talent for selling and sold ads for the school newspaper and ascended to the position of advertising manager. Later, he sold ads for a local phone book and made so much money that it took years after graduation to reach that income level again. A businessman was in the making.

Steve eventually took a sales job working for his biological father's company in Chicago. He did well, selling silver-related products, but felt that there were better choices than working for his father. Steve found himself out of a job after the Hunt brothers failed to corner the silver market, which saw the price spike to $52 per ounce. Next up was a sales job in the pharmaceutical business. Once again, Steve did well, but the internal politics of the large company grated on him. In one specific case, he hired a Black woman despite discouraging moral suasion from his manager. She was the best candidate but had a subpar credit report because of her sister's imprudent ways. For Steve, things were never quite the same. He started work on an MBA degree with an accounting concentration. Following some part-time accounting work and filled with confidence in his hard (accounting) and soft (sales) skills, he quit his pharma job and opened his own shop. He ran his own show until his recent semi-retirement in the desert.

Steve married in his early 30s while still in the pharma business. In his mid-40s, he and his wife traveled to China with a group and returned home with a daughter. That's how I met him. I was in the same group. Today, his only child is a highly responsible young woman studying and working as a part-time paramedic in Las Vegas. He acknowledges the experience of adopting his daughter as his life's high point.

In his vocation, Steve has worked with many wealthy individuals. For some, he says, people see their self-worth inexorably linked to their bank account. But as merely their accountant, he is hardly there to provide moral counseling. This long-term exposure has undoubtedly left an indelible, positive imprint on his egalitarian philosophy of life.

Steve surmounted the childhood challenges of chaos and isolation. His value-driven life began a successful career as an entrepreneur and the blessings of an enduring marriage and adoptive fatherhood.

THE DEPRESSION ERA GIRL AND WARTIME NURSE

A story from Florida (written by Lois in the third person)

Lois is one of the few people today who can vividly remember the Great Depression. She was born in 1925, four years before the stock market crash and subsequent repercussions such as 25% unemployment, soup kitchens to feed those in need, and men going door to door asking for any job in exchange for food.

Lois recalls overhearing her parents talking about their inability to pay the rent on their tiny house. Her mother asked, "David, will they put our furniture on the sidewalk?" Luckily, he found a home in bankruptcy and could buy it with a small sum borrowed from a close friend. Lois was six years old at the time. Her parents, five children, an aunt, and her grandpa lived in a three-bedroom house with one bathroom. Families doubled up in those times. David had been a real estate broker, but with no money available to buy property, he had to close his office.

Since she lived 75 years in the 20th century, Lois wanted to tell what it was like to live in that period. Antisemitism and racial discrimination were rampant in the years before and during WWII. It was a time when celebrities like Henry Ford, Charles Lindbergh, and Father Coughlin spewed hatred on the radio. Radio was America's leading entertainment, and families gathered around the radio after dinner to listen. Television was not widely available until the 1950s. Racial discrimination in grade school was the reason Black children were taught in what everyone called the "shacks," shabbily built structures on the grounds of the big school where white children attended. In her senior year of high school, Japan bombed Pearl Harbor, and America was at war.

Lois joined the Nurses Cadet Corps to relieve her father's financial pressure. Since all the nurses were joining the military, the government had to do something to ease the acute shortage of nurses in local hospitals. The Cadet Corps offered full tuition, uniforms, and a $15/month stipend.

The war ended in August 1945, and the men returned home. They got jobs, married, bought homes, and the economy was booming. In 1945, Lois received a call from Phil, a fellow who lived next door to her when they were children. He was a tank driver in the Marine Corps in the Pacific battles. It was a brutal experience, especially the battle of Iwo Jima. Phil had been dating a girl before the war, and they corresponded while he was away. He expected they would marry when he returned, but she had fallen in love with another man and told him upon his arrival. Phil's sister suggested he call Lois. They were married for 69 years until Phil died in 2014.

Lois's loving family includes her caring older daughter and her significant other, her lovely middle daughter and her husband, her talented son and his wife, her sweet grandson, and her fabulous granddaughter and grandson-in-law, who are expecting a baby girl. She keeps in touch with her many wonderful nieces and nephews. Lois said that when her great-granddaughter arrives, her life will be complete.

GO-WITH-THE-FLOW TO FINDING A LIFE PURPOSE AFTER AGE 60

A story from Nova Scotia

Paul has been my best friend since we met in seventh grade. When our paths diverged after high school and then university, we stayed in touch via the proxy of sports and a long-lasting chess game that took over 20 years to play. Writer's prerogative: I won. Sorry, Paul, I could not help myself. Before COVID-19, we had somewhat lost touch but reconnected as many did when the scourge befell us. Much had changed in Paul's life.

Paul and his younger brother were raised in a responsible and stable family he described as distant. His father was an avowed atheist, and, for some reason Paul could never discern, his agnostic mother had him clandestinely baptized in an Anglican church. His father was utterly incommunicado on the matter. Despite the baptism, he has no recollection of ever attending church. His parents separated while he was still in school, and his brother left the home shortly after graduating from high school. It was just Paul and his mom. A mature father/son relationship never really materialized.

Following high school, Paul was uncertain about what he wanted to do. Without familial encouragement to continue his education, he was adrift. At some point, cooking dawned on him as a potential career. He figured he would find something else if it didn't work out. Over time, Paul graduated from being a short-order cook at a fast-food establishment to sous-chef at an elite golf course, from which he recently retired.

In his 20s with no girlfriend and perhaps symbolic of his take-life-as-it-comes persona, Paul had not yet acquired a driver's license. Like Forest Gump, if he had to go somewhere, he was running. He eventually completed a marathon and posted a respectable time that would have been remarkable (projected 2:45) had his legs not died at the 20-mile mark. It is around 20 miles, otherwise known as *the wall,* when a runner's glycogen is often depleted.

Paul was also an active basketball player, and through this sport, he met Nancy, a devout Catholic. This spiritual water and oil emulsion soon had two children. After his children were grown, things got interesting for him in a very unexpected way.

While Nancy never forced Paul to become an active Catholic, he did start to attend church. Now a fervent Catholic, Paul ascribes to the view that the Holy Spirit works through a slow conversion. That was his experience. Today, he leads prayers and worship for a men's group, helps feed the needy, and referees basketball. He relates the story of a mentally and physically challenged kid who participated but couldn't compete with the other boys. Witnessing this, Paul quietly told both coaches that he would call a phantom foul that would put the kid on the free-throw line. The kid swishes the first, and the crowd goes nuts! As my best friend told me this story, I welled up. Paul, the formerly consummate go-with-the-flow guy, had found his purpose.

FORMER SPORTS STAR, A CALIFORNIA DREAM, HITTING ROCK BOTTOM; A NEW LIFE?

A story from Kentucky

The world is replete with sports stars who peak in high school or university and then disappear into the ether. Keith could have found a home in that club except for his indomitable spirit. He was the youngest of three children and had the misfortune of having a hoops star brother whose accomplishments he superseded despite being overlooked growing up. A scrappy kid with an affinity for physical confrontation, Keith constantly needed to prove himself worthy of attention.

Born near Philadelphia into a nomadic family, Keith lived in six states before age ten. That ceased upon their arrival in Cincinnati. There, the multi-sport athlete became an All-State hoops and soccer star in high school and then played basketball at Bellarmine University in Louisville. There, he started to study psychology but, with family encouragement, soon switched to business as it seemed more practical. Just before his senior year began, a summer fling came with a consequence: Keith was about to assume financial responsibility for his daughter upon graduating college.

Keith's religious parents took the mother and daughter in, and Keith found himself an outcast. After his graduation, he found work in the legal services industry but also experienced fear, resentment, anger, and depression. Ever the achiever, he did his best to repress those percolating feelings. Professionally, Keith performed exceptionally well and, in his mid-20s, moved to San Francisco for an extraordinary opportunity with the added benefit of extricating himself from the psychological predicament in which he was mired.

Over the next several years, Keith's career flourished, and he entered a serious relationship that led to marriage and a move to Seattle, where they had a son together. After a move back to San Francisco, Keith's rocky marriage with a wife who was by now a borderline alcoholic hit rock bottom during a fight that saw him spend a night in jail. He recalls being overwhelmed as he tried to take his son away in an event that escalated into a physically severe altercation between Keith and his wife. The marriage was over, and Keith was not without his share of issues that led to his demise.

A new relationship with a younger woman did not alleviate Keith's problems. She was terrific to his son, and even his ex-wife recognized that. But Keith's hard-living ways, including excessive drinking, continued to take a toll. Anxiety and panic attacks started to plague him. In addition, he discovered he was living in a biologically toxic dwelling. Ultimately, Keith was diagnosed with post-traumatic stress disorder and bipolar disorder. Keith's life was spiraling out of control. With his relationship over and help from an ex-girlfriend, he headed to familiar ground, Cincinnati.

With his health deteriorating, he spent 13 days in a hospital, eluding death. Ostracized by his family, Keith admitted himself into a rehab facility for 21 days. It was the intervention he needed.

Now living in Louisville, where he went to university, Keith is making a comeback. Money had come to him quickly in the past, and with a sober and newly enlightened disposition, there is no reason to believe it will not happen again.

DISADVANTAGED KID FROM A LARGE FAMILY RISES ABOVE IT ALL

A story from Mississippi

Shujaa grew up poor, with outhouses and no running water in rural southern Florida, where racist attitudes prevailed. His extended family lived on one plot of land with multiple houses, and dinner was often served based on what was shot or caught and what they grew on the farm. His mother's sister, who lived on the same land, had 15 children, and he had eight siblings in his nuclear family. Life did not hand Shujaa a silver spoon.

Work started early for Shujaa as a six-year-old picking peanuts. That effort represented seasonal income for the destitute family. When he was about seven, with his father already absent, his mother decided to leave the family for California. About a year later, his mother sent for her children, who had been staying in a crowded, small house with her sister's 15 children. Since his mother did not send a ticket for Annie Gene, his cousin who was to accompany them on the bus, she took Shujaa's ticket, and he was forced to stay behind with his grandmother. This event left Shujaa devastated, feeling abandoned and unloved, shaping the remainder of his life. It was a full year later, at age eight, when his grandmother took him to rejoin his family, but he never got over feeling like an outsider.

Although not the eldest, by 14, Shujaa was the man of the house. He worked and kept his siblings in line. His price—a solemn vow to never have children. Married late in life, that became his destiny. Today, he wistfully cogitates on the path not taken.

It comes as no surprise that the educational system can catastrophically fail certain people. Shujaa was one of those failed by the system. After high school, he spent two years in a community college to learn how to read and write the English language. His mother had extricated the family from the deep South for a reason, and Shujaa was driven to rise above his lot. One fateful day, he attended a presentation about an Iowa university that taught not only academics but also about the spiritual awakening that transcendental meditation imbues. Still an angry young man, on May 9, 1981, he gave TM a 10-minute audition, and his life was forever changed.

That fall, he enrolled at Maharishi International University, a school founded in 1973 by Maharishi Mahesh Yogi, the developer of TM. His first real-world experience following enlightenment occurred in suburban Chicago when his car was pulled over by white cops while driving with a white woman in the passenger seat. Despite being roughed up and enduring hateful racial epithets, Shujaa remained tranquil and even felt a kind of Christian love for the cops whom he had been taught to hate. He was no longer an angry man, and nor was he a victim.

While working on his Ph.D., after acquiring a Master's degree from Arizona State University, Shujaa was asked to teach business classes in Beijing, China. His decision to do so was life-altering as he met his future wife there at age 45. He has enjoyed a long career teaching TM to children at various locations in the United States before retiring just before the arrival of COVID-19.

Shujaa has exceeded society's expectations for someone with his early background of poverty and as one of only three from his extended family to attend university.

THE ADVENTURER AND DEPUTY COMMISSIONER RETURNS HOME

A story from Nova Scotia

By some accounts, Allen was a unique character in high school who aspired to be a Mountie. So, naturally, he became Deputy Commissioner (second by rank) in the Royal Canadian Mounted Police (RCMP) before retiring in 2012. But it was more challenging than it sounds. Allen, you see, was ¼ of an inch too short and had his initial application on his 18th birthday to join the world-renowned brigade rejected.

Born seventh into a highly supportive family of nine, Allen saw many of his immediate and extended family join the Mounties. He was enamored by the RCMP's dress code; remember Dudley Do Right? Following his rejection, he investigated ways that might enable him to add that ¼ inch. He was directed to the Boston University Athletics Department and was told that people are up to ¾ of an inch taller after they get out of bed in the morning. Allen had a plan. After waiting for six months, he applied again and had an afternoon meeting set up. He remained horizontal for the day and laid down in the back seat of a buddy's car as they drove to his appointment. Much to his chagrin, the officer wanted to conduct the entrance interview first. Allen's solution was to stretch his legs out and lean back as far as possible. Picture that from the interviewer's perspective! When it came time to be measured, just as the Boston University advisor told him, he was ½ of an inch taller than regulation. Allen was in!

His first assignment was in Newfoundland for ten years as a general duty policeman and then as an investigator. Seeking a new adventure with his nurse wife, they moved to a remote village of about 300 people in Labrador. In one almost tragic incident, Allen flew to a crash site in a blizzard to extract victims. After loading the chopper, the pilot told Allen there was no room for him. With no communication equipment in temperatures as low as -30°C/-22°F, Allen used his survival training to build a lean-to and hoped the pilot would return. He did, 28 hours later.

To move into the upper echelon of the RCMP, Allen studied French and landed a job in Ottawa, which he considers a turning point in his life. Eventually, as superintendent, he oversaw security for significant events, including those with international dignitaries, and planned responses to terrorist attacks. While you may perceive an exquisitely self-assured man, Allen initially felt slightly anxious about each promotion, as each role involved considerably more responsibility and a steep learning curve. Considering the highly talented source, that admission is one from which we can all take heed.

Allen avows that he has had a great career and life. In his various roles, he has witnessed devastating tragedies and, remarkably, experienced the best of people in some of those. Philosophically, he unequivocally identified compassion as humanity's preeminent value.

Finally, to quote Allen, "where there is a will, there is a way." Allen lived that credo by finding a way to join the Force, surviving perilous adventures with life and death implications, and continuously improving his human capital, which led to his final post as Deputy Commissioner.

GET UP. DUST YOURSELF OFF. PRESS ON WITH LIVING. AND HOPE.

A Story from Illinois

Wayne was the second of four born into a supportive and especially adventurous extended family environment that turned upside down when he was only 14. The turmoil involved the loss of his maternal grandparents within months of each other and the insidious impact of his father's increasingly problematic alcoholism. Unsurprisingly, the latter had the most significant impact, resulting in an all-too-common familial downward spiral. Such is its nature. The ripples from his family's demise would have far-reaching consequences on Wayne's life in the decades to come.

Distraught at the loss of her parents, the strain of caring for a special-needs child (the youngest), and a disintegrating marriage, Wayne's mother mentally checked out. With the family parentally rudderless, Wayne's high school career was punctuated by falling grades, risky behavior, and emotional detachment. Wayne's world was upside down. He left home at 18 to attend college and, after graduating, returned to the area to begin work in the landscaping business. That led to entrepreneurship, but things, even with counseling, needed to be addressed. Around age 26, Wayne decided to try something new.

While returning to community college to study chemistry, Wayne met his future wife, who was studying business. Over the next few years, they alternated working and studying to support each other in getting their four-year degrees. Wayne curtailed his less-than-responsible extracurricular activities and returned to church. Life began to look up following his marriage at 33.

Forging one's path while extricating oneself from the turmoil of family drama can often come at a cost. For Wayne, relations with his siblings, who seemed blind to the truth of their upbringing, eventually became non-existent. Following his mother's death at 63, a sibling schism began that lasted almost two decades. It was three-against-one. Wayne was the one. But life went on, and at age 36, Wayne became the father to a baby girl and then, a couple of years later, to a son. By this time, he was working in Big Pharma, and dreams were coming to fruition.

During his son's high school tenure, cracks in the family structure began to appear. Wayne was apprehensive about his son's obsession with electronic gaming and had other issues with both children, while his wife seemed oblivious to his concerns. Although both kids did well in school and eventually attended a Christian university in Michigan, the communication breakdown in the family resulted in divorce after 27 years and another unfortunate three-against-one dynamic. Wayne, again, was the one. Today, six years after the divorce, this man of faith stoutly awaits a communication breakthrough with his children beyond the obligatory Christmas wishes.

Now retired from the pharmaceutical industry and after recently losing his special needs brother, Wayne has blissfully found love again and was married late in 2023. His optimistic yet realistic approach to life led him to this new phase at age 66. He remains effusive about life and looks forward to this unexpected and unfolding chapter. After all, whether his children eventually have the epiphany that their father was a good guy remains to be seen. One can only hope.

A FRANCO-AMERICAN CHRONICLES HIS CULTURE

A story from New Hampshire

Robert B. Perreault is a one-man gang writer and proselytizer about New England's long-standing French/Québécois heritage, particularly in Manchester, New Hampshire. After graduating from his hometown's liberal arts college, Saint Anselm College, Robert's career has encompassed research assistant/oral history interviewer, librarian/archivist, freelance writer, historical tour guide, public speaker, photographer, and conversational French teacher. He presently serves on the faculty of his alma mater.

Manchester became a major textile center in the 1800s, and almost one million French Canadians migrated to it and other New England mill towns between 1840 and 1930 in search of a better life. While his influential maternal grandfather, Adolphe Robert, immigrated to the area from Quebec, he was not interested in the mills. He wanted to be a journalist and writer. Robert B's future was shaped even before he was born. Growing up on the east side of Manchester, his parents spoke French at home, and Robert was fluent in two languages by the time he started school, where further instruction in both languages awaited him.

The Québécois brought with them an esprit de corps known as la survivance. Simply put, they had considerable pride in their *foi, langue, et institutions* (faith, language, and institutions) that they were unwilling to relinquish for the welcome economic advancement they found in their adopted country. Robert has upheld that spirit and is well-known in the Franco-American community today.

Robert spent his first year of high school in Massachusetts at an elite prep school. Although his father did well as a Linotype machinist, it was ultimately a fish out of water story, so he returned home for the rest of his school days. However, even in the 1960s, Robert experienced the resentment of other ethnic groups that dated back to the early industrial days when the French would ostensibly undermine the economic advancements the others had made. Surviving that, he studied in Paris as part of an exchange program where he and a buddy were rock stars to the other American students, 33 women. It was a rough life in Paris! Robert considers that experience a tremendous validation of his French heritage.

It was in March 1973 that Robert got his big break. He was offered a job as a research assistant for Tamara K. Hareven and Randolph Langenbach to interview people who had worked at the famous Amoskeag textile mills that closed permanently in 1936, a Great Depression fatality. His French skills proved vital, and he parlayed that experience into the other roles noted earlier that defined his eclectic career.

Robert B. Perreault, the author of *Franco-American Life and Culture in Manchester, New Hampshire: Vivre la Différence*, believes knowing one's heritage is crucial to understanding oneself. He is an exceptionally proud Franco-American who has written and spoken elegantly about the French experience. I, Canadian-born, learned a great deal from him. As time inexorably marches on and technologies act as a pseudo-hegemonic influence on tradition, his job is even more critical lest many Franco-Americans forget from whence they came. If they know not that, how can they understand themselves?

A CHILDHOOD INCIDENT, MOTHER TO TWO CHALLENGED SONS

A story from Illinois

As a baby of nine siblings with a high-ranking Army Colonel father and a former model as a mother, Erica's early life was chaotic. Always expected to toe the line responsibly, she often sought adventure as a respite from her home life. Being one of many growing up in a highly dysfunctional, competitive setting while dealing with remnants of sexual abuse, she taught herself how to survive.

Erica talks about the battle within. She left home at 18 to pursue higher education, which resulted in multiple degrees in different fields. After attaining a graduate degree from Syracuse University, she moved to Illinois, met her future husband, and married four years later. Two years hence, she was blessed with a son who gradually began exhibiting tendencies similar to autism, a developmental disorder in which the individual struggles in social situations and is prone to thinking patterns that can be rigid and repetitive. Six years later, unable to conceive again, she and her husband adopted a boy from Eastern Europe, aged five. He also had special needs, unrealized at the time of adoption, which became more apparent as he acclimated to society. Superimpose the demands of two children with special needs onto the realization that her marriage was showing signs of trouble, and the battle within was raging. Life was not going according to the playbook.

Erica's search for answers led her down many paths. Counseling. Meditation. Yoga. Redefining faith. One of the most exciting paths came after adopting her son. Although her birth son had special needs, Erica never saw herself as especially adept at dealing with them. While working as a substitute teacher, the school district called and asked if she would consider teaching kids with special needs. Sometimes, destiny seeks you. She now believes that time under the tutelage of a mentor was a genuine growth event and, indeed, a turning point in her life.

After 19 years of marriage, Erica entered a new chapter: acceptance. Despite knowing it was the right thing to do, divorcing her husband was not easy because of how it violated the societal expectations upon which she was raised. While caulking the tub one day, Erica broke down crying as she wondered how she would raise two challenging boys on her own. Conscience can sometimes be a ponderous adversary.

Following our interview, Erica emailed me to explain how she would like to be remembered. "I would want people to be inspired by my desire to get out and do different things, embrace change, and know that, no matter how bad things seem, things will get better— they can always be worse, so stay grateful for what the present brings." Erica is a strikingly contemplative person. When asked about future life projects, she could not identify one. However, she worries about how her sons will navigate the future when she is gone. To that end, Erica has always done her utmost to prepare them. That, seemingly, *is* her project.

A CLASSIC LOVE STORY AND AN OFFER DECLINED

A story from California

Joanne's life began somewhat inauspiciously when she was diagnosed with rheumatoid arthritis as a young child. She missed a school year but had the good fortune of having a mentor who worked with her to make up for that missed year. She also had the benefit of eventually meeting a doctor who defied customary medical advice. He suggested that to protect her body, she engage in fluid activity to help the joints rather than remain sedentary. Later, another doctor, who was ahead of his time, had her incorporate some simple dietary guidelines. By following these wise insights, Joanne's life with arthritis became more bearable.

Engaged at 19, she met another man from her work, Jerry, who, coincidently, was also seeing someone else. Well, some things are just meant to be. Following their marriage, they made a down payment on a house in Queens, New York, to begin their lives together. Except… there was the issue of an employer's bounced check. After begging for a second chance, Jerry won over the sellers, and their journey began.

Joanne carved out a career in the travel business, while Jerry was a successful sales executive. They visited about 50 countries and found the time to raise a family of five children. The New Yorkers retired to Palm Springs to partly mitigate New York's damper climate's impact on Joanne's arthritis. In 2019, just a few months before COVID-19, Joanne's beloved passed away.

On one trip to Jordan, Jerry entertained a lavish proposal from one of the sheiks. Apparently, the sheik took quite a shine to Joanne and offered Jerry two camels so she could become his fifth wife. After some profoundly introspective contemplation, Jerry politely declined the generous offer. Besides, his wife provided much more utility than two camels in New York City.

Joanne's life, like everyone else, was not without its challenges. Her successful salesman husband descended that slippery slope of overindulging in spirits as he entertained clients. His drinking eventually became so excessive that Joanne thought it might threaten their marriage. With her support, Jerry enrolled in Alcoholics Anonymous. She identified that as the low point and turning point in her life. About a year later, he had kicked the habit, and they never looked back.

A devout Catholic, Joanne was, and is, a faithful churchgoer. Her faith was such that it imbued her mate, a primarily secular soul, with a sense that he needed to give back. She relates that as the years went by, he evolved into a spiritual being committed to giving others the greatest gift of all: his time.

Joanne's life is about the love story and how she impacted her family. A successful entrepreneur in the travel business, she imparted a sense of travel adventure to her children and grandchildren. A devoted wife, she inspired her husband to become a better version of himself. Today, widowed, she retains a youthful optimism about seeing her descendants navigate life and is committed to being there whenever her sage advice is needed.

RURAL, RELIGIOUS, HARVARD GRAD FINDS A CALLING VIA "FAILURE"

A story from New Brunswick

Bill is a recently retired Professor of Gerontology from Saint Thomas University in Fredericton, New Brunswick, and an acknowledged pioneer in *narrative gerontology*, which studies how stories, by which we understand our lives, thicken and change over time. How apropos that I had the privilege of learning about his life.

A small-town New Brunswick boy with two sisters whose authoritarian father was a minister in the United Church of Canada, Bill was encouraged to apply to the elite American universities of the Ivy League. As it turns out, the only application he could get his hands on was one from Harvard University. The day the acceptance letter arrived from that venerated institution was one of the greatest moments of his life. Upon his cum laude graduation from Harvard in 1972, Bill acquired a Master's degree in Divinity Studies from the University of Toronto, was a Divinity Ph.D. candidate at Cambridge University, and finally acquired a Master's degree in Theology from Princeton Theological Seminary with the ambition of following in his father's footsteps. Bill's ministerial journey began in 1979 in rural Saskatchewan, a Canadian province near Montana.

In 1988, after several years of ministering at different locations within the United Church, Bill found himself in Toronto working on a special project for that same institution. With encouragement from individuals he considers very special in his life, in his late 30s, he enrolled in the Education doctorate program at the University of Toronto. Following the book publication of his Ed.D. thesis, Bill accepted a post at Saint Thomas University in his home province.

The trip home was entirely unexpected, even somewhat unwelcome, and involved immersing himself in a subject in which he felt academically unqualified. Saint Thomas University wanted him to be a visiting professor of gerontology. That unanticipated post resulted in a partnership and friendship with Gary Kenyon, the department's founder, that continues today. As Bill says, it also established a small university on the continent's periphery as a center of excellence in narrative gerontology.

Upon reflecting on his life, Bill acknowledges his "failure" at Cambridge University as a seminal moment, even if he did not understand it then. He attributes the lack of funds and even focus as factors that led to his inability to complete his Ph.D. Theology program. Had he succeeded, it is a virtual certainty that Bill would not have found what he now considers his true calling; teaching about and helping others navigate the aging process.

Bill's entire nuclear family was stricken with polio. One sister has only experienced the world with braces or while sitting down. As she ages, perhaps it is comforting for her to know that Bill is an expert in cognitively aging with grace.

CHEMIST, TEACHER, CHEMIST, TEACHER, CHEMIST, TEACHER?

A story from Illinois

Rob is a chemist. No, teacher. No, chemist. No…Where will it end? Rob grew up in New York but moved around a lot. His father was a noted jazz musician who played with some of the biggest names in the business, while his mother was a teacher. His parents divorced when he was 11, but this was surprisingly more relieving to Rob than anything. Even though he was relatively young, he had seen the writing on the wall for quite some time.

Rob was raised in an environment he described as adventurous, responsible, and chaotic. Following his parents' divorce, he lived with his mother on Staten Island while his father, employed by Columbia University at the time, remained in Manhattan. By the time he started junior college, Rob was living with his father in Connecticut. After one unsuccessful year, he decided to join the Navy. Following his military duty tour, Rob returned to the same school and completed two successful years. At age 28, he pursued a Bachelor's degree in Chemistry from the University of Connecticut. Following graduation, the first of his two careers would start with an offer in Illinois at one of the country's largest pharmaceutical companies.

While living in Illinois, Rob, who suffers from ADHD symptoms, moved several times, and pursued an MBA degree. After six years, he accepted a Big Pharma job in Michigan. Less than two years later, he moved to New Jersey to work for another Big Pharma company.

Three years later, Rob started his second career as a teacher in New York City at age 40. Six years after that, the pharmaceutical industry called again, this time from New Hampshire. He later moved to Boston while still working in NH. But teaching was not out of his system. He started to teach in New York City for the second time, living first in NYC and later in New Jersey. As much as Rob seemed to truly enjoy teaching, he was on the move again after less than a two-year teaching stint. This time, he landed in Wichita, Kansas, for another job in Big Pharma. Following a consolidation at that location, Rob moved to Illinois for the second time while keeping the same position. However, Rob admits that he still thinks about teaching and may return to the classroom someday.

Rob never married but has wondered how life would have been different had he done so. Would he have found more stability? Would he have learned that his true passion was teaching and stuck with it? "Scientists are teachers," Rob says. The lowest point in Rob's life was when his mother died. He was devastated as he informed his father of her demise.

Rob's destiny is still being forged. Will he move again to be closer to his girlfriend in New Jersey? Rob will tell you understanding is the single greatest aspiration a human can have. With that stated, will he ever teach again, which I, as a mere chronicler, believe is his passion? Regardless of what he does next, one thing is obvious: it has been an oscillating adventure.

THE DALAI LAMA'S AND SAKYA TRIZIN'S FRIEND

A story from California

Marilyn Ravicz grew up thinking girls were dull. Born in Illinois to supportive parents, she would enter the nearby woods with her father to shoot at game: not your typical girl stuff. She was taught to be independent in thought and to not live up to the expectations of a woman, especially as they were in her day (1940s). Marilyn was destined to forge a unique path.

After graduating from Augustana College, Marilyn was ready to take on the challenge of studying at Harvard University. Unfortunately, the environment was not particularly welcoming to women (in fact, women were enrolled at Radcliffe until 1999), prompting young Marilyn to quit and sail to Morocco by herself. She spent two years there, living with the Berbers and studying their way of life. Upon returning home, she again enrolled at Harvard and met her future husband, Robert, who was studying anthropology. During her second Harvard stint, she met the encouraging Paul Tillich, a renowned philosopher, who instilled in Marilyn an intent to pursue her dreams.

Following marriage, she and Robert traveled to the East to learn more about its philosophy, notably Buddhism. However, traveling in some regions of the world can incur unwanted risks. While on a bus in mountainous Nepal, Robert had to physically throw Marilyn off the bus and then jump off himself just before it plunged into a ravine. During more tranquil times, she met the 41st Sakya Trizin, Ngawang Kunga, and the 14th Dalai Lama, Tenzin Gyatso, upon whom she bestowed an honor from Harvard. While traveling in the East, she ensured her children received the intellectual stimulation she had always valued by having them study at an elite Swiss boarding school.

Marilyn, who obtained her Ph.D. in anthropology from UCLA, developed a love of original American Jazz and even started a jazz society in Boston. She wrote 11 books on various topics, including an anthropological discourse titled *Erotic Cuisine: A Natural History of Aphrodisiac Cookery*. Hmm...(just the author musing). She became an avid art collector and has personally signed work by Andy Warhol and works by his contemporary, Roy Lichtenstein, among others. In addition, when the Ravicz Collection of Japanese woodblock prints was repatriated, it was considered the most extensive private collection outside Japan.

After settling in California with her professor husband, Marilyn ran the International College, Los Angeles. This trailblazing school was ahead of its time with no classrooms but operated by pairing students with highly credentialed tutors. Sadly, despite having degrees recognized by major universities such as Harvard and Johns Hopkins, it never achieved accreditation and closed its doors in 1986. Following that, Marilyn started a business catering to the needs of people with disabilities and, at its peak, ran five offices.

Marilyn broke the mold of her day. She refused to be pigeonholed (be an artist, she was told—yes, she was talented), especially by men of high intellectual stature. She merely wanted to pursue her passion. Her mentor, the esteemed existentialist Paul Tillich, and her husband, intrigued by her chutzpah, inspired her to achieve that. [**Author's note:** Marilyn died at 91, just a few months after telling her story.]

THE SEMI-PERMANENT STUDENT, A WORLD CLASS ETHICIST

A story from New Delhi, India

Darryl has two Ph.D. degrees from the University of Southern California and has studied or worked in institutions of higher learning in at least five countries worldwide. I have known him since high school when we played on the chess team (Darryl played board #1, of course, and I #2) in the '75 Nova Scotia high school championship. Forever an intellectual, I often wondered if he would always be a student.

One of six siblings born into a Canadian military family, Darryl was constantly on the move (Nova Scotia, New Brunswick, Northwest Territories, British Columbia, and Ontario) in his youth. Growing up without a television and sometimes in sparsely populated areas, Darryl was creative about exploring his environment and soon took to sports. After graduating high school, where he wrestled and played chess, he enrolled at Dalhousie University in Halifax to study kinesiology. He was thinking about a career in physical education. He transferred to the University of Alberta for year two, but after his third year, he had a change of heart. After transferring back to Dalhousie University, he completed a degree in the classics. Darryl had experienced his first career vectorial adjustment.

His next foray into academia took him to Cincinnati to study theology at Xavier University. He followed that experience by attending the Catholic Theological Union in Chicago, now one of the largest Catholic graduate schools in the English–speaking world. This association eventually led him to work in a parish in Los Angeles, where he was inspired to apply his theological training in Latin America. Naturally, while in Los Angeles, Darryl enrolled at another school, the Claremont School of Theology, to finish some required work.

While living in Los Angeles, a fellow Canadian asked Darryl where he would get a Ph.D. Oh, there's an idea. Since he lived close to USC, he decided to drop in and say hello. He enrolled in a Ph.D. program for Social Ethics (grad. '97). His goal remained to work in Latin America, but not as a theological leader. This meant he needed something more than a background in ethics. He required training in economics. So, Darryl switched to the Ph.D. program in Political Economy and Public Policy (grad. '95). Between Chicago and USC, he studied in Germany (present when the Wall fell in 1989) and taught in Budapest, Hungary. Post USC, he taught in India and Canada as a long-time professor at York University in Toronto and then briefly at the University of British Columbia. He is presently a Distinguished Professor at Shiv Nadar University in Delhi, India, where his wife, whom he met at USC, is the Vice Chancellor.

When the Berlin Wall came down, so did Darryl's academic path. He had earlier decided that Latin America was no longer a good place to live and that the discipline of comparative economies in the West and East offered some exciting opportunities. Serendipitously, he and his wife landed jobs at York University, where he was commissioned to start a program well suited to his political, economic, and ethical academic background.

Despite experiencing his version of entropy following high school, unlike the second law of thermodynamics, Darryl's career finally coalesced as he has been recognized as one of the world's most highly published academics in economic ethics. He has contributed an academic legacy by studying local economies and co-ops in the spirit of The Antigonish Movement[10] of the Coady Institute at Saint Francis Xavier University in Antigonish, Nova Scotia, which has been exported to many developing nations.

---

[10] https://en.wikipedia.org/wiki/Antigonish_Movement

THE INSPIRED SCIENTIST, A RELIGIOUS CONVERSION

A story from Illinois

Doug is one of the most intensely detailed people you will ever meet. Therefore, it is no surprise that his high school science teachers were two of the most influential people in his youth.

Growing up in Indiana, he was raised in a highly religious family, such that his father was a deacon in the Lutheran Church. Both parents provided encouragement and love. In seventh grade, Doug had a major falling out with religion, resulting from an event that he described as one of his worst childhood memories. Doug's close friend, David, was a devout Catholic. One day, Doug approached his Lutheran religious studies teacher at school to inquire about his friend who had beliefs other than what he was taught. Doug was told in no uncertain terms that David would go to hell and that no reconciliation was possible unless he converted. This hurt Doug profoundly, and he started to turn his back on organized religion. He now considers himself agnostic, believes deeply in the universal order, and has pursued intellectual readings into other faiths.

High school started ominously, as he was required to attend school in a town with which he was unfamiliar and knew nobody. Right on cue, two teachers helped give Doug a sense of purpose. Mr. Rose, chemistry, and Mr. Jennings, physics, encouraged him to delve deeply into the subjects. He ultimately chose to attend Purdue University, a school well known for its technical fields. His path was set.

Upon graduating, Doug entered General Electric's Manufacturing Management Program, moving to multiple states. By 30, he had landed a position at Baxter, where he met his future wife, had two children, and enjoyed the best time of his life. While at Baxter, he made a significant technical contribution to an apheresis project that laid a foundation for future life-saving medical breakthroughs and marked the pinnacle of his technical contributions to society.

Scientists and other technical people can sometimes endure an entire career without such an impactful accomplishment.

Then, while working in Georgia as a director for a sizable urological company, Doug's marriage began to unravel. One night, tucking his son into bed, he started to cry. How do you explain that to a child? Following a contentious divorce, he endured the most significant pain of his life for ten years. After his ex-wife remarried, the emotional relief of reconciliation came from recognizing their enduring bond of shared parenthood.

Because of his humanist approach towards life, Doug identified community as humanity's preeminent value. To that end, he is now involved with the green movement in his hometown. Although he still faces challenges with his two sons who live far away (in Hawaii), Doug has made it his mission to forge ahead and make whatever contribution he can to improve the world. A scientist at heart, his work is never done.

FATHER A TRIBAL LEADER, TRIBAL LEADER HIMSELF, SON A TRIBAL LEADER

A story from Wyoming

Ben was the youngest of five children. His father was a rancher and a Northern Arapaho Tribal Leader. In his youth, there were about 4,000 members of the tribe. His parents grew up without electricity or running water and lived in tents. They stressed to Ben that education was the only way to a better life. While his entrepreneurial father led the family, his mother reinforced good habits and discipline. Both taught him to be proud of his heritage.

From an early age, Ben learned to look after the land, use irrigation, and sustain crops. His grandparents told him stories and did their best to engender laughter in their grandchildren whenever possible. This was a shield of sorts from the hardships Native Americans are often forced to endure. Ben spent eight years in Catholic school and learned that some children, like him, were different. He played basketball, which tended to be an equalizer, as talent mattered more than background.

Ben got a guitar at age seven, and as he wasn't old enough yet to get a formal job, he freelanced and began to parlay his musical talent into income. With that exposure, however, came alcohol. Later, after quitting drinking, Ben met an influential professor at the University of Wyoming who stressed the importance of history. That inspired one of his most significant achievements. Ben was destined to tell the world about the tragic Sand Creek Massacre, of which his great-great-grandfather was a survivor.

His activism around the 1864 murder of the Arapaho and Cheyenne people by the United States Army under Col. John Chivington facilitated the expansion of a National Park Service site that will forever remain a testament to the inglorious aspects of frontier history. In 2007, the Battle of Sand Creek was officially relabeled as a massacre. That was one of the highest points in Ben's life. Since then, Ben has been a consultant to the federal government and testified in Washington, DC, on matters concerning Native Americans. He has met Presidents and other high-ranking members of the federal government, all in the name of furthering the interests of his people.

Ben was recently appointed to the Saint Stephen's Indian School Board on the Wind River Reservation. Recent corruption in the system led him to take on that role, and his future holds the opportunity to secure reparations for past injustices. If successful, it would be a boon to the education of the youth on the Wind River Reservation.

When Ben lost his mother to cancer, he remembers her last words as being about taking care of the family. After his father's passing in 2004, he was determined to continue the tradition of service to his people. He claims that respect is humanity's preeminent value in homage to his parents.

Today, Ben is the director of the Tribal Historic Preservation Office in Riverton, Wyoming. Like his father and like himself, Ben's son has assumed a leadership role within the Northern Arapaho Tribe. If his son is anything like him, the legacy and traditions of his people will be well-preserved. His other children are also important to him and have excelled in basketball (two were state champions) and track and field. His daughter, a high school All-American, was 16th in the nation in the Foot Locker National Championship cross-country meet in Fresno, California, in 1994. In addition to being an accomplished tribal leader, Ben has raised a wonderful family.

FINDING PEACE IN SOLITARY LIVING AFTER A LIFE OF CHAOS

A story from Nova Scotia

Betty was born into a large francophone military family but endured considerable anguish growing up, and then again in her marriage. Following a divorce at age 36 and with two children, she eventually sought therapy and began to embrace her independence.

Betty's mother was an understanding, empathetic teacher who promoted education in the family. At the same time, life with Québécois roots in Nova Scotia meant the family engaged in many activities together. When she was about seven, her father left the military to run his own business, and shortly after that, the era of tranquility ended. Sadly, her father suffered a severe accident that left him in constant pain. That, coupled with his alcoholism, took a toll on the family, resulting in increasingly chaotic years for her between the ages of 7-15. Following her parents' divorce at age 15, she and four of her five siblings moved with their mother to a new dwelling, during which life improved significantly. Estrangement from her father ensued.

Betty, however, was precociously finding trouble on her own by age 15. She started hanging out with older boys who were already drinking. Naturally, she engaged, and this behavior ultimately resulted in a date rape for which she blamed herself and which she never told anyone about. By university age, Betty realized the hazards of becoming an alcoholic and concentrated on books while still enjoying the university experience. Ironically, her future husband, whom she met at university, was himself becoming an alcoholic, his family affliction. Sometimes, reaching escape velocity from a deleterious life pattern is challenging. In Betty's case, the total price was yet to be extracted.

Betty's career first took her to teaching, followed by other vocations, including federal work and pharmaceutical sales. Eventually, she returned to teaching, her true passion. Following her return to education came infertility treatment and a move to Montreal, followed by pregnancy. However, teaching in Quebec was not enjoyable for her, given that she needed to be sufficiently fluent in French. Another child, a physically abusive husband traveling a lot, two house fires, and the death of a brother were all followed by a move to Ontario that she hoped would lead to a reprieve from her exacting life. Regrettably, it was not to be, even though she and her husband engaged in couples counseling.

Following her divorce, Betty began to heal even as she was suddenly financially challenged. Her children were happy, and she found the support she needed. By age 40, Betty was free.

What can be taken from Betty's challenging life? During her recovery, she learned that love was humanity's preeminent value—specifically, self-love. She has witnessed her children's growth and has become a grandparent. Living alone, Betty does her best, with some physical limitations, to contribute to society when she can. During COVID-19, she made masks from home when there was a real shortage. She never gave up. That is the ultimate lesson her story can impart to others.

GEOLOGIST MEETS GORBACHEV AND OTHER FORREST GUMP STUFF

A story from Alberta

Fred is a story teller extraordinaire. Naturally, he does more than that, such as working in the Canadian oil patch as a geologist, which has taken him to numerous exotic international locations. In addition, the would-be Mafia Don has collections from some of the most infamous hoods, such as Ben "Bugsy" Siegel, Charles "Lucky" Luciano, Frank Costello, Myer Lansky, and George "Bugs" Moran. But perhaps his most prized treasure is the only authenticated cheque allegedly endorsed by Al Capone. Fred once walked down a street in Moscow, Russia, dressed in all-black clothes. The shopkeepers just voluntarily started to give him things. Fred soaked it all up!

Fred's life began humbly in a small Manitoba town that lacked the amenities found in larger cities but in which people looked after each other. It was a classical small-town existence. Friends were a cornerstone during his youth, and he was with a good crew as many pursued university careers. For Fred, his first year at the University of Manitoba was beset by his father's death as first-semester exams got underway. Despite the tragedy, he graduated on time in 1974 and moved to Thompson, Manitoba, with his wife, whom he had married in his third year.

Fred drove to Calgary in 1979 to seek work and to better support his wife and two children and hooked up with a major energy pipeline company. For the next 19 years, he applied his scientific skills during the various economic vicissitudes of the oil business. Following a divorce in 1998, he moved to work in Muammar Gaddafi's Libya. There, Fred learned about how small generosities could go a long way in making life easier. After he moved back to Calgary in 2000, Fred continued to work for different entities and eventually traveled to Russia on business. Seeing how a Libyan servant reacted after receiving $20, kneeling to kiss Fred's hand, and seeing life in rural

Russia, Fred was overcome with gratitude for all we have in North America. He now considers himself to be semi-retired. Full retirement does not sit easily with Fred, who remarried eight years ago. And, so, his future remains uncharted.

Fred's stories include an accidental meeting with Mikhail Gorbachev because Fred's friend, the politician, failed to show. So, Gorbachev introduced himself to Fred, assuming he was the politician. Then, there is the story about landing in Moscow and being greeted by two menacing-looking officers brandishing AK-47s. They escorted him away to a limo—all set up unbeknownst to him by his politician friend. His NASA traveling companion thought he was on his way to the modern gulag. He met Bill Clinton, Wesley Clark, and Michael Bloomberg during his travels. But the *pièce de résistance* was when he walked up to a stationary limo in Rome and peered inside, only to have the window rolled down. Pope John Paul II then blessed Fred.

Fred is the real Forrest Gump. Or Chauncey Gardiner, take your pick. But like those characters from the eponymous *Forrest Gump* and *Being There* movies, he has also lived the gamut of life—death of a father way too early, divorce, children, remarriage, career success. The cycle of life eventually meets everybody. It did with Fred.

EARLY FAMILY DISRUPTION, HOCKEY STAR/CAR GUY MAKES GOOD

A story from Nova Scotia

Born fifth into a family of seven, Bill became one of the youngest automobile dealership owners in the country at age 27, despite seeing his father forced to abandon his dealership at age 12. By some measures, Bill's dealership was one of the most successful in the country. That led to a good life for him and "retirement" as a golf course owner with plans to transform it into an American-style golf course/luxury home haven.

Bill recalls his childhood in Cape Breton until he was 12 as a wonderfully memorable time playing hockey and baseball and experiencing special moments at his family's cottage on Bras d'Or Lake. When his hometown experienced an economic catastrophe, and the car dealership was shuttered, the family moved to the largest metropolitan area in Nova Scotia in anticipation of a new start. During his school years, Bill added paddling to his sports repertoire while dabbling in buying, fixing, and selling cars.

Although that entrepreneurial industriousness portended big things to follow, Bill pursued a career as a pilot after school. However, that ended not long after his job of flying over the Atlantic Ocean to monitor the intercontinental communication cables almost put him to sleep with boredom. Bill needed to find something else to do and was soon in the car business.

Following some early success at his uncle's dealership in Cape Breton, he moved to Halifax to work for a prominent car dealer. There, Bill's ingenuity in creating new income streams led to his becoming a co-owner of a dealership in a small town about 100 miles outside of the city. After buying his partner out eleven years later, prosperity ensued for much of the next two decades, with one excruciating exception around 1997. During those years in Middleton, he and his girlfriend married and had two children. He started to coach hockey again after a fortuitous knock on his door, and in what he ironically considers the turning point in his life, he turned down an offer to become involved in the automobile business at a much more visible level. For him and his family, it was about lifestyle and appreciating what they had in a small town.

Upon retiring from the car business, Bill and a partner acquired a failing golf course in another small town on the ocean. Bill now envisions his next chapter as he seeks to combine real estate ambitions with his golf mogul tenure.

Bill has lived life's highs and lows. A great career. A son's law degree. A daughter's marriage to an upstanding young man whom he knew via hockey. But then came his sister's recent euthanasia via Canada's Medical Assistance in Dying Law. No life is without the lows, as Bill knows all too well.

The competitive nature instilled in Bill from his early involvement in sports, juxtaposed with the setback he witnessed his father endure, has served Bill well, as has his conviction on the merits of reading positive-thinking books. In deciding to stay ensconced in small communities and eschewing the big-time offer, he has lived the values he learned on his journey.

HIRED A CONSTABLE, RETIRED A CONSTABLE; WHY?

A story from Alberta

Steve is a man of myriad talents. A football and hockey star who played football in college, he also has a highly tuned ear for music and started in that business as a teenager with his band. Steve was primarily a keyboard guy. Late in his high school career, Steve's parents became increasingly argumentative and eventually divorced. The stress at home and music performance demands manifested in academic underachievement, prompting him to drop out of the band. Nonetheless, he added another skill to his repertoire shortly after high school as a cub reporter for a local newspaper.

Following university and a stint as a substitute teacher, Steve joined the Halifax Police Department in Nova Scotia. While there, he and a few other policemen started a band known as Blue Thunder, a platform they used to play music regionally and as an instrument of goodwill with the community. It even took them to Slovakia, as Canadians helped the Slovaks build a Western-style force following communism's demise.

However, Steve's 34-year police journey was unusual in another way. Although he was the subject of television and print media coverage at his retirement, extremely rare for a cop in a mid-sized city, he never received a promotion. How odd was that for one so highly admired by the community that he served?

Steve endured significant financial hardship at university as his paternal relationship soured, and his mother eventually remarried. This experience bequeathed him perspective and an understanding of the inherent value in something hard-won. When he began his career as a street cop, he would occasionally clash with his superiors from the old school. Steve held his ground, refusing to yield to the prevailing winds. Where he saw injustice, he acted, such as in his role as a founding member of the Halifax Police Union. Steve was the first Halifax officer to become a community-based constable. In doing this, he helped change the face of policing in Halifax. But there was that union thing...

The untimely tragic loss of his mother, who was in the hospital for something that should not have ended in death, marked the lowest time of his life. In his grandchildren, however, Steve sees life slowing down, and at the same time, he senses a reconnection with his mother. Today, he continues to give back to his adopted community in Alberta as a high school football coach. Coaching is familiar to Steve as he coached football in Nova Scotia for 25 years and led the Saint Mary's University women's hockey team to that sport's inaugural national championship. In coaching, Steve finds an outlet for expressing what he considers essential values to which we should all aspire.

Steve is convinced that his failure to be promoted to sergeant was due to his union activities and his unyielding commitment to serving the community in a way that occasionally clashed with unwritten norms. His wife, Barb, was the first female officer to receive a promotion as a member of the Halifax Police Department, where she served for 33 years. The day of his media-celebrated retirement was his daughter's first day of service in the Calgary Police Department. She will undoubtedly enjoy a stellar career if she is anything like her father. Finally, his son, Sean, has served in the Calgary Police Department for ten years. Steve's lifetime of service cascades.

TENNESSEE KID, HARVARD GRAD, M&A GURU, DE&I CHAMPION

A story from Georgia

Chris is a veritable force of nature. Born into a family of six children and celebrated as the first boy after two girls, he was a star in the making. Encouraged by his inspiring parents, Chris performed exceptionally well in school and was a voracious reader. He even began reading newspapers and following political developments very early in life. Given his prodigious talent, he decided that there was only one school he would attend following high school—Harvard University. The Black kid from the South would be a mover and shaker.

Following completing a Bachelor's degree in Economics, Chris hit the corporate world with IBM. He returned to Harvard for his MBA after deciding that a law degree did not fit his ambitions, even though he and others always suspected that he would make a great lawyer. Law, for many, is a stepping stone into politics, so that dream withered and ultimately died upon his decision to pursue business. After graduating, he entered the Mergers and Acquisitions Finance group at Bankers Trust's Atlanta office. His acumen for influencing others was about to be put to the test.

One of the most motivational moments in Chris's life came when Sidney Portier delivered the line, "They call me Mr. Tibbs," in the movie *In the Heat of the Night*. To Chris, it meant no boundaries to dreams, regardless of race. Depending on the situation, he decided to outwork, outthink, and outperform everybody, including all the "white guys" channeling either George Bailey or Michael Corleone, as both personas form the core of his personality. And thus, it unfolded at Bankers Trust.

With deals beginning to evaporate following the Wall Street junk bond scandal of the early '90s, Chris decided it was time to conquer another world. That world turned out to be at Price Waterhouse, one of the big accounting firms expanding its horizons beyond bean counting. There, he met an outstanding mentor, a Southern good-ole-boy. Naturally, they hit it off. With the backing of Larry and later others, Chris relentlessly climbed the corporate ladder to senior positions, including Managing Partner of a 3,000-person professional unit. Then, in 2004, a new opportunity was presented to him; senior management wanted him to head up a diversity team. Not one to shrink from a challenge, he was all in.

Despite what some observers might view as a dead-end opportunity, Chris was determined to make this new role come alive. He endeared himself to people of all backgrounds and even convinced the skeptics to address LGBTQ issues much earlier than other corporations. Chris's approach to diversity, racial relations, and gender conflicts is embodied in his two mantras: "We're All a Little Screwed Up" and "Let's Learn to Give Each Other a Break." It has paid off big time for the gifted public speaker. He has successfully parlayed that role into speaking engagements and other consulting endeavors in his retirement, which came in 2014.

Chris's life was not without disappointment. When one of his sisters died, his beloved mother became a recluse until her death years later. A divorcee, he has three sons, including one with whom he has infrequent interactions. Even the most gifted ones cannot escape life's tribulations. Despite this, Chris will have left a significant legacy when the curtain falls.

A MOTHER'S DILEMMA, AN UNFATHOMABLE DECISION; A FUTURE?

A story from California

Amy had reached the end of her rope and faced an existential decision. When the judge asked if she would follow through on her plans to move from Philadelphia to California should she not be granted the right to move with her two boys, she responded, "Yes."

Her ex-husband was awarded full custody, and Amy moved to Los Angeles *sans* children. What would prompt a rational, intelligent woman whose friends will testify that she is a great mother to make such a gut-wrenching decision? Sometimes, life presents one with no good options.

Born into chaos, Amy felt lonely and inadequate growing up. Having a three-time divorced father and a four-time divorced mother meant there was a revolving door of humanity in the household during her formative years. She had an older, gifted brother who was always doing his own thing, frequently leaving young Amy alone at home. She also seemed academically slow, although it was later determined this was not representative of her innate intellectual abilities. Amy saw her father regularly for about 12 years until, at age 13, she wrote him a long letter informing him of her feelings of estrangement. With that, her father ceased visiting Amy and her brother, a consequence of which she felt profound guilt.

Amy studied Business and Accounting at university. Her eldest son was autistic, was repeatedly kicked out of different schools, and, over time, became aggressive towards his petite mother. In addition, not knowing what a healthy relationship looked like, Amy suffered abuse at the hands of her husband for much longer than many women would endure. Unable to pursue a meaningful career because of her son's issues that found him in and out of treatment centers, Amy was enduring severe psychological duress. To better understand her son, she earned a Master's in Education and started teaching elementary school. Amy wanted to *Primal Scream* throughout those stressful years, probably unaware of its legitimate academic roots (Arthur Janov). How could she escape her torment?

Ironically, her "escape epiphany" occurred after her son asked what she wanted to do when she was young. Already divorced, this is when Amy's life instinct started to stir inside her. She decided that if she was to prioritize safety, change her legacy, and discover her inner self-worth, she had to physically remove herself from the torment.

Amy knew that was her only option, and sadly, that meant leaving her children. For her, staying would be tantamount to a death sentence.

Upon her arrival in Los Angeles, Amy, then in her late 30s, started a business that catered to the tourism industry. In 2022, her business partner bought her out, leaving her flummoxed as to what would come next. The chapter Amy calls "Spread Your Wings and Fly" began. In this chapter, she becomes a flight attendant, travels, and lives in the moment.

Amy has endured a lot in her life. A lost girl. An abused wife. An autistic child. A forced choice that others struggle to comprehend. Today, she seeks to self-actualize and manifest her true self. To Amy, the journey is the thing.

BRAIN DRAIN FROM THE USSR, AMERICA'S GAIN

A story from Illinois

If you looked up the definition of "family" in the dictionary, you might find a picture of Alex. Alex is the son of a Russian mother and a Ukrainian father who lived in Kharkiv. As I write this, Kharkiv, along with other Ukrainian cities, are, for unfortunate reasons, well-known to the world. Growing up, however, Alex enjoyed a childhood that he foundationally described as adventurous, stable, and supportive, all buoyed by well-educated parents. But in his heart, Alex, brother to a younger sister and her pseudo-father figure that continues to this day, fancied himself a rebel. He was active in sports during his school years and performed well academically, particularly in mathematics and physics.

Alex met his future wife at university and married her by the age of 21. Before long, they were blessed with their only child, a daughter. After pursuing a Ph.D. in engineering physics, Alex published technical articles in important publications that were noticed in the Western world. But he was in the USSR, facing a limited future. He wanted better for his family. Following up on an offer in the United States, Alex made an arduous escape from the Soviet Union. Although he was not a defector, it was not without adventure. Extricating himself from a bleak intellectual and financial future controlled by the state (read, KGB) was a vicarious peek into part of Alex's rebel persona for those who know him.

Alex began to make his life in the new world by applying his considerable talent to software development rather than pursuing a postdoc position. He was eager to provide a better life for his wife and daughter. His second job, in Big Pharma, lasted several years before it was time to move on and up the technical/management ladder. Alex has had a successful career. However…

Cancer can be excruciating for those who are left behind. In Alex's case, he was left behind three times. Mother, ovarian in 2005; father, pancreatic in 2016; wife, stomach in 2017. All gone. How does one process that? In his mother's case, he traveled to Ukraine to say goodbye. His wife, Natalia, was gone 6-7 months after being diagnosed. Sometimes, there are no words, so I shan't continue.

When asked about his high point in life, Alex could not name just one. Instead, he noted there were two born of the same ilk. The birth of his daughter, now a gastroenterologist, and the birth of his first grandchild, who is now the light of his life, along with his other three grandchildren. Following his wife's death, Alex found strength in the family life of his daughter, although it was not always easily won. Today, several years after Natalia's death, he feels he is returning to life and has recently met a beautiful woman from Tehran with two terrific boys.

Alex has lived a great deal. He says empathy is humanity's preeminent value. Given what he has experienced, Alex is the epitome of grace in living up to that value. With a mission to use the word "love" more often, it is easy to conclude that Alex has lived a remarkable life.

THE KID WITH CEREBRAL PALSY LIVES HIS DREAM AS A FARMER

A story from South Dakota

With apologies, here is a motto I have tried to live by since I was a teen: "There are no excuses." That said, Harlan Temple is an indefatigable soulmate in this philosophy. Cerebral palsy is caused by an abnormal brain development that affects movement, muscle tone, and posture. This was Harlan's cross that he had to bear. He did, however, have the fortune of being born into a highly supportive family with an older sister and a younger sister with Down syndrome. Harlan's enlightened parents enabled his journey in whatever manner he needed.

Surgeries, surgeries, surgeries. That theme encompassed Harlan's early childhood in a chapter he called "Uncertain Times." Unfortunately, they were largely ineffective. He started school at the typical age, and his older sister, who attended the same country school, was a pseudo-caretaker for him for a few years. His middle school and early high school years were harrowing for Harlan. He attended a school associated with a hospital and could only go home on the weekends. It was an excruciatingly lonely time.

His last two years of high school were typical for any teenager, and he began to dream of being a farmer like his parents. As time went by, Harlan could take on more responsibilities as his parents always provided the requisite paraphernalia for him to perform his farming chores.

An insurance agent at age 33, Harlan found love and married after breaking off a relationship with another woman. Throughout the years, he has enjoyed many things that those unhindered would. He fished and hunted and, on one memorable excursion, bagged a "5/6 deer." The 5/6 describes the number of antler points on the animal. Being a farmer, it should come as no surprise that he finds a particular comfort whenever nature is nearby. It provides the tranquility he seeks as one challenged by the world in ways most of us cannot fathom.

Despite his challenges, Harlan and his wife, Rita, give back via involvement with the Special Olympics and dedicated time to the University of South Dakota School for Occupational Therapy. As a childless man, this gave him a nurturing feeling from which he had benefited growing up. His inspirational story and treasured guidance led to multiple commencement speaking engagements at the school. Overwhelmed by the honor of serving, this humble man distinguished himself.

The final chapter of his autobiography, *The Best is Yet to Be*, is titled "Sunset." The book's cover depicts him from behind, sitting in his wheelchair, looking into a beautiful bright light on the horizon with a small picture of his Savior, Jesus Christ, just off to the right. Harlan is now in a senior citizen's home, and his farming life is over. The present, for him, represents one of the two low points in his life, the other being the school period noted earlier. Nonetheless, his faith is strong as he envisions his biological life eventually eclipsed by his eternal spiritual life.

Despite a lifetime of physical challenges and the ignominy of his current internment, Harlan feels blessed. It is from his deep faith that we can all be inspired.

FORMER BRAZILIAN POLICEMAN MAKES A NEW LIFE IN CANADA

A story from Saskatchewan

GKT received his first job offer in Canada one month after emigrating from Brazil and less than 24 hours after completing his life story interview with me. The former Brazilian policeman had been subjected to such ruthless treatment from his superiors that he felt the only way to extricate himself from the pain was to leave his homeland and make a new start elsewhere. After he and his professor-wife had considered both the United States and Canada, they concluded the latter offered the best opportunity for them to succeed.

GKT grew up with a father who used to beat him and a mother who never really wanted him: she'd wanted a girl. Upon his father's death from a heart attack when GKT was only 18, his mother developed psychological issues with which he had to deal. He survived, and after high school, he enrolled to study technology. Several months later, he joined the military, a mandatory requirement in Brazil. After dropping his technology schooling, GKT became involved in what turned out to be a permanent relationship with his future wife. Following one year in the military, it was time to think deeply about his future. For GKT, that meant policing. He took the requisite exams, but before being accepted into the Curitiba force, he spent three years as a corrections officer in a prison. Finally, in 2016, the call came, and GKT's dream job became a reality. His real life had begun, or so it seemed.

It did not take long for GKT to inexplicably assume some of the darker aspects of policing. Although he did not become mired in some of the destructive behavior he observed in his older colleagues, he found himself inflicting physical abuse onto others. GKT's conscience bothered him so much that he sought to perform other duties that might alleviate the stress he was experiencing, and which was beginning to impact his home life. Unfortunately, his situation continued to deteriorate in the form of multiple brutal beatings at the hands of his superiors. It seemed ominously familiar. GKT was once again a victim.

To cope, GKT sought psychological counseling and was transferred to another division in which he performed perfunctory administrative duties. But he recognized that this was only a brief palliative respite, and that real change was needed. He and his professor wife, who was also experiencing doubts about her future, began considering starting a new life in another part of the world.

When a situation for his wife in Canada manifested itself, the die was cast. GKT was ready.

GKT's life began with and continued with physical abuse that ultimately led to a clarion call compelling him to move from his home country. Thus began his journey to make the unpleasant memories of victimhood a thing of the past. Perhaps destiny intervened in that his loving wife, faced with an analogous situation, also sought the exact profound change in her life.

As GKT adapts to his new country and with his dignity restored (humanity's preeminent value, according to him), he will undoubtedly succeed in his 20-year plan to build a solid financial foundation and achieve the desired future that eluded him in Brazil.

A GEOLOGIST'S TRANSFORMATION, A MAN IN HIS ELEMENT

A story from British Columbia

Pete is one of those lucky people who eventually discover their life's true calling. For him, it occurred after pursuing the world of geology for over two decades. This into-the-weeds, father-of-three scientist is a veritable people person. And finding that out was pure luck.

Pete grew up in a loving middle-class environment with parents who immigrated to Canada from England. While not wealthy, he never felt deprived and found passion in soccer. His father, a true Englishman, was prominently involved in the sport as a referee. His parents provided stability and support, and Pete was never pushed to overachieve despite showing academic promise from an early age. Just before his university career was to begin, his father suddenly died. Undeterred by the financial uncertainty his father's death wrought and being highly self-motivated, he enrolled at Dalhousie University in Halifax, Nova Scotia. Pete found great camaraderie in the close-knit geology department as he settled in. Upon completing his Bachelor's degree, he moved to Ontario and studied for his Master's at the University of Ottawa. Pete's ex-Nova Scotia journey had begun.

The Canadian West was his next port of call, where he continued working in the mining business, earned an MBA degree, and started a family with Wendy, a teacher he had met in Ottawa. Life was good. Then came the Bre-X scandal in the late 1990s. That company's impact on mining changed the landscape for Pete even though he had nothing to do with the company. In an industry facing hard times, he answered a cryptic ad in The Toronto Globe and Mail that mentioned project management. The company that ran the ad was RLG International, a group of performance improvement specialists based in Vancouver. They were looking for talented people from various industries who could communicate effectively with clients, and Pete's geology background, by their reckoning, fit the bill perfectly. Initially skeptical, he was eventually convinced to join their team. A new Pete was about to emerge.

In his new role, which has lasted for 25 years, Pete has coached leadership teams all over North America in many different industries. He calls himself a "positive feedback guru" and has instilled this philosophy in the minds of his clients. Pete had his epiphany: he was a people person, albeit one with a panoply of technical talents.

The recent COVID-19 plague brought trying times for many, and Pete was no exception. Working from home rather than constantly traveling had benefits and drawbacks, as the challenges of coaching people from a distance had to be fundamentally addressed. It's been a change requiring personal growth and flexibility, but it's working.

Interestingly, we sometimes define ourselves narrowly and miss the bigger picture. For Pete, once he took a chance and stepped out of the "I'm a geologist" comfort zone, a new world opened for him. In it, he learned a lot about himself, discovered talents that he has used to impact the lives of others, and, in the process, closed the gap in achieving the elusive self-actualization experience.

KLUTZ/OLYMPIAN/SURGEON/FATHER/VETERAN/ ECKIST/SCULPTOR

A story from Arizona

Hugh, to date, has lived a long and accomplished life. The arc of achievement was tilted in his favor at an early age as the eldest of three siblings raised in a supportive, adventurous, and intellectually stimulating environment.

Born in Albany, New York, Hugh struggled with asthma as a young child. His father was a pediatrician who knew the desert air would suit his son, so the family moved to Tucson when he was three. Thanks to his father's generosity, life in the desert was a wonderfully explorative experience with summer camps and other experiential opportunities. At age 16, he boarded a train bound for one of the East Coast's most famous prep schools, Phillips Exeter Academy, in New Hampshire. Despite achieving average grades, he was admitted into Yale University, the third with the same full name to attend that venerated institution.

As a kid, Hugh was non-athletic, though he dreamed about participating on a team. At his dad's 25th reunion, he watched Yale beat Harvard in crew and envisioned himself rowing in the Olympics. Amazingly, after rowing at Exeter and Yale, he did go to the 1956 Melbourne Olympics in Australia (as an alternate) for the Olympic team, Yale (and the United States), winning the Gold Medal in the eight-oared shells! Incidentally, 1956 was the last year the United States sent a collegiate rowing champion to the Olympics that stood on the top of the awards podium.

After graduating from Yale and then Yale Medical School, Hugh began five years of training in orthopedics. He chose this path over other specialties because his father referred to Orthopedists as "carpenters," and the young doctor loved working with his hands and wood. It turned out to be a perfect fit. Immediately following this training at Columbia Presbyterian Hospital in New York City, he served his country in the Army with tours in Vietnam and at Fort Huachuca, near Tucson, where he joined a small Orthopedic group.

His medical school marriage ultimately failed 19 years later because of long work hours and Hugh's lack of awareness of a woman's needs. He enjoyed co-parenting his three boys, sadly losing Seth to melanoma at age 36. Seven years after his divorce, Hugh was emotionally ready to try marriage again but knew it must contain a spiritual path. Following a fall off the roof, in which he broke both ankles, and after several unusual coincidences, he was led to the Path of Spiritual Freedom, *Eckankar*. The goal of Eckankar, an individual spiritual path, is to learn to give and receive Divine Love as a co-worker with God.

In retirement, Hugh was nudged to explore art forms, ultimately ending up in the world of stone sculpture. As a sculptor, he works with the calcium carbonate of marble instead of the calcium carbonate of bone while still using the big tools that orthopedists use. His works grace various venues in Tucson. Hugh has many other passions, including Rotary, Literacy Mentoring, Travel, and Outdoor Adventures.

Some peoples' journeys always maintain their intensity and meaning. Hugh is one of those lucky individuals.

THE RESILIENT ONE FINDS PEACE IN WESTCHESTER COUNTY

A story from New York

The oldest of three sisters, Lauren is a bright, enigmatic woman ahead of her time who seemingly could have done anything she wanted in life. Following high school, she convinced her parents to allow her to take a gap year before that term was used, and she never went back home. Instead, she started her year off as a waitress on Cape Cod and developed an interest in the hospitality industry. Following a trip to Italy with her dad and more hospitality-related work, she enrolled at the University of Massachusetts to study Hotel Restaurant Travel Administration. She also found time to be a photojournalist and later a restaurant reviewer for the Daily Collegian. Lauren married the sweetheart she met at UMass on the weekend she graduated.

While her birth family was a responsible one, Lauren felt her parents were somewhat preoccupied with work and younger sisters. So, moving to New York was an adventure. While working at Rockefeller Center for Royal Viking Cruises, she modified certain office practices that made sense to her but was fired for her creativity. From there, it was on to making serious money. A serendipitous meeting with a gentleman she asked to speak at an alum event led to a job in the investment industry at Merrill Lynch and later at E.F. Hutton and Prudential Bache. That lasted for seven lucrative years until 1987 when, while following corporate strategy, she exposed her clients to uncovered options during unprecedented volatility when investors got whipsawed (i.e. losing money on long and short positions). Lauren lost her job in 1987 and feels remorseful about her client's losses despite following company policy. By 1989, after selling wine cellars, Lauren had worked for her last employer.

An entrepreneurial period began for Lauren as she worked in disparate ventures such as a wholesale jewelry business and corporate product naming. As times changed, she moved on, believing work should be enjoyable. Lauren's newest entrepreneurial enterprise is a Paint Party called *TwiftiesPaint,* where guests may paint Van Gogh's *The Starry Night* or other projects simplified by Lauren. She's partnering with a friend who runs wine tastings and envisions providing entertainment at events and parties. She also runs a successful Airbnb, recently had an ophthalmic laser rental business, and is an Amazon third-party reseller. Her creation of "Twifties, The Fun People Over 50" concept is a plan and a brand to fulfill the needs of a cohort overlooked by Madison Avenue.

Lauren's relationship with her parents was complex. As the firstborn girl, her father loved her dearly as she vicariously replaced a sister he lost early in life. Lauren's mother was a positive inspiration, although their worldviews and temperament differed. Ostensibly married for over 30 years (she thinks, as they never got a license), Lauren never had children. Her former husband likely lives with undiagnosed autism, and this prevented them from fully connecting. Following an amicable divorce, she lives in a house nestled in a forested, tranquil setting. A snowboarder since age 43, she met her new love of ten years at a Vermont ski event. She and her two sisters keep a warm, respectful, familial relationship to honor their mother and, from personal experience, recommend family therapy.

Lauren says the best things in her life happen organically. Life unfolds for Lauren when she is not pressing things and knows the success of her Twifties idea will follow.

YOUNGEST ONE ASSUMES FAMILIAL BURDENS, RISES TO SERVE

A story from West Virginia

Laurie's childhood was characterized by the considerable freedom of being the youngest. That freedom, however, gave way to four years of horrifying night terrors and chaos. Her mother, a piano teacher, had three children from a previous relationship, as did her father, a pharmacist. Following her parents' divorce when she was five, she and her mother moved in with her maternal grandparents. Laurie's mother would often be teaching piano until late in the evening and, at other times, could not meet her teaching obligations due to her affinity for the bottle. Laurie's grandparents were the saving grace.

While some in Laurie's family, other than just her mother, struggled with alcoholism, music was something they all seemed to have in common. Music provided Laurie with a way to express herself, which continues today. In addition, as a youth, she worked at her father's pharmacy to help the family, given that he was slowly going blind. She also started to drive (illegally) at age 13 to help both her mother and father. Laurie learned to think of others first.

Laurie enrolled in nursing school after high school, but her plate had much more on it than studies. She ran the pharmacy as time permitted while helping her father and mother keep appointments. Furthermore, her mother attempted suicide, and her father died before her second year of nursing school. Life was full of challenges for the budding nurse.

Laurie married upon graduating and had two children following two miscarriages. She eventually divorced but enjoys a healthy relationship with her ex-husband, which is undoubtedly a manifestation of her deep faith in God. She remarried and remains so to this day. Finally, she has overcome some serious health problems, such as the time doctors proposed removing part of her lungs to combat *mycobacterium avium complex* (MAC).

After 40 years as a nurse, Laurie decided it was time to call it a day. Nursing has been good for her both inside and outside the clinical setting, as one day, she saved a person's life in a restaurant by administering the Heimlich Maneuver. However, she did have one traumatic nursing experience in the natal care unit. During a shift change, the pharmacy mistakenly prepared an adult dosage of antibiotics for infusion. But it was Laurie who, unfortunately, administered the drug. She found out about it the next day, and upon learning about the potential impact and feeling suicidal, she never returned to that unit despite her love for caring for babies. In retirement, she has enjoyed grand mothering, traveling, and dancing—a passion her husband shares. She has also been more involved in church affairs and is a kitchen volunteer at The First Presbyterian Church at Saint Albans.

Much of Laurie's life has been spent thinking about others before attending to herself. During the journey, the theme of faith sustained her. Her abiding faith has gotten her through challenges such as MAC, a heart operation, and the burden of being the one to whom others look for support. She continues in that latter role today at her church.

THIRD WORLD BORN, FIRST WORLD IMMIGRANT, A LIFE OF SERVICE

A story from Ontario

Harry is the youngest 83-year-old you will ever meet. Born in British Honduras, now known as Belize, he began working at age eight. He lived in a one-room dwelling with his mother, three brothers, and two sisters. Harry's father was absent. While they divided the room into three pseudo bedrooms, life was challenging for the low-income family. Harry began his entrepreneurial activities by getting up every morning at 5 a.m. to sell the 18 Johnny Cakes (biscuits) his mother started to prepare at 4 a.m. After he was done with his first customers, he would return home 30 minutes later, just as the second batch was ready. Harry was learning resourcefulness.

As resourceful as he may have been, Harry acknowledges he has never accomplished anything on his own. For him, mentors along the way facilitated his journey, and some acted as de facto father figures. One was a Canadian man he met while working in Montego Bay, Jamaica, who repeatedly told him, "Harry, I think you should go to Canada; you can find work there!" Six months later, Harry did just that. After landing in Toronto, he sought work at several architectural firms, a profession in which he was autodidactically talented. He ultimately found a position in Montreal while boarding with a cousin and his wife. Harry's fiancé, meanwhile, was still waiting back home. After returning to his homeland to marry and bring her to Canada, destiny awaited him in the form of two influential Montreal brothers. Mentors, again.

While working with the brothers on a project of mutual interest and simultaneously pursuing an engineering degree part-time for six years, they asked Harry how much money he would need to complete the degree program full-time. The philanthropic duo subsequently paid for him to attend what is now known as Concordia University full-time for three years. It is straightforward: what you give, you receive. Harry is a consummate giver.

Like all of us, Harry faced many challenges in life. In addition to growing up in dire economic conditions and fatherless, he is a two-time cancer and one-time heart attack survivor. Although he considers enduring chemotherapy for colon cancer the most arduous time of his life, he has co-authored a self-help book about prostate cancer. Finally, the thought of being fatherless, despite sagacious guidance from father-like mentors, evinces a subtle, emotional regret in Harry.

Harry identified service as humanity's preeminent value. The final line in the Jaycee Creed reads, "And that service to humanity is the best work in life." Harry is a former Jaycee, a service organization that imposes an upper age limit (40) on membership. He serves on multiple boards, including my alma mater, the University of Western Ontario, and was a city councilman for 18 years. Harry, a man of faith, is a disciple of servant leadership. [**Author's note:** Harry has served me wonderfully by being the first with whom I had no prior relationship, to agree to an interview.]

COMING TO AMERICA: THE "UNWORTHY," ACCIDENTAL CHEMIST

A story from Illinois

Mohan grew up in India with a deep sense of inadequacy and no aspirations, as he was repeatedly told that he would make nothing of himself. So, of course, he earned a Ph.D. in chemistry from an American university. Organic chemistry, no less! You know, the super geek stuff. However, his stellar academic career belies a childhood filled with challenges.

While Mohan uses the word affectionate to describe his family ethos, he also sees it as harsh and unsupportive. While his father was a good man, he shouldered considerable childhood baggage, making the father-son relationship complex and problematic. His father endured abuse as a child from his father, and this was passed along to Mohan in an unimaginable way. His father sent him to live in his grandfather's house in another city for ten years. The separation, particularly from his gentle mother, was painful for Mohan, and they endured long periods without seeing each other. During those years, the abuse Mohan's father suffered as a child was experienced by him.

Mohan needed to escape and chose to do so with books. In books, he learned that others thought and lived differently so that he could temporarily be transported to a better place. It did not, however, relieve the extreme self-doubt when he had to deal with the real world. He did enjoy another escape. That was when, for one brief moment as a child, he spent time with his mother's family. That family was the antithesis of his father's. One can only speculate what a dearth of positive experiences means to one's development. Despite the odds, Mohan succeeded in achieving both a Bachelor's and Master's degree and was looking for a job.

Although Mohan was still mostly uninspired, he was blessed with a manifestation of Adam Smith's *invisible hand*, ready to intercede at critical moments. That manifestation took the form of people. One key influencer who impacted his life's trajectory was someone he knew for only a few days. While interviewing for a job, an electrical engineer befriended Mohan and convinced him to pursue a Ph.D. offer in The United States. That gentleman told Mohan he could get a job offer anytime but only had one chance at a Ph.D. Mohan's journey to his new home was taking shape with the generous influence of others.

While pursuing his Ph.D., Mohan met another significant influencer, Beth, who would become his wife. He related the story of his return from a trip to his home in India and seeing Beth cry at the airport because she was so happy to see him. This emotional support was something he had never known. Mohan was truly home. Despite the childhood chaos, his greatest regret is not telling his father that he forgave him before he died of cancer.

Mohan repeatedly stressed the importance of people in his life at key inflection points. There were more than those mentioned above. As important as they were, it was Mohan who ultimately triumphed over a repressive upbringing and is now, and has been for some time, a highly respected chemist.

MISSISSIPPI'S YOUNGEST FREEDOM RIDER (1961) EDUCATES

A story from Mississippi

Hezekiah Watkins' picture is hung on a wall in the Mississippi Civil Rights Museum in Jackson. It is in the Freedom Rider's room; he was only 13 years old. He had unintentionally walked through the wrong door, was arrested, and sent to a notorious Mississippi prison where he was placed on death row. Some days later, under pressure from President Kennedy, the governor had him pardoned. It's hard to believe that that's the way it was for some Americans in those days.

Before he was born, Hezekiah's parents had moved the family from Mississippi to Milwaukee during The Great Northward Migration to seek a better life. At age three, following the death of his father, his mother decided to move him and his two much older brothers back to be closer to kin. She did her best to shelter the young lad from certain realities for Blacks in the South. Interestingly, he lived in a neighborhood with white people who lived across the street. There was, however, very little interaction. By the time he was 13, Hezekiah was becoming more aware of the realities of the day and begged his mother to allow him the freedom to partake in agitator activities. His mother finally consented, and he soon found himself ostracized by people, both Black and white.

Not long after starting at a junior college, the school president approached him and told him to cease his activist ways. Hezekiah refused and was forced to deal with the consequences. One day, a military man knocked on his classroom door and escorted the confused young man to an induction ceremony. Just like that, Hezekiah was a soldier. After going AWOL and being read the riot act following his discovery and arrest, he was an exemplary soldier until he was dispatched at age 21. True to his core, he immediately re-engaged with the activist movement.

Hezekiah knew all the players. Martin Luther King. Jesse Jackson. John Lewis. And so on. However, as the movement progressed, he realized something surprising. His attitude towards white people evolved as he realized that they, too, had played an important role in effecting change. The white Freedom Riders were enduring the same ignominious treatment as their Black colleagues. Furthermore, as the awful treatment of those white people percolated in society, a voice arose among some demanding that government leaders take heed. This, he believes, helped accelerate long overdue action.

Following a five-year marriage that ended in divorce, Hezekiah married again in his late 30s and bought a store that he felt could prosper with the right leader—him. Although getting the loan was difficult, he made it work for over 30 years. While his doctor used moral suasion to retire him, his second wife helped him change his life in significant ways for which he is grateful. She was very strait-laced, and he was drinking too much. That changed, and he has not looked back since. Without her, it is unlikely he would be in his current role.

Today, Hezekiah is a public speaker and often presents to groups attending the Mississippi Civil Rights Museum, where his picture is prominently displayed. He believes it is vital to help educate those with little knowledge of the angst he endured as a pioneer in the civil rights movement. To that end, he has published an autobiography titled *Pushing Forward* to convey his plight.

A DIAMOND IN THE ROUGH ULTIMATELY DISCOVERS HIS TALENTS

A story from Alberta

Andrew Werner was born in Calgary, Alberta, into a loving home. Unfortunately, life became turbulent in his teens as his parents fought often, ultimately leading to divorce. This made life at school and home complex, and he eventually dropped out of high school. He soon found a job insulating houses and used the money to party incessantly. Some of his friends became increasingly negative influences, so he moved to Banff to get away. While working at the famous and beautiful Banff Springs Hotel as a valet, Andrew made the most of it as he hiked, skied, and began a photography hobby. While working there, he met several famous people, such as Steve Winwood, Brooke Shields, and Bobby Hull. However, his continuous partying took a heavy toll on his health until he realized that he needed to do something. Andrew moved back to Calgary and got his GED with straight A's. He toiled for DC Comics for six years and met the girl of his dreams. Andrew became engaged, only to be heartbroken, and eventually they broke up.

As his photography became more serious, he merged this with a passion for the outdoors. Andrew hiked numerous trails in the Rockies and was obsessed with the West Coast Trail as he trekked this arduous and dangerous terrain thrice. He did this primarily to experience its rugged beauty and photograph its true essence and wild nature. He loved the West Coast so much that he moved there, but again, life led him to a dead end. After returning to Calgary to pursue his education, he enrolled at Mount Royal College and settled on business and marketing. While studying, Andrew was hired by a large transportation company. Upon realizing this would become his lifetime career, he left Mount Royal College before graduation.

Andrew's love of photography and the outdoors continued to grow. He also loved live music and learned to play guitar while becoming friends with many musicians. His photography talents led him to do on-site shoots for musicians and weddings, taking him to many remarkable events and places, such as the Rocky Mountain Music Festival in Merritt, British Columbia, and a Napa Valley, California wedding. He also continued to hike more amazing trails, such as Cape Scott, Juan de Fuca, and the Chilkoot trails. Andrew eventually got into ocean kayaking and paddled to Gwaii Haanas and the Broken Group Islands, the latter twice. His fantastic photography was displayed in two galleries and sold a few thousand prints. He also wrote a stunning poem titled *Photo Quest*, for which he won an award. It was also published in a book of poetry called *Dawn's First Light*.

Andrew eventually bought a house and landscaped the backyard into a magnificent flagstone garden with a pond and waterfall. He continued to develop the home with a cedar deck and a custom basement. Andrew ultimately built a man cave with an arcade machine, pinball machines, art, fossils, antiques, native artifacts, and his photography.

Eventually, smoking and partying habits caught up with him, resulting in two near-death experiences in his 50s. Undeterred, he continued to thrive and pursue his love of the outdoors. Although his life started inauspiciously and he never married, with determination and resilience, Andrew realized his talents.

MILITARY MAN CLAIMS DEGREE, SURVIVES TREACHEROUS HIKE

A story from Alabama

Fletcher's dream was to be an Air Force pilot. He enrolled at Virginia Tech University to acquire the mandatory degree but dropped out after his second year. Not one to succumb to failure, he did achieve a Bachelor's degree later in life. After leaving Virginia Tech, he joined the Army and became a helicopter pilot, flight instructor, and maintenance officer. That career took him to myriad locations worldwide during his ten years of active duty and later as a reservist.

Fletcher grew up in a highly supportive family in Dayton, Ohio, with two sisters and moved to Florida at age 16. On the move to Tallahassee, his father entrusted him to sail the 30-foot family sailboat the entire way. For Fletcher, it was a huge confidence builder. One of his sisters, the youngest, suffered cognitive damage that resulted from a complication at birth. Her devoted brother became her guardian when she was in her 40s. As the father of two daughters, he was always there for them during their youth and often passed up on activities such as spending time with his colleagues at the officer's club to ensure that was the case.

As time progressed while in the Army, Fletcher was always willing to take on challenges to improve the future for himself and his family. He became a highly respected instructor and eventually took that to the next level with demanding training on the Black Hawk helicopter. His can-do attitude led to selective opportunities while in the reserves.

One of Fletcher's most exhilarating memories involves a recent pilgrimage to Italy with an old high school friend who is now a Buddhist. The excursion they diligently trained for required hiking between 10 and 12 miles daily over rugged terrain. That was not a trivial feat for a former heart attack patient, Fletcher, or for his less well-conditioned friend, who also has ADHD. One day, they were forced to alter their plans as an earlier earthquake had blocked the intended route. Before long, they were perambulating an expert trail, not exactly what the doctor ordered for two men in their 70s.

Furthermore, they had to return to camp by 5 p.m. or risk being in the wilderness after dark. Darkness eventually enveloped them while navigating a particularly treacherous section on the precipice of a mountain cliff before they finally emerged into a meadow. But the duo still faced a 6k walk back to camp. He laughs at it now but appreciates the quest's quixotic (foolish?) nature.

The Golden Rule drives Fletcher's philosophy. He is religious, stays out of the limelight, and would prefer supporting any initiative. That outlook integrates well with his role in the service and reserves as a behind-the-scenes guy. His goals today are to play the guitar and relaxingly enjoy the fruits of a long and productive career.

Fletcher, the consummate family man who was always there for his teacher wife, his two daughters, and a special-needs sister, also volunteers for the Rotary International organization. Knowing that he can contribute to societal well-being after spending 37 years serving his country gives him great personal satisfaction.

THE WEST OPENS THE EYES OF A CHINESE BIOMEDICAL ENGINEER

A story from Shanghai, China

Sean was raised in the Hunan province of China as an only child to supportive parents: his father, an engineer, and his mother, a librarian, encouraged him to seek the best education available. He started school earlier than most children and studied English from the outset. His paternal grandparents were both teachers and tutored him so he could pass the demanding junior high school and high school entrance exams. In China's highly stratified university system, matriculation from a prestigious high school with a highly competitive academic Olympics curriculum is almost essential for admission into a Tier 1 school. Sean succeeded on every count and entered Shanghai Jiao Tong University to study biomedical engineering.

In some ways, Sean's childhood was similar to that of children from North America. He played sports and took a memorable vacation to the province of his maternal grandparents. At university, he also played sports and dabbled in the financial markets with the ¥30,000 gifted to him by his father. That experience was a precursor of things to come.

Following graduation in 2010, a summer exchange program at UCLA in Los Angeles introduced him to life in the West. Subsequently, he went to IIT in Illinois to work on his Ph.D. He graduated from IIT in 2015 after acquiring valuable collaborative industry experience in helping heart failure patients get back on their feet and receiving the high honor of a Young Investigator Award. A 2015 trip to Croatia yielded important contacts and his first job at Saint Jude Medical of Minneapolis, a company later bought by the multinational healthcare company Abbott Laboratories. Remembering his trading experience in China, Sean started work on the Chartered Financial Analyst accreditation in his spare time. In 2023, his employer, Pfizer, announced a significant transition out of Illinois operations that impacted his future. Today, he envisions working independently in the financial world due to his stellar 2022 trading performance (48% return).

Sean's personal life did not have the same gilded trajectory as his educational and professional ones. Married in 2015 and settling in Boston, his wife was unsuccessful in finding suitable work and moved back to Chicago two years later. Sean eventually followed, but the relationship deteriorated, resulting in divorce, cementing the lowest point of his life. Nonetheless, while in quarantine during a 2022 trip to China, he swiped right on a dating app and is now in a new relationship with a pianist. Although she also studied in the United States, her current domicile is China, which is a logistical dilemma for them. Stay tuned…

Sean has found the experience of living in the United States transformational. In China, where the *greater good,* as defined by the Chinese Communist Party, is the driving narrative, there needs to be more individual thought and action. Individualism is not encouraged, and worse, it can be severely punished. The opposite, for the most part, is true in the West. Sean recently moved back to China, but because of his exposure to Western experiences, he feels free to indulge in the thought of more significant financial and emotional security by entertaining an about-face in his career.

Sean has achieved much throughout his life and will undoubtedly succeed in his next chapter, including an impending marriage.

FARM GIRL BREAKS FAMILY MOLD, PURSUES HIGHER EDUCATION

A story from Saskatchewan

Leonora, the second youngest, grew up with eight brothers and sisters and recalls performing farm chores as early as age five in the 1930s. Education was not stressed as especially important, as her family was mostly noncommunicative with little parental support. Besides, there was a farm to keep the family busy. But Leonora had other ideas for her life and, perhaps just as importantly, she had a role model. Her educated Aunt Natalie was a highly respected nurse. Leonora had her eyes on a prize at an early age.

Following graduation from high school, she moved to the city (Regina), where she attended a nursing school run by nuns. Her father's needless death of appendicitis during that time marked the lowest point in her life. He required surgery but refused because he disapproved of the doctor Leonora had found for him. Following that tragic loss, her mother moved to Regina with Leonora's youngest sister. Upon graduation from nursing school, she stayed in Regina to live with her mother and sister and helped support them by working in the public health system. Two years later, she was on the move to British Columbia as a member of the Canadian Navy. That, unfortunately, lasted only two years as her mother became ill. After moving back to Regina, Leonora found her career calling as a hospital nurse. She met her future husband at a golf event and was married at age 29, which was very late for a woman in that era.

Leonora's life was beset by tragedy once again as, like her father, her mother died at a relatively young age. Nonetheless, her life unfolded nicely, and she was blessed with three children. She identified the marriage of her eldest daughter as the most joyous moment of her life. Despite being married to a husband who did not have the affinity for travel that she had, Leonora did, on one occasion, find her way to Europe with a sister, a brother, and his wife. She expresses regret that her husband was a homebody and that she did not get to see more of the world.

Raised Lutheran, Leonora's life is anchored by an abiding devotion to God. Philosophically, she believes that simple kindness is humanity's preeminent value. Her calling to be a nurse embodies that value and is something of which she is very proud. Perhaps not surprisingly, she describes herself as conservative. This is undoubtedly an extension of her self-reliant experience growing up, where everybody had to pitch in to survive.

Leonora's husband died just before her retirement. She maintained the family home by herself until her 80s when she moved into a senior citizen living community. She expressed inner happiness about being with others her age and said there always seem to be plenty of activities to occupy her time. Her primary goal these days is to keep her mind as sharp as possible. It is interesting, is it not, how the simple things in life take on increasing importance as we age.

Leonora has lived a very fruitful life. In defying parental expectations, she became an educated woman and carved out a career embodying service to others while living up to her most cherished value, kindness.

SECTION 4

THE JOURNEYS

"The journey of a thousand miles begins with a single step."

Lao Tzu

INTRODUCTION

I wonder what it might have been like to have had the eyes of Marco Polo or Ferdinand Magellan. I will never know, but I had an exciting adventure. During my travels, I found people exceptionally open to conversation when they learned of my quest. I talked with about one thousand people while delivering 19 speeches to approximately 500 (mostly) Rotary Club members. The knowledge that others saw value in my message was indeed an honor. I traversed the United States and Canada, encompassing 53 destination cities, 39 states, and eight provinces, while driving 26,403 miles. I beheld the evolving landscapes, researched local histories, and had my boundless curiosity fulfilled. Most importantly, I formed connections with individuals who will forever hold a place in my heart (and on my contact list).

As the initial journey unfolded, I primarily aimed to encounter individuals willing to share their life narratives. However, over time, my focus transitioned. I increasingly immersed myself in urban attractions and engaged in casual conversations unrelated to formal interviews. My strategies for connecting with people also underwent an evolution. In my first 26 cities, I gave just six speeches. In the ensuing 27 cities, that number surged to 13. Additionally, I progressively engaged in more spontaneous man/woman-in-the-street conversations. The four journeys originating from my continentally central base in Illinois transpired as follows:

- Eastern Journey: 17 cities, 84 days, May 1, 2022, to July 23, 2022
- Western Journey: 16 cities, 82 days, September 1, 2022, to November 21, 2022
- Southern Journey: 11 cities, 58 days, January 23, 2023, to March 21, 2023
- Great Plains Journey: 9 cities, 47 days, April 23, 2023, to June 8, 2023

Between each of these four journeys, I embarked on trips to Europe. During the initial excursion in late August, I assisted my daughter in settling in Paris for a year of study at the University of Paris. A second visit to Paris occurred during Christmas, allowing us to partake in a traditional festive *dinde* dinner. A third journey in April fulfilled a commitment to my daughter made in 2017 when we endeavored to dine at the Anthony Bourdain-endorsed Cervejaria Ramiro restaurant in Lisbon, only to find it closed. Back then, I assured her that we would return for dinner someday—a pledge now fulfilled.

Although there were 53 destination cities, I stayed in 64 different locations, as some long drives between cities necessitated overnight stays along the route. My lodgings included:

- 56 Airbnb homes (some solo, some shared)
- One tiny Airbnb tree home (a one-night pitstop to live a boyhood dream)
- Four homes of family members
- Two homes of friends
- One hotel

In the ensuing paragraphs, I provide general commentary with specifics on some of the more riveting experiences.

EASTERN JOURNEY

Of the first 17 destination cities, I had visited 11 earlier. Furthermore, I was well acquainted with the eastern landscape. Except for New York City, my primary focus during the Eastern Journey was all business. Surprisingly, despite my extensive global travels, I had never been to The Big Apple. So, there, I embraced the role of a tourist. Elsewhere, the natural beauty of places like New Brunswick, Maine, New Hampshire, and Pennsylvania left an indelible mark on me.

After an uneventful visit to my first destination, Lansing, MI, I crossed into Canada to visit three cities in Ontario. These included London, where I attended the University of Western Ontario (UWO), a school noted for its world-class business school (Ivey's case-study library[11] is second only to Harvard's); Toronto, where I began my investment banking career; and Ottawa, where my daughter was studying at Carleton University. In London, I conducted my first interview with a stranger, a gentleman named Harry. The thrill was electrifying! In Toronto, I met up with a couple of UWO buddies. In Ottawa, I prepared dinner for four 21-year-old university women bewildered by the term *bull session*.

---

[11] https://www.ivey.uwo.ca/

From Ottawa, it was onto French-speaking Quebec and Montreal. It was there that I attended my first Cirque du Soleil performance.

One particularly vivid memory stands out from the morning I entered New Brunswick, following a pitstop in Quebec's whimsically named Saint-Louis-du-Ha! Ha!. The lush and undulating landscape was draped in a dense, almost ethereal white fog, creating a breathtaking vista. After pulling off the highway, I managed to capture a few pictures. Yet, as they say, photographs often fail to capture the genuine experience—a sentiment that indeed held here. For the rest of my journey to Fredericton, I opted for the leisurely route along the meandering banks of The Saint John River. In a nod to John Steinbeck, I paused for lunch at a charming café in Perth-Andover, where I spoke with an American family from neighboring Maine. Our connection was sealed after the waitress enlightened me about the locally renowned fiddlehead soup. As it turned out, the couple were former urban dwellers who had sought solace in small-town life, escaping the inherent chaos of metropolitan areas—he hailed from Philadelphia, she from New York City.

The visit to my birthplace, Halifax, NS, was marked by a bittersweet memory. Despite having little in common and seldom spending time together, I unexpectedly shared a hug with my brother-in-law before departing for Maine. The previous night, during a family reunion where all ten Leesons (three siblings, six cousins) gathered for the first time (ever!), he had playfully teased me about my mission. Following my response in front of the others, he fell silent. The following morning, his request for a hug pleasantly surprised me. It appeared that I had managed to win him over. Regrettably, this poignant moment became my final memory of Kevin as he passed away on January 1, 2023.

While in Maine, I resided in a remote area outside Portland where Amish communities utilize horse-drawn carts. My Airbnb hosts were a couple of intellectuals (anthropologist and biologist) who largely dropped off the grid to plant vegetables and raise animals.

American flags graced the landscape more abundantly in New Hampshire than in any other state. While trying to find my Airbnb deep in the woods outside Manchester, the movie *Deliverance* came to mind. It was an unsettling feeling as I surveyed the place where I would spend four nights. Ultimately, my burly, bearded host was an incredible young man with a remarkable story. Journeying from Manchester, I explored Boston, MA, Providence, RI, and New London, CT, before arriving in the gleaming city of New York. It was my third visit to Boston, and I somehow survived without getting lost in the Combat Zone (1975), or having a heart attack and being rushed to Massachusetts General Hospital (2012). I did visit Harvard Yard without incident. New London allowed me to get reacquainted with a former Pfizer colleague.

Unsurprisingly, I could write about my first visit to New York City forever. To keep this section succinct, I will relate two personal experiences and then account for the surreal. My first experience began in a Manhattan Subway sandwich shop restaurant. There, a young man generously offered to pay for my water at the register, leading to a conversation on the streets. Slightly lost, he offered to accompany me when I told him I was going to Ground Zero. Along the way, he shared the tragic stories of his two uncles, whose names are now engraved on the Memorial. Elion's empathetic nature left an ineffaceable mark on me. Two days later, I visited the Ground Zero Museum and saw his uncle's pictures to fulfill my promise to him. In a related story, I saw my first Broadway play, *Come From Away*. That play is about the incredible generosity of the people of Gander, NL, who hosted about 6,600 guests for several days during the 9/11 catastrophe as planes landed at the airport of the former airplane gas station during the 1940s, 50s, and 60s.

For the surreal, I saw:

- In Times Square, a man with a sign reading, "Need money for weed, why lie?" I gave him five dollars.

- Also in Times Square, the Naked Cowboy and, in an unexpected surprise, The Naked Cowgirl.

- Numerous people engaged in fascinating conversations—with themselves.

- An eight-foot-tall cyclist (well, slight hyperbole, but not much).

- A woman in pajamas.

- Spider-Man and The Hulk discussing supply chain problems of the pandemic.

- An older gentleman strolling down 42nd street with his pants at his ankles. A young woman let out a startled shriek upon nearly colliding with him. Obviously, she was not a New Yorker.

As I departed the East Coast to return to Illinois, I marveled at the lush, thick green forests covering rolling hills and mountains, a sight unlike any I had witnessed before. That drive through Pennsylvania, from Philadelphia *en route* to Cleveland, OH, left me in awe of the state's natural beauty. In Philadelphia, I snapped pictures of The Liberty Bell and Independence Hall, while in Cleveland, I (figuratively) rubbed elbows with music elites at the aptly named Rock and Roll Hall of Fame Museum.

Commencing any distinctively novel project is always a struggle, as credibility can be elusive. Nevertheless, I found people were receptive, and some were willing to engage in deep conversations about their lives. I viewed the East as a promising start to the project and harbored an eager anticipation for my upcoming exploration of the relatively uncharted (for me) West.

WESTERN JOURNEY

Having previously served as the President of The Libertyville Lions Club in Illinois, I contacted at least one Lions Club in each Eastern city for potential speaking engagements. Unfortunately, my efforts yielded limited success. The only offer I received came from The

Lions Club of Toronto Central, and the audience consisted of merely five attendees. Between my travels in the East and those in the West, a former colleague informed me about his membership in a Rotary Club in Chicago and extended an invitation for me to speak. I enthusiastically accepted the offer, seizing the opportunity to learn more about the Rotarians. I discovered their scope of service was generally broader than that of the Lions, prompting me to contact Rotary Clubs in the West. Lamentably, my inquiries were belated, and several clubs had already secured speakers for the specific date I would be in their city. Nonetheless, I was privileged to address clubs in Portland, OR, and Los Angeles, CA.

After visiting Milwaukee, WI, and Minneapolis, MN, where Bob Dylan and Prince came to life in substantial wall murals, the journey across the prairies of North Dakota, Manitoba, Saskatchewan, and Alberta *en route* to Calgary, AB, could be likened to watching paint dry, as the scenery remained essentially unchanging. Many years ago, at the Newport Folk Festival, Ian Tyson once remarked that romanticizing Saskatchewan was challenging. Yet, he penned the renowned love song "Four Strong Winds" about the prairies. This ode to that landscape stands as a remarkable exception. Nevertheless, I encountered good-natured individuals who embodied the independent spirit that defined the North American West.

However, similar to the United States, the settlement of the Canadian West was not without conflict, as European influences collided with the cultures of the First Nations, Métis, and Inuit peoples. Recent revelations about the residential school system serve as a stark reminder that history is multifaceted and experienced from various viewpoints.

I met Elvis in Regina, SK, where he is known as "Memphis." As a resident of the Chicago area, I am compelled to share my brief experience in Moose Jaw, a small town outside of Regina. While it might bewilder non-Canadians, the sense of nostalgia tied to Moose Jaw is linked to hockey and a connection to Al Capone.

This connection earned Moose Jaw the moniker "Little Chicago," attributed to the town's role in facilitating Capone's alcohol shipments via rail. Rumor suggests that Capone even visited the town. This revelation unfolded before me through a mural depicting the story. It was an "Aha!" moment when I mentally connected the town with a scene from *The Untouchables*, starring Kevin Costner and Sean Connery, in which they intercept illicit alcohol intended for Chicago in Saskatchewan. Now, it makes sense.

During my visit to Calgary, I found a respite from Airbnb homes as my brother graciously hosted me for several days. This provided a terrific opportunity to reconnect and meet some of his friends. Additionally, I had the pleasure of meeting Forrest Gump's twin, catching up with a cousin, and sharing dinner with two former high school classmates, Thelma Melanie and Louise. As I traveled approximately an hour west of Calgary, the landscape transformed first with the Foothills and then the majesty of the Rockies. Following a night's stop in Kamloops, BC, my journey through the Rockies towards Vancouver, BC, continued on secondary highways. Despite my arrival in the coastal city being later than expected, the mountain scenery, especially after days on the flatlands, was a refreshing sight.

While in British Columbia, I embarked on a ferry to picturesque Vancouver Island. There, an old high school friend named Pete introduced me to the stunning beauty of his hometown, Victoria. It would be remiss of me not to mention the surreal scene of homelessness on the West Coast. Vancouver's East Hastings Street presented a striking scene reminiscent of nothing I had witnessed before except, perhaps, in Chennai, India. Stretching for about half a mile, tents and makeshift shelters lined both sides of the street. Although I was aware of the West Coast's homelessness issue, nothing could have prepared me for the sight before me.

Transitioning from British Columbia to Washington involved a tedious four-hour border crossing. In Seattle, WA, where I learned how to juggle (okay, I tried), the area known as East Duwamish Greenbelt was similarly, though perhaps less dramatically, affected by tent camps, as in Vancouver. In Portland, OR, the homeless were concentrated in a park where one individual delivered a speech about social justice. My Portland highlight was meeting up with a former schoolmate I've known since second grade. Mike, also a former college roommate, became Pittsburgh's Head Coach in the National Hockey League in 2014 and is now the Vice President, General Manager, and, until recently, the Head Coach of the Portland Winterhawks Junior team in the Western Hockey League.

While the homeless community certainly includes individuals with mental illnesses, I also encountered those who, due to circumstances, had become vulnerable to some of the harsher vicissitudes of life society can mete out. Their simple aspiration was to have an opportunity to regain their footing. This experience of encountering homelessness persisted as I journeyed to the California cities of San Francisco and Los Angeles. Although the issue seemed more acute on the West Coast, its presence was evident in numerous cities in both countries. While dismissing these individuals as expendable or attributing their circumstances to poor decisions would be easy, their impact on society is more profound than we might realize.

On the way to San Francisco from Portland, I experienced the horrendous impact of late summer wildfires as I made a pit stop at the University of Oregon to see the mural of a childhood hero, the great distance runner Steve Prefontaine. The drive along Big Sur from San Francisco to Los Angeles surpassed my expectations and was my second great-ocean-drive. I had previously driven The Cabot Trail, which winds along the Atlantic Ocean cliffs of Cape Breton in Nova Scotia and was named after the explorer John Cabot (1497).

San Francisco and Los Angeles shine as two of the most remarkable cities in the United States to explore. From the iconicity of Haight and Ashbury to the allure of nearby Napa Valley, Hollywood, and the Santa Monica Pier, these destinations offer a plethora of exhilarating experiences. In San Francisco, I got invited to my first California beach party, a nighttime affair with music and a bonfire. I walked the Hollywood Walk of Fame in Los Angeles and entered the Hollywood Bowl, from which one has a great view of the iconic Hollywood sign. During my time in these locales, I also met a diverse range of people, two of whom stood out. In San Francisco, I met Frederick, a 46-year-old Gibson-guitar-playing throwback to the hippie era, who was released from a New Mexico jail after his wrongful murder conviction was overturned. Regrettably, he never agreed to an interview. At a speech I gave in Los Angeles, I met Ken Atchity, CEO of Story Merchant Books, the publisher of this book.

Following my departure from San Francisco (let's avoid calling it "Frisco"), I entered Henry Cowell Redwood State Park to marvel at the colossal trees. During this visit, I met three brothers in their 60s, one of whom was a classically trained musician. A few years earlier, he had visited my birthplace in Nova Scotia to perform with The Atlantic Symphony Orchestra. Small world.

Transitioning from the lush landscapes of southern California, the scenery gradually transformed as I embarked on my journey through the desert, making stops in Las Vegas, NV, Palm Springs, CA, and Tucson, AZ. Arriving in the desert during late October ensured that while the weather was sunny, the temperature remained pleasantly moderate. An unexpected challenge arose when my GPS appeared to falter, directing me onto an obscure trail leading to a dead-end in the California mountains. For nearly an hour, I encountered no other vehicles. Eventually, I retraced my route and found my way back to a highway, allowing me to continue the expedition. Subsequently, I was caught in a fierce sandstorm in Arizona between Phoenix and Tucson.

In addition to taking in a Rich Little show in Las Vegas (among other interesting experiences that will stay there) and reconnecting with my brother in Palm Springs, where I interviewed Marilyn, a personal friend of The Dalai Lama, I was fortunate enough to be in Tucson during the *All Souls' Day* parade. My Airbnb host, Joe, asked if I was in town to celebrate the event. Puzzled, I inquired further. That day is a remembrance for the departed, observed by certain Christian denominations in November. In Tucson, this was marked by a grand celebration, reputedly the largest of its kind in North America, with over 100,000 participants. People don festive attire and march along a designated parade route for two miles, culminating in a park where music, dance, and a ceremonial burning of letters to the departed occur. It was an otherworldly experience. I met several bereaved people that night.

The landscape gradually transitioned as I left the desert behind and headed towards San Antonio, TX. While it might not have possessed the same visual grandeur as the Rocky Mountains, the journey was uniquely engaging. The desert terrain gradually gave way to small shrubs, then larger ones, followed by more lush vegetation and trees. As the desert scenery faded from my rearview mirror, I approached the historic city of The Alamo. I savored this Tucson to San Antonio drive, making two overnight stops on the journey. However, I suspect the Arizona State Patrol officer I encountered saw things differently. Thankfully, I only received a warning after explaining I had lost my wallet, which accounted for my temporary driver's license, on the last day of my August trip to Paris. Perhaps he felt a twinge of sympathy. That incident marked the sole occasion law enforcement stopped me.

I distinctly remember exercising extreme caution while driving in Texas, given my awareness that many individuals stored firearms in their vehicles' glove compartments. My suspicions were confirmed when my San Antonio Airbnb host informed me that approximately 70% to 80% of cars in the region contained guns. This cultural penchant starkly contrasted with my experience in Canada, where I grew up, and Illinois, where I live. My host also treated me to the Texas double hitter. After attending a mega-church service on Sunday morning, he, an Air Force retiree and avid hunter, took me to a military base to shoot guns for the first time. I shot:

- Springfield XDM
- Springfield Hellcat
- FN SLP 9-Round Shotgun
- Ruger AR-15 Semi-automatic Rifle

Leaving Texas, I continued my journey through Oklahoma and Missouri, making stops in Oklahoma City and Saint Louis before finding my way back to Illinois. In OKC, I met the director of The Oklahoma Sports Hall of Fame, Mike James, who explained why Nadia Comaneci, a Romanian, was an inductee. Nadia was the first Olympic athlete to be awarded a 10.0 score[12] for an event. That happened at the 1976 Montreal Olympics, and I recall seeing it live. She and her American husband, Bart Conner, are doing great things in the state.

In Saint Louis, I was met with something no man wants to hear in public, "Sir, zip up your fly." I'm retired now, so I guess it was just a matter of time. Apparently, I had been parading around town and entered the Arch of Saint Louis with the barn door open. It took a National Park Security Ranger to set things straight.

This western expedition was quite extensive, much like the journey I previously undertook in the eastern part of the continent. Despite being unable to return to my own house for another six and a half months—as I had rented it out for thirteen months to embark on this mission—I eagerly anticipated the familiarity of my home state. I recognized myself as a person without a permanent residence, albeit a fortunate one compared to the many homeless individuals I had met.

---

[12] https://en.wikipedia.org/wiki/Nadia_Com%C4%83neci

SOUTHERN JOURNEY

As I began my Southern Journey in late January, I had already scheduled six speaking engagements at Rotary Clubs. The first occurred in Louisville, KY, with an audience of almost 100. Following my speech, a gentleman approached me and asked if Dr. Bill Randall, whom I had referenced, was the same Bill Randall he knew as a student at Harvard. Indeed, it was the same fellow. Bill, then a Visiting Fellow at Emmanuel College, Cambridge University, and a retired Canadian professor, is the author of this book's Foreword and had earlier nominated me to give a TED Talk. This episode was just another small-world phenomenon. Following my speech, The Louisville Rotary Club gave me a certificate that affirmed a $500 donation to the Rotary West Louisville Housing Fund in my name. A true honor.

In West Virginia, I made a stop at Marshall University in Huntsville to visit a memorial to the fateful plane crash in 1971. The football team perished, and in 2006, a movie starring Mathew McConaughey titled *We Are Marshall* was made about the events. While at my Airbnb in Saint Albans, WV, Forbes magazine released a list of the top 50 tourist destinations in the world. Tiny Saint Albans made the list, and although not explicitly noted in the article, the waterways likely played a role in achieving the honor. I interviewed the gentleman, Bill Currey, who was most responsible for turning the West Virginia waterways in the area from the worst in the country to arguably the best. Between interviews, I stopped in Drummy's Bar & Grill for lunch, where a local bought lunch for me upon hearing about my project. Ah, the people of West Virginia.

I spent my time in Washington, DC, primarily taking pictures and visiting landmarks and museums. My visit coincided with the State of the Union Address.

As my travels progressed, the weather gradually warmed up, reaching delightful temperatures by the time I arrived in Richmond,

VA, where I attended a reenactment of the "Give Me Liberty or Give Me Death" speech at Saint John's Church by the Revolutionary War hero, Patrick Henry. Remarkably, Henry gave that speech in the same church. While in the pew, the woman beside me told me to contact Bill Lohmann of the Richmond Times-Dispatch newspaper about my project. Bill interviewed me remotely while I was in Raleigh, NC, and the editors approved a front-page story on February 17, 2023.[13]

Raleigh offered me the opportunity to interview students about the country's future at three prominent schools in the area: Duke University, the University of North Carolina, and North Carolina State University. Their perspectives were revealing.

On my journey from Raleigh to Atlanta, GA, I crossed into South Carolina and paused for lunch. Outside the restaurant, fate introduced me to four long-in-the-tooth memorable characters: Joker, Donkey, Lightning, and a regular guy with no moniker. They were part of a biker club. The loquacious Joker, anointed the leader by Lightning, expressed interest in a remote interview, though it never materialized.

During my stay in Atlanta, I prepared jambalaya as a gesture of gratitude for the delicious shrimp meal the other Airbnb guest had cooked the previous night. After Atlanta, I had the privilege of staying in the residence of my former boss, Debbie Dufresne, who had relocated to Saint Augustine, FL. Being the oldest permanent settlement in the United States, that small town attracts many tourists. I was also invited to a house party where the locals relieved me of a few dollars at the pool table.

While exploring the Deep South—encompassing Alabama, Louisiana, and Mississippi—I had experiences that closely echoed

---

[13] https://richmond.com/lifestyles/lohmann-man-retires-travels-the-country-talking-to-people-and-telling-their-stories/article_13e03a7c-ad31-11ed-8e76-27cfeaaffa30.html

the region's history. Southern hospitality was extended to me, allowing me quality time with a select group of individuals. In Mobile, AL, I enjoyed a gorgeous sunset on the Gulf of Mexico with an equally gorgeous woman whom I had met while giving a Rotary Club speech in Fairhope, AL. We then went to a restaurant for a delicious dinner. When I gave my speech, I think the Alabamians were surprised to hear I was a fan of Alabama Crimson Tide football back in the day.

Then, there was New Orleans, LA, where I encountered a slightly inebriated gentleman with a French name and accent. I was in a public square, enjoying the surrounding music, when he sat down at the other end of the bench. We initiated a conversation; he was quite the flibbertigibbet. I inquired if he was Cajun, and upon confirming my suspicion, I mentioned I hailed from Nova Scotia, the ancestral home of the Cajuns. His enthusiastic response quickly faded when I revealed that my heritage was British. With a chuckle, he said, "Well, perhaps I ought to shoot you right now." Setting aside that humorous anecdote, I must note my deep foray into Cajun territory and provide a brief history of the Nova Scotia/Louisiana connection.

In the mid-1750s, just before the British triumph over the French on the Plains of Abraham (now Quebec City) in 1759—a pivotal moment in North American history—the British Crown began the expulsion of the Acadians from Nova Scotia and its surrounding areas. Many of these individuals eventually found their new home in the region previously settled by the French, now known as Louisiana, and came to be recognized as the Cajuns. The heart of Cajun culture resides in Saint Martinville, where a historical park honoring Henry Wadsworth Longfellow, the author of the epic poem *Evangeline*, is located. Furthermore, the rich heritage is augmented by an Acadian Museum, a monument dedicated to Evangeline, Saint Martin de Tours Catholic Church, and a local legend that echoes the tale of Evangeline and her betrothed, Gabriel. Engaging discussions with individuals tracing their lineage back to Nova Scotia, some of whom still maintained connections with relatives there, were enlightening experiences for me as a *Bluenoser*.[14]

In Jackson, MS, I met and interviewed the state's youngest *Freedom Rider* from the early 1960s. Hezekiah Watkins is an impressive man. He just happened to be giving a presentation at the historic Mississippi Civil Rights Museum when I was there. You can't make that stuff up. It was an honor to meet a figure who played a role in the maelstrom known as The Civil Rights Movement. A local banker I met at my speech in Flowood bought me breakfast the day before I left Mississippi. As I said, Southern hospitality!

Much like my previous two journeys, I eagerly anticipated my return home by the time I reached my final destination, Memphis, TN. Naturally, I visited Graceland and paid my respects to the authentic Elvis. However, for devoted Elvis enthusiasts, the experience was over the top for my taste. Nevertheless, I can now check it off my bucket list.

GREAT PLAINS JOURNEY

My odyssey's fourth and final leg to the Great Plains was relatively short, encompassing just nine cities. My first stop was in Wichita, KS, where one of my London, ON, interviewees and his girlfriend just happened to pass through on their way to Omaha, NE. He is a shareholder in Berkshire Hathaway and was trekking to Omaha to attend Warren Buffett's annual meeting. It was great to have lunch with them.

The journey from the flatlands into Denver, CO, was inspiring as I again enjoyed spectacular vistas. One can stay entertained by Sirius XM for just so long. Until that point, the landscape had stirred

---

[14] https://www.cbc.ca/news/canada/nova-scotia/bluenoser-makes-it-into-the-oxford-dictionary-1.1402642

memories of the prairies on my Western Journey—flat and uneventful, except for that tornado I witnessed from the highway in Kansas. I'm from Chicago, so my story is that I experienced a tornado, and I'm sticking to it. In Denver, I visited the RiNo district and delivered the first of the five planned speeches for the trip, a day that aligned with my birthday.

I found the landscape between Denver and Salt Lake City, UT, novel and fascinating, particularly as I navigated the rugged terrain of Wyoming *en route* to Utah, where I fully engaged in authentic Mormon experiences at Temple Square. Furthermore, I embarked on a day trip to Brigham Young University in Provo, UT, where a BYU woman invited me to a Mormon testimonial service. After leaving Utah, I re-entered Wyoming and spent several days in Casper. And that's where my Great Plains journey got interesting. Where were my pants? They didn't make it to Casper. Then it hit me: I left my pants in the dryer at the home of my Salt Lake City host, Petra. She mailed them and a hoodie to my next Airbnb stop in Billings, MT. In Casper, I got by on one pair of pants. Thank goodness I had underwear.

But that wasn't the end of my travails and tribulations in Wyoming. On the drive from Casper to the Wind River Reservation in Riverton to interview a Northern Arapaho Tribal Elder, my car's warning light flashed, and I found myself driving in *limp mode*. That mode limits a car's functionality due to a sensed malfunction. I had no clue. After making it to the town and interviewing Ben, he took me to a repair shop that told me they had an opening in ten days. Oh, Oh!

Luckily, the technician referred me to a competitor, Gunner's Automotive Center. Raenell and Chuck had me running the next day with a recommendation to see a Hyundai dealer as soon as possible in Billings, my next planned stop. Before I left Casper, my Airbnb host prepared a delicious eggplant parmesan dinner. Perhaps she felt sorry for me.

Although the car reverted to limp mode during the drive, I made it to Billings. Before entering the city, I got acquainted with George

Armstrong Custer at the field where The Battle of Little Bighorn occurred in 1876. Meanwhile, the car needed a part that had to be ordered. I paid a surcharge for a rush order and went without a car (and $800) for two days. After that, I embarked on a day trip to Yellowstone National Park to visit Old Faithful. For the record, seeing a bison walk past your car just six feet away is surreal. Just don't jump out of your vehicle and get close to the behemoths as some ~~tourists~~ idiots do.

As I departed Billings for Bismarck, ND, I was relieved that my car troubles were over, except for the flat tire that occurred just two miles out. Fortunately, roadside assistance arrived in about 30 minutes, installed the donut, and advised me that the tire was repairable. I drove to a repair shop and was on my way in 45 minutes. The road to Bismark took me through The Badlands (known by the Lakota people as *Mako Sica*), which eventually gave way to verdant flatlands.

Before driving to my next destination, Sioux Falls, SD, Mount Rushmore in Rapid City, SD, beckoned. The mountain engravement, a tribute to four presidents (c'mon now, you can name them), looked better than in the pictures. After arriving in Sioux Falls, I met a fascinating young man and his boyfriend at my Airbnb. Although only in his early 20s, Milez has experienced some troubling times. To my astonishment, I learned that he had read Dan McAdams's book, *the stories we live by*, which contained the interview protocol I had been using. He said that it led him to Buddhism. Secondly, because he is unable to drive due to a physical affliction and is estranged from his parents, daily life is challenging. When we met, he was preparing to travel to South Korea, where his partner had secured a teaching position scheduled to start in the fall of 2023. The problems Milez was facing were related to finances and documentation. His mother held key identification documents that prevented him from obtaining a passport. He needed money to circumvent her obstructive ways. As I listened to his story and reflected on my fortune in life knowing that this thirteen-month odyssey was nearing an end, I went to my room and removed $300 from my wallet. Sometimes, an act of faith can set off a positive chain of events. I hope it does so for Milez. He was overwhelmed. I wished him and Anthony the best. And no, I did not feel duped for one minute.

In Omaha, NE, I drove by Uncle Warren's home (Warren Buffett) to snap a picture and then made a day trip to the University of Nebraska in Lincoln. Once again, as this project has been replete with coincidental experiences, I met a gentleman on campus who was taking the same picture as me. We started a conversation, and he mentioned that his adopted Chinese daughter, a student at the University of Pennsylvania, was on campus for the summer. Chinese daughter, you say? He had two, and I have one. Amazed, we talked about our mutual experiences in China, particularly our stays at The White Swan Hotel in Guangzhou, where we both have the famous *red couch pictures* of our daughters. As I alluded to earlier, these things happened time and time again.

Des Moines, IA. Destination city 53 out of 53. Before starting these epic journeys, I envisioned having dinner with someone on my last night. Well, Stephen Covey was right; things do happen twice. On my last night on the road, I shared dinner with two gentlemen from a Rotary Club: Eddie, a Republican State legislator, and Bruce, a retired tech businessman. I also gave two speeches and, in perhaps the most bizarre coincidental meeting of all, on Day 403 of my epic adventure, I visited Pappajohn Park for a photo shoot and decided to have one last random conversation. A gray-haired man was enjoying the sun on a nearby bench, so I approached him to introduce myself. During the conversation, he mentioned his age, and I casually commented it was the same as mine. A moment later, I told him I set out on May 1, 2022, to conduct research for the book I envisioned. That's when he blew my mind.

"May 1," he uttered, "that's my birthday."

Wait. Same age! Same birthday! For the record, I now know two people born on the same day as me in 1957. The other was a classmate with whom my daughter, Jennifer, shares the same name. That, my dear reader, is not a coincidence. I'll let you figure that one out.

On June 8, 2023, I arrived home and slept in my bed for the first time in one year, one month, one week, and one day. I woke up on June 12th ☺.

AFTERWORD

"Do not be afraid of death so much as an inadequate life."

Bertolt Brecht

MOUNT SOAPBOX

In my biography below, I will recount how my mother taught me an invaluable lesson: *Life is what you make it—there are no excuses.* I will also write about how reading biographies helped shape my philosophical outlook on life. This prolonged immersion into the lives of others during my formative years indelibly shaped my perspective and likely sowed the seeds for my four journeys and writing this book. Rooted in my background and through thorough research, I learned that delving into the experiences of others enhances our own lives and fosters empathy.

No one else on this planet shares my exact journey, nor does anyone share yours. However, this distinctiveness does not consign us to perpetual miscommunication and disconnection. This is the crux of empathy—a bridge that fosters connections. When we unveil shared themes binding us to others, barriers crumble, and empathy flourishes. It is my goal to share that lesson with you.

DISMOUNT SOAPBOX

WHAT WOULD YOU DO?

What should we believe? Are we currently living in an era of intertwined social, political, and economic crises that could reshape established institutions, leading to an entirely different national landscape, as has occurred in the past? Historical instances of such crises include the 18th-century American Revolution (externally focused), the 19th-century Civil War (internally focused), and the dual challenges of the 20th century, the Great Depression and WWII (the former internal, the latter external). If we're experiencing a crisis, one manifestation of this (up to the present, primarily internal) is the heightened sense of division, as expressed by many anonymous respondents. Although most were optimistic about the eventual outcome by a seven to three ratio, that still leaves a statistically significant number of less sanguine people. The remainder of the decade will undoubtedly reveal much.

I would now like to ask you a question. One question was my favorite during my in-depth life interviews with 71 brave souls. Interestingly, this question demanded a one-word answer. My answer is "service." This query, directly from Dan McAdams' book, *the stories we live by*, reads:

What is the single most important value in human living?

The most prevalent response, as you might expect, was love. Number two, I bundled together as it was empathy/compassion; three was respect. However, while writing this book, another question came to mind. Therefore, I challenge you to contemplate the question in the next paragraph.

Imagine on your final day on Earth, you are granted perfect cognitive clarity but must spend the entire day alone before embarking on your next journey. What thoughts would occupy your mind besides pondering what that new adventure might entail? Please indulge my speculation on this matter.

Initially, one might reminisce about the joy experienced throughout the years and how enriching life was. In essence, initial thoughts revolve around what one *received*. Subsequent reflections may encompass personal and professional accomplishments. It's at this juncture that the final day becomes intriguing. Our achievements can never be viewed solely from a self-centered perspective. Invariably, our life experiences and accomplishments impact others. For a fortunate few, such as Thomas Edison or Dorothy Hodgkin, the extent of this impact is beyond comprehension. But what about the average individual who never achieved fame yet played the roles of son, brother, husband, father, grandfather, daughter, sister, wife, mother, and grandmother?

Who have you influenced? Throughout my interviews with mostly unsung individuals, a clear message emerged, either explicitly or implicitly. This message echoed, "My life matters!" Without exception, interviewees always found a way to underscore their contributions to the world, however modest. The scale is not the crux of the matter. Every reasonable individual yearns to believe that their existence serves a purpose. Hence, I deduce that when this fictional day comes to a close, the solitary soul won't dwell on self-serving contemplation but rather on the legacy one bestowed upon humanity. In other words, individuals will go out contemplating what they *gave*.

I traveled the continent for over thirteen months. People bought me lunch. People cooked for me. People listened to what I had to say. People invited me to parties. People brought me gifts. People gave gifts to charities in my name. People=strangers. You know the Irish poet William Butler Yeats's quote about strangers, right? Now that you've delved into these mini-biographies, consider the shared bonds that connect us all. The empathy we draw from learning about others' lives is a precious gift from which we can draw hope (the only thing that never escaped Pandora's Box) as we collectively navigate this exceedingly challenging historical juncture. With steadfast faith, our society will emerge stronger, wiser, and empathetic.

ACKNOWLEDGMENTS

"No one can achieve success alone;
it takes the hands of many to build a dream."

Unknown

Success is always a shared journey. I have been fortunate to have had many incredible people share in this moment as I gave several presentations during my travels. I want to acknowledge the following for making those presentations happen.

Name	Venue	Location
Ed Duffy	Lions Club of Lake Forest & Lake Bluff	Lake Forest, Illinois
Ray Carbonneau	Lions Club of Toronto Central	Toronto, Ontario
Roger Lee	Pfizer	Lake Forest, Illinois
Bill Sampson	Osprey Ridge Golf Club	Pine Grove, Nova Scotia
Mike Theodore	Rotary Club of Chicago Lakeview	Chicago, Illinois

Name	Venue	Location
Ron Gullberg	Rotary Club of Central East Portland	Portland, Oregon
Joyce Kleifield	Wilshire Rotary Club of Los Angeles	Los Angeles, California
Walt Kanau	Louisville Rotary Club	Louisville, Kentucky
Gene Durman	Rotary Club of McLean	McLean, Virginia
Booth Kalmbach	Rotary Club of the Capital City	Raleigh, North Carolina
John Bowman	Rotary Club of Fairhope	Fairhope, Alabama
Jennifer Hyde	Carrollton (New Orleans) Rotary Club	New Orleans, Louisiana
Blake Chance	Flowood Rotary Club	Flowood, Mississippi
Janace Fischer	Rotary Club of Wheat Ridge	Wheat Ridge, Colorado
Tom Rupsis	Billings West Rotary Club	Billings, Montana
Rebecca Wimmer	Rotary Club of Sioux Falls West	Sioux Falls, South Dakota
Blair Overton	Rotary Club of Johnston	Johnston, Iowa
Kent Patterson	Rotary Club of Ankeny	Ankeny, Iowa
Bob Holert	Bellevue Breakfast Rotary Club	Bellevue, Washington

You will undoubtedly note the numerous Rotary Clubs in the above list. I formed a pseudo-partnership with them on this project. Rotarians abide by the following pledge:

- *Is it the TRUTH?*
- *Is it FAIR to all concerned?*
- *Will it build GOODWILL and BETTER FRIENDSHIPS?*
- *Will it be BENEFICIAL to all concerned?*

The third and fourth of these get to the heart of this book's message. So, should you ponder my earlier challenge to reach out, joining a Rotary Club (or any other worthy service organization— Lions, Kiwanis, etc.) would be a great place to start.

Others also played a role in creating my first book. To Dr. Dan McAdams of Northwestern University, Evanston, Illinois, and Dr. Bill Randall, Professor Emeritus Saint Thomas University, Fredericton, New Brunswick, and a Visiting Fellow at Emmanuel College, Cambridge University, Cambridge, England, I am deeply indebted. Dr. McAdams's interview protocol was instrumental in extracting the life stories, and Dr. Randall's enthusiasm for my project was more than encouraging. To the interviewees, I am profoundly grateful. I was extremely privileged to hear about your journey, and your openness and vulnerability were genuinely inspiring. That included dear reader, 30 of the 71 interviewees who cried during the telling. A few early manuscript readers, Faiek Mahmud and Christine Podgorski, provided key input that significantly improved the book. There is, of course, my publisher, Story Merchant Books, and its leader, Dr. Ken Atchity. Without his belief in my project, this book does not happen. Samantha Skelton and Charlotte Drummond ably assisted Ken in shepherding the process.

Finally, my young daughter, Jennifer, who is just embarking on her career, has always been an inspiration. Never forget the two rules by which to live that I taught you, Jen.

TO MY READERS

If you loved this book, *Ordinary Lives, Extraordinary People: A Path to Reconciliation in Our Divided Times,* please write a telling review on Amazon.

—Gregory J. Leeson

APPENDIX A

℘

THE INTERVIEW PROTOCOL

*"And the good life story is one of the most
important gifts we can ever offer each other."*

Dan McAdams

INTRODUCTION

The interview protocol I employed below draws from Dr. Dan McAdams's book, *the stories we live by* and *The Life Story Interview* paper. I am deeply grateful to Dr. McAdams, a professor at Northwestern University, for permitting me to share this protocol. As he suggests in his book, I strongly encourage readers to utilize it. Please note that I crafted each question in sections 1 and 10 of the protocol, while questions in sections 2-9 I derived from McAdams' work.

I did not include one question in the interviews, but, in retrospect, I wish I had. It is a question about which one interviewee voluntarily offered her opinion. That question, *"How would you like to be remembered?"* has the potential to elicit profound responses, and I think it adds a layer of depth and significance to the protocol.

I met Professor McAdams for the first time in February 2024 after I had submitted the book's first draft to my publisher. He informed me that few researchers were involved when he started exploring psychology from a narrative perspective in the 1980s, even though Walter Fisher introduced the concept in the 1960s. However, it was not until 1986 that Theodore R. Sabin coined the term "narrative psychology." Today, thanks to the pioneering efforts of McAdams, clinicians use the approach to help patients, a testament to the profound influence of his work.

To add moral suasion to my above invitation to use the interview protocol, consider the well-known New York Times columnist and best-selling author David Brooks, who penned his most recent book, *How to Know a Person*, that was, at least in part, influenced by the work of Dan McAdams. I was stunned when I heard about Brooks's book, released in October 2023. Knowing I was on the same page as such an eminent author like Brooks validated my thinking. So, one more time, please use the protocol in your life. Have someone interview you. Interview a friend. Interview a cousin, aunt, or uncle. Interview (yikes!) a parent, sibling, or child. And read Brooks's book.

INTERVIEWEE FEEDBACK

Finally, here is feedback from one interviewee, Amy, about the interview and its impact. After reading the protocol and pondering how you would respond, I leave it to you to discern its merit.

They say things happen for a reason, and this is a perfect example.

I met Greg randomly in Seattle. I live in Los Angeles but visited Seattle for two days for a job interview. In line at a chocolate store, we said hello and did some small talk, then went our separate ways. Later, we bumped into each other two more times. By the third random meetup, something told me we needed to talk more, but I had no idea why. I just went with it.

When we were about to say our last goodbyes, I briefly shared a little more about my life with the hopes he would ask to interview me, as I know my life story is a unique one to share. It turned out the timing couldn't have been any better. Greg's travels brought him to Los Angeles three weeks later, so we planned to meet then.

From the pre-interview homework question of breaking my life down into chapters and naming each chapter (a great retrospective exercise) to the last question, each was meticulous, had a purpose, and was well thought out. Greg took me on a journey of my own life while gathering everything he needed to write my story. My interview lasted about five hours.

The questions covered many different topics, and the answers to his questions brought out all types of emotions, from happiness to sadness, guilt to shame to regret, moments of pride, and everything in between. Not once did I feel judged or uncomfortable sharing.

When I first met Greg in Seattle, he mentioned some people he had interviewed later reported back to him that they had healed or were able to process parts of their lives that they never had before. I didn't think I would have the same outcome.

But I was speechless when Greg emailed me my short story after turning my five-hour interview into 500+ words. He understood! He GOT MY STORY! Someone finally heard me, understood my journey, and could tell it in a way that allowed me to release so much of the pain I had been carrying for years. For that, I am forever grateful to Greg.

THE PROTOCOL

This is an interview about the story of your life. The process is selective and, as such, we will not cover everything that has happened in your life as that is simply not possible in the time we have set aside. Instead, your task is to tell me about the most important things that have happened in your life and to provide some insight into how you see your future. There are no right answers. There are no wrong answers. There are no judgments. I am simply interested in learning about your life.

1. Childhood Family Life

Please check four boxes that best describe your family life growing up. Add your own word(s) if you wish, but keep to the four-word limit. The four words may come from both sides of the ledger.

Positive	Negative
Adventurous	Arrogant
Affectionate	Chaotic
Generous	Distant
Responsible	Harsh
Stable	Irresponsible
Supportive	Selfish
Unassuming	Unsupportive

2. Life Chapters

Please begin by thinking about your life as if it were a book or novel. Imagine that the book has a table of contents containing the titles of the main chapters in the story. To begin here, please describe very briefly what the main chapters in the book might be. Please give each chapter a title, tell me just a little bit what each chapter is about, and say a word or two about how we get from one chapter to the next. As a storyteller here, what you want to do is give me an overall plot summary of your story, going chapter by chapter. You may have as many chapters as you want, but I would suggest having between about 2 and 7 of them. We will want to spend no more than about 45 minutes on this first section of the interview, so please keep your descriptions of the chapters relatively brief. [**Author's note:** I found that most people, while abiding by the seven-chapter limit, tended to spend more than 45 minutes answering this question].

3. Key Events

Now that you have described the overall plot outline for your life, I would like you to focus in on a few key scenes that stand out in the story. A key scene would be an event or specific incident that occurred at a particular time and place. Consider a key scene to be a moment in your life story that stands out for a particular reason— perhaps because it was especially good or bad, particularly vivid, important, or memorable. For each of the eight key events we will consider, I ask that you describe in detail what happened, when and where it happened, who was involved, and what you were thinking and feeling in the event. In addition, I ask that you tell me why you think this particular scene is important or significant in your life. What does the scene say about you as a person? Please be specific.

1. **High point.** Please describe a scene, episode, or moment in your life that stands out as an especially positive experience. This might be *the* high point scene of your entire life, or else an especially happy, joyous, exciting, or wonderful moment in the story. Please describe this high point scene in detail. What happened, when and where, who was involved, and what were you thinking and feeling? Also, please say a word or two about why you think this particular moment was so good and what the scene may say about who you are as a person.

2. **Low point.** The second scene is the opposite of the first. Thinking back over your entire life, please identify a scene that stands out as a low point, if not *the* low point in your life story. Even though this event is unpleasant, I would appreciate you providing as much detail as you can about it. What happened in the event, when and where, who was involved, and what were you thinking and feeling? Also, please say a word or two about why you think this particular moment was so bad and what the scene may say about you or your life.

3. **Low point.** In looking back over your life, it may be possible to identify certain key moments that stand out as turning points—episodes that marked an important change in you or your life story. Please identify a particular episode in your life story that you now see as a turning point in your life. If you cannot identify a key turning point that stands out clearly, please describe some event in your life wherein you went through an important change of some kind. Again, for this event please describe what happened, when and where, who was involved, and what you were thinking and feeling. Also, please say a word or two about what you think this event says about you as a person or about your life.

4. **Positive childhood memory.** The fourth scene is an early memory—from childhood or your teenage years—that stands out as especially positive in some way. Please describe this good memory in detail. What happened, when and where, who was involved, and what were you thinking and feeling? Also, what does this memory say about you or about your life?

5. **Negative childhood memory.** The fifth scene is an early memory—from childhood or your teenage years—that stands out as especially negative in some way. This would be a very negative, unhappy memory from your early years, perhaps entailing sadness, fear, or some other very negative emotional experience. Please describe this bad memory in detail. What happened, when and where, who was involved, and what were you thinking and feeling? Also, what does this memory say about you or your life?

6. **Vivid adult memory.** Moving ahead to your adult years, please identify one scene that you have not already described in this section (in other words, do not repeat your high point, low point, or turning point scene) that stands out as especially

vivid or meaningful. Please describe this scene in detail: tell what happened, when and where, who was involved, and what you were thinking and feeling. Also, what does this memory say about you or your life?

7. **Religious, spiritual, or mystical experience.** Whether they are religious or not, many people report that they have had experiences in their lives where they felt a sense of the transcendent or sacred, a sense of God or some almighty or ultimate force, or a feeling of oneness with nature, the world, or the universe. Thinking back on your entire life, please identify an episode or moment in which you felt something like that. This might be an experience that occurred within the context of your own religious tradition, if you have one, or it may be a spiritual or mystical experience of any kind. Please describe this transcendent experience in detail. What happened, when and where, who was involved, and what were you thinking and feeling? Also, what does this memory say about you or your life?

8. **Wisdom event.** Please describe an event in your life in which you displayed wisdom. The episode might be one in which you acted or interacted in an especially wise way, or provided wise counsel or advice, made a wise decision, or otherwise behaved in a particularly wise manner. What happened, when and where, who was involved, and what were you thinking and feeling? Also, what does this memory say about you and your life?

4. Significant Influences

Every person's life story is populated by a few significant people who have a major impact on the narrative. These may include, but not be limited to parents, children, siblings, spouses, lovers, friends, teachers, coworkers, and mentors. I want you to describe two or three such people. At least one of these should be a person to whom you are not related. Please specify the kind of relationship you had or have with each person and the specific way he or she has had an impact (positive or negative) on your life story.

Describe other key influences on your life. By this I mean things such as books, magazines, movies, TV shows, music, art, and so on. Tell me about your favorite stories from this domain. What impact, if any, did each story have on your life?

5. Future Script

Your life story includes key chapters and scenes from your past, as you have described them, and it also includes how you see or imagine your future. Please describe what you see to be the next chapter in your life. What is going to come next in your life story? Please describe your plans, dreams, or hopes for the future.

Do you have a life project in your future? A life project is something that you have been working on and plan to work on in the future chapters of your life story. The project might involve your family or your work life, or it might be a hobby, avocation, or pastime. Please describe any project that you are currently working on or plan to work on in the future. Tell me what the project is, how you got involved in the project or will get involved in the project, how the project might develop, and why you think this project is important for you and/or for other people.

6. Challenges

This next section considers the various challenges, struggles, and problems you have encountered in your life. I will begin with a general challenge, and then I will focus on three particular areas or issues where many people experience challenges, problems, or crises.

1. **Life challenge.** Looking back over your entire life, please identify and describe what you now consider to be the greatest single challenge you have faced in your life. What is or

was the challenge or problem? How did the challenge or problem develop? How did you address or deal with this challenge or problem? What is the significance of this challenge or problem in your own life story?

2. **Health.** Looking back over your entire life, please identify and describe a scene or period in your life, including the present time, wherein you or a close family member confronted a major health problem, challenge, or crisis. Please describe in detail what the health problem is or was and how it developed. If relevant, please discuss any experience you had with the healthcare system regarding this crisis or problem. In addition, please talk about how you coped with the problem and what impact this health crisis, problem, or challenge has had on you and your overall life story.

3. **Loss.** As people get older, they invariably suffer losses of one kind or another. By loss, I am referring here to the loss of important people in your life, perhaps through death or separation. Looking back over your entire life, please identify and describe the greatest interpersonal loss you have experienced. This could be a loss you experienced at any time in your life, going back to childhood and up to the present day. Please describe this loss and the process of the loss. How have you coped with the loss? What effect has this loss had on you and your life story?

4. **Failure, regret.** Everybody experiences failure and regrets in life, even in the happiest and luckiest lives. Looking back over your entire life, please identify and describe the greatest failure or regret you have experienced. The failure or regret can occur in any area of your life; work, family, friendships, or any other area. Please describe the failure or regret and the way in which the failure or regret came to be. How have you coped with this failure or regret? What effect has this failure or regret had on you and your life story?

7. Personal Ideology

Now, I would like to ask a few questions about your fundamental beliefs and values and about questions of meaning and morality in your life. Please give some thought to each of these questions.

1. **Religious/ethical values.** Consider for a moment the religious or spiritual aspects of your life. Please describe in a nutshell your religious beliefs and values, if indeed these are important to you. Whether you are religious or not, please describe your overall ethical or moral approach to life.

2. **Political/social values.** How do you approach political or social issues? Do you have a particular political point of view? Are there particular social issues or causes about which you feel strongly?

3. **Change, development of religious and political views.** Please tell the story of how your religious, moral, and/or political views and values have developed over time. Have they changed in any important ways?

4. **Single value.** What is the most important value in human living?

5. **Other.** What else can you tell me that would help me understand your most fundamental beliefs and values about life and the world? What else can you tell me that would help me understand your overall philosophy of life? What have you learned?

8. Life Theme

Looking back over your entire life story with all its chapters, scenes, and challenges, and extending back into the past and ahead into the future, do you discern a central theme, message, or idea that runs throughout the story? What is the major theme in your life story?

9. Other

What else should I know to understand your life story?

10. The Little Stories

Here is a little story from my life. A little story is one from your life that, in the big scheme of things, has little impact but, for some reason, endures in your mind and may tell the world something important about you. Do you have a little story?

Greg's Little Story

A fortnight after winning the provincial 1500-meter championship for 14-year-olds, I eagerly entered another track meet, which presented an opportunity to distinguish myself. Here, I would compete in a track/cross country race featuring Brian Malone, the provincial 16-year-old 1500m champion. Open to those under 17, this event held tremendous potential for my growth as a runner. Shortly after the starting gun fired, I found myself in a familiar position: in last place, a strategy I had learned from my athletic idol, Kip Keino, the 1968 Mexico City Olympic hero.

The first runner I prepared to pass was a young boy, hardly more than eight years old. Just as I was about to overtake him, a profound sense of purpose overcame me, guiding me toward a greater mission that day. I stayed by the young boy's side as the race progressed, offering continuous encouragement. As we made our way back into the stadium for the final stretch of 120 meters, the vibrant cheers of the crowd resonated. Some among them undoubtedly recognized me and comprehended the unfolding scenario. I urged the young runner to unleash his best effort for the last 50 meters. Ultimately, I finished in last place.

Upon crossing the finish line, I paused momentarily before returning to congratulate him. However, I never got the chance.

The boy's mother emerged from the spectators and enveloped her child in a warm embrace. With a contented smile, I walked away, confident I had fulfilled the purpose set before me that day. Later, Brian confided in me, expressing that he had searched for me during the race, curious about my whereabouts. He had been eagerly anticipating the competition, as had I. I explained I had other obligations to attend to. This anecdote resurfaces in my thoughts whenever I encounter moments of self-doubt as a reminder of my inherent value as a human being.

The inspiration behind my actions that day stemmed from the biography *I Am Third*, which recounts Gale Sayers's life. The book's core philosophy—prioritizing God, Others, and Self in that order—resonated deeply with me.

APPENDIX B

MY STORY (A TEMPLATE)

"Start a huge, foolish project, like Noah… it makes absolutely no difference what people think of you."

Rumi

MY LIFE – INTERVIEWED BY DR. BILL RANDALL

I initially intended to leave my story out of this book. However, the question about my life arose numerous times on my journeys, so I have included an appropriately detailed accounting. In saying that, I imply an accounting significantly shorter than any full biography but sufficient to impart a sense of my story to the reader beyond the mini-stories recited above. It will give you an insight into the most critical events in my life, both good and bad, and the people who played the most significant roles. In doing so, I hope you see that writing your own story is manageable.

The question was about how to get this done. During a meeting with Bill Randall, he suggested that he interview me and use that output as the basis for a brief autobiography. I prepared meticulously for the interview as, unlike the people I interviewed, the questions were well known to me, other than those extemporaneously posed by Bill.

I read an article about 30 years ago that resonated with me then and still does today. The writer asserted, "Some people live with a sense of destiny." I felt this since my youth, even if the "what" related to that destiny did not crystalize until my 20s. As I see it, three fundamental factors will determine someone's destiny. You have no control over the first one. You have partial control over the second one. You have complete control over the third one. They are, in order:

- Luck
- Ability
- Attitude

Of these, the most important is attitude, which is rather convenient since it is the only factor over which we have complete control. A metaphysical link between attitude and luck exists and I have experienced this in my life. Ability consists of the innate and the nurtured. Once again, attitude is connected, as it will govern the willingness to augment your human capital. This understanding empowers us as it firmly puts the reins of our destiny in our hands.

As you will learn in these pages, people, books, and circumstances shaped my attitude, which led to my writing this book. In it, I urge readers to open their minds empathetically to the journey we all share and the implications therein.

So, for those who asked or wondered how and why a kid from the far northeast corner of the continent (Nova Scotia) made it to Lansing, MI, Des Moines, IA, and the 51 communities in between to engage with strangers and to tell a story of hope, I trust that you will find the answers in the narrative below.

Youth—"Living in his own world."

I was raised with three siblings, guided by dependable parents who provided everything we needed. My father, a civil engineer and city planner at Bell Aliant, a division of Bell Canada, began his career as a telephone man and retired as a telephone man. Remarkably, I recall him missing only one day of work due to illness, a testament to his dedication. Meanwhile, my mother, hailing from a blue-collar background, dedicated herself to homemaking after marriage, a common practice at the time. My father's family valued intellectual pursuits, while my mother's family embodied the blue-collar work ethic. Together, they represented the convergence of hands-on labor and intellectual engagement in our family narrative.

My introverted parents kept to themselves, rarely interacting with the community or expanding their social circle. Affection, encouragement, and celebration were scarce in our household. With one exception, birthdays were never celebrated, and graduations came and went without acknowledgment. On the night of my high school graduation ceremony, I was shooting hoops on the playground. This distant upbringing perception is a sentiment shared by my siblings as well.

When I was 19, I had my first meaningful conversation with my father; it wasn't until I turned 20 that I had a similar talk with my mother. That conversation with my mother gave me profound insights into my father's life. In his youth, while his two brothers headed to McGill University in Montreal for higher studies, my father chose a different path, opting for forestry sciences at the University of New Brunswick. His decision likely stemmed from McGill not offering his preferred discipline. However, his academic journey was interrupted by rheumatic fever, a debilitating illness which forced him into a prolonged period of convalescence, preventing him from completing his studies. This illness, with its potential heart complications, instilled in him a perpetual fear for his health, shaping his cautious approach to life. Consequently, he steered clear of risk-taking and rarely deviated from his narrow professional trajectory. Despite his evident intelligence, he never actively pursued promotions, appearing content with whatever came his way. This cautious demeanor inadvertently influenced our upbringing. While he provided for our family diligently through hard work, he likely never fully realized his potential.

My mother's life took a significant turn following her mother's passing when she was just ten. Instead of pursuing education beyond ninth grade, she assumed the caretaker role for her father, sister, and two brothers, who later found success in the construction industry. I vividly recall her dedicated efforts every Friday, meticulously clipping coupons in preparation for her weekly shopping trips to several different grocery stores. She prioritized deals, buying bananas from one store if they were on sale and milk from another if it offered a discount. Thanks to my father's consistent employment and my mother's unwavering domestic support, my siblings and I experienced remarkable stability during our upbringing. While we were spared the struggles of alcoholism, drug abuse, and other societal issues endemic in some families, emotional engagement was notably lacking. Reflecting on my upbringing alongside others I've encountered, I see it as a mixed bag, with stability on the one hand but a deficit of emotional support on the other. My sister once shared our upbringing with her therapist, who commented on how she essentially had to "raise herself," a sentiment that deeply resonated with me. But who was I?

My life journey began auspiciously. Before formal schooling began, my mother became my first teacher, introducing me to the wonders of the alphabet and numbers. I vividly recall the day she attempted to unveil the mysteries of addition and subtraction through flashcards. Years later, in that conversation to which I alluded earlier, my mother informed me about asking my father, upon his return home from work that day, whether he had taught me math, only to find out he hadn't been involved in my math education at all. This revelation puzzled them before concluding I had autodidactically taught myself those fundamental skills. As I embarked on my primary grade journey later that same year, my report card bore a succinct yet meaningful statement: "Gregory throws himself wholeheartedly..." These words resonated with me, becoming a beacon for the person I aspired to become and the attitude I aimed to cultivate. I held onto that report card and another until my twenties, occasionally revisiting them to reflect on their encapsulated ideas.

Shortly after I began first grade, the phone rang at our home. The principal called to inform my parents that, following an evaluation, the school recommended that I move to a class with second grade students. Despite their initial reluctance, my parents eventually agreed, as my mother later disclosed to me. I vividly remember being escorted out of my classroom, walking down the hallway, and directed to take a seat in my new classroom. However, beyond that moment, I have no recollection of that academic year. If I hadn't recalled that day and subsequently inquired about it during that conversation with my mother, I would have remained unaware of my skipping a grade, as my parents never broached the topic. The Leeson children were not encouraged to excel. The following summer, after my father's three-year assignment outside the city concluded, we returned to the city, and my parents reenrolled me in second grade. During our enlightening conversation, my mother explained that upon further consideration, they believed it was essential for me to be among children my age.

When I was six, I returned home from school in tears, having been bullied by an older boy. My mother came over, looked down on me, and inquired about what had happened. After I told her, she informed me she would not always be there to solve my problems and that I needed to stand up for myself. With those words, she turned and walked away. In never picking me up, never hugging

214

me, or consoling me in any way, she imparted a valuable lesson I have carried throughout my life. *Life is what you make it—there are no excuses.* My mother confirmed that memory during our conversation years later. From this early lesson, I would soon learn to shape a world for myself.

In third grade, one noteworthy moment helped shape my outlook on life. Our teacher, Mrs. MacDonald, suggested we exchange Valentine's Day cards. The night before, I addressed cards to everyone in the class except one little girl, questioning whether to give her one. We placed our cards on the teacher's desk the following day, and she began calling out the names. That little girl received a card from the teacher and one from a fellow girl, making it just two cards in a class of approximately 25 students. And then she received one more. It was from a boy. I remember the night before wondering what other kids, especially the boys, would think of me if I gave her a card. When it was over, not only was there no backlash, but I felt good about myself because I dared to be different, especially from the other boys. It was my first real experience with that. Being different was certainly nothing that my parents would have encouraged. I still possess the class picture from that year, and that little girl unmistakably stands out. I occasionally wonder how her life unfolded.

The fourth grade brought four significant events, one laying the groundwork for my philosophical journey. To begin, I experienced my inaugural epileptic seizure early in the year – a grand mal episode that signaled an anomaly in my brain's development. Even now, I hold onto the 1968 doctor's report from the electroencephalogram, which starkly labeled my brain activity as "abnormal," evoking echoes of Mary Shelley's narratives.

Secondly, I purged fictional books from my reading repertoire, save for those obligatory selections mandated by schools. Fictional works seemed inadequate for fostering the knowledge I craved. The last fiction I willingly read before adulthood was likely a Hardy Boys mystery.

Thirdly, between the ages of nine and eighteen, I immersed myself in biographies, reading more during that period than most would read in a lifetime. These books depicted accounts not only of perseverance, triumph, and love but also of disillusionment, failure, and loss. My focus gravitated toward two distinct categories of individuals: Athletes, symbolic of action, and Coaches, emblematic of contemplation. Through these biographies, I gleaned insights into pivotal historical events: from the Great Depression to WWII, Jim Crow to the Civil Rights Movement, and the FLQ to the Counterculture. I traversed narratives chronicling the harsh realities of poverty, whether in the heart of Texas, the plains of Alberta, or elsewhere, all while absorbing the ethos of accountability and resilience. Stories recounting the indignities of racial discrimination, such as being denied entry to a restaurant based on skin color, were among the many eye-opening revelations. Within these narratives, the scaffolding of my philosophical outlook on life began to form while reinforcing my mother's no excuses lesson.

My fascination with philosophical inquiries led me to delve deep into John Wooden's renowned *Pyramid of Success*, meticulously studying its principles as elucidated in his literary masterpiece, *The Wizard of Westwood*. Through Gale Sayers's *I Am Third*, I embraced the profound notion that life's purpose extends beyond oneself. Rod Gilbert's *Goal, My Life on Ice,* vividly embodied the virtue of perseverance. Roy Campanella's stirring narrative in *It's Good to Be Alive* illuminated the power of finding gratitude amidst adversity. Sandy Koufax's moral stance, as portrayed in his eponymous book, during the 1965 World Series Game 1, falling on Yom Kippur, left a lasting impression on me. Muhammad Ali's unwavering integrity was personified throughout *The Greatest: My Own Story*. This diverse collection of books, spanning basketball, football, hockey, baseball, and boxing, intricately weaved a tapestry of inspiration.

They often say meeting your heroes can be disappointing, but when I met Rod Gilbert at age 12, it was a moment I'd never forget.

It happened during an exhibition game in Halifax, where the New York Rangers faced off against the Montreal Canadiens. Gilbert, a hockey legend, scored a goal, and the game ended in a 3-3 tie. After the game, amidst a crowd of rambunctious boys outside the dressing room, I patiently awaited my hero's arrival, determined to get his autograph. As players emerged, they brushed past the crowd, paying little attention to the boys. Then Gilbert stepped out of the dressing room. Despite the chaos around him, Gilbert signed every piece of paper thrust his way. I vividly recall his graciousness, especially when he responded to a gentleman's gratitude with a sincere "My pleasure, sir," spoken in his distinctive French-Canadian accent. I made sure to wait until the end to approach him. Walking out of the stadium, I shared my admiration for his resilience, having read about his return to hockey, defying doctors' prognostications after two spinal cord surgeries at the Mayo Clinic. Rod Gilbert embodied perseverance and humility in every aspect of his life. Sadly, he passed away in 2021, and I never had the chance to express my gratitude to him directly. But his selfless actions that day left an indelible mark on me, reminding me of the qualities that make a true hero.

The fourth significant moment stemmed from my teacher, Mrs. Dolan, whose words on my report card stayed with me well into my 20s. She tersely noted, "Gregory often appears to be living in his own world." This was a warning to my parents, I surmise, and was echoed by my siblings when I recently asked them about their perceptions of me growing up. In fourth grade, it marked the beginning of a journey. As my sister's therapist once remarked about her, it was the commencement of self-determination. Mrs. Dolan's insight was astute; within the pages of books, I found refuge from a family dynamic characterized by detachment, cultivating a distinctly different mode of thought and action. Interaction with my parents was minimal; I cannot recall a single argument and only one instance of discipline. My mother's recollection of a parent-teacher meeting in seventh grade speaks volumes—one teacher informed her that her presence was unnecessary, as there was nothing to discuss. She told me it represented her last time talking to my teachers and that she ceased worrying about my educational journey.

During my transition from fifth to sixth grade, I was captivated by the 1968 Mexico City Olympics. Among the iconic moments etched in my memory are Bob Beamon's record-breaking jump and the historic Black Power salute by John Carlos and Tommie Smith. However, Kip Keino's remarkable victory in the 1500m race left the most profound impression on me. Despite starting from the back of the pack, Keino clinched the gold medal, inspiring me in ways I couldn't foresee. Little did I realize then that this memory would later shape the most significant achievement of my youth.

In sixth grade, I got into a fight in the schoolyard, which ended with me fracturing my right hand from a punch I threw. The next day, I had to miss school for X-rays and to get a cast. That same day, the class voted to go on a field trip that, for some reason, required a unanimous vote. Upon my return to school the day after that, a friend told me someone had said, "I'm glad Greg isn't here." They say that kids are more aware of things than they are given credit for. Apparently, in an odd affirmation of Mrs. Dolan's observation, those twelve-year-olds realized I was an unlikely passenger on a bus. I had to be the bus driver. During the next three years, I would have a handful of experiences driving.

During my formative years in school, I was fortunate to encounter two extraordinary educators who recognized my potential and served as invaluable mentors, steering me toward my goals. The first of these mentors was Charles Weatherby, my physical education teacher and coach throughout junior high school, spanning grades 7 to 9. This relationship extended into high school, where I continued to benefit from his guidance through his Thursday night basketball clinics. Mr. Weatherby eventually got to know me better than any other teacher. He actively encouraged my participation in cross-country running, which commenced in September. By the time I completed junior high, I had transitioned from a mere participant to a consistent winner of city cross-country races, ultimately achieving recognition as the top 14-year-old 1500m runner in Nova Scotia. I clinched the Nova Scotian Track and Field 1500m title in what I later discovered was a record-breaking time (unconfirmed). My competitive running journey was defined by last-place starts, reminiscent of the lesson I gleaned from observing Kip Keino in 1968. Those successful running experiences, particularly when I started in last place but still won, profoundly empowered confidence in my abilities and spilled over to other aspects of my life.

A fortnight after winning that provincial 1500m championship, I eagerly entered another track meet which presented an opportunity to uniquely distinguish myself. Here, I would compete in a track/cross country race featuring Brian Malone, the provincial 16-year-old 1500-meter champion. Open to those under 17, this event held tremendous potential for my growth as a runner. Shortly after the starting gun fired, I found myself in a familiar position—in last place.

The first runner I prepared to pass was a young boy, hardly more than eight years old. Just as I was about to overtake him, a profound sense of purpose overcame me, guiding me toward a greater mission that day. I stayed by the young boy's side as the race progressed, offering continuous encouragement. As we made our way back into the stadium for the final stretch of 120 meters, the vibrant cheers of the crowd resonated. Some among them undoubtedly recognized me and comprehended the unfolding scenario. I urged the young runner to unleash his best effort for the last 50 meters. Ultimately, I finished in last place.

Upon crossing the finish line, I paused momentarily before returning to congratulate him. However, I never got the chance. The boy's mother had emerged from the spectators and enveloped her child in a warm embrace. With a contented smile, I walked away, confident I had fulfilled the purpose set before me that day. Later, Brian confided in me, expressing that he had searched for me during the race, curious about my whereabouts. He had been eagerly anticipating the competition, as had I. I explained I had other obligations to attend to. This anecdote resurfaces in my thoughts whenever I encounter moments of self-doubt about who I am.

The inspiration behind my actions that day stemmed from the biography *I Am Third*, which recounts Gale Sayers's life. The book's core philosophy—prioritizing God, Others, and Self in that order—resonated deeply with me.

During junior high school, I was deeply involved in other sports, playing on the soccer, volleyball, and basketball teams. Beyond the school teams, I also participated in a national fitness competition backed by the Canadian government to promote physical activity among students. This competition was no ordinary affair; it comprised six distinct athletic challenges, each testing various aspects of fitness such as speed, endurance, upper body strength, core strength, explosiveness, and agility. The ultimate prize was a prestigious award endorsed by the Prime Minister of Canada himself. To secure the Prime Minister's Award of Excellence, one had to rank in the top 5% nationwide in each of the diverse fitness categories. To this day, I keep both the scorecard signed by Mr. Weatherby and the certificate bearing the signature of Prime Minister Pierre Elliot Trudeau as cherished mementos.

In the early days of ninth grade, Mr. Lacy, my math teacher, approached me with an intriguing proposition. He recognized my enthusiasm for tackling math problems and offered unlimited questions to solve and tests to take. Moreover, he encouraged me to engage in self-directed learning, empowering me to approach problem-solving in my unique way. Unlike the conventional methods outlined in our textbooks, Mr. Lacy didn't confine me to a set path. That school year, I immersed myself in endless mathematical challenges. My experience in Mr. Lacy's class starkly contrasted with the lack of encouragement and recognition I experienced at home. In the nurturing environment Mr. Lacy fostered, I discovered the transformative power of support, igniting a newfound passion for creative exploration.

To better understand the inner workings of numbers, I dedicated some solitary weekend evenings that year to inventing scenarios and then setting out to crack them. While I can't recall the exact number of attempts, I managed to conquer two riddles. The first involved devising an equation that swiftly calculates the sum of a series of structured, ascending numbers. Interestingly, this formula was in my math textbook by 12th grade. I later discovered that Carl Gauss, the renowned German mathematician, tackled this problem during his youth. However, his solution relied on just one variable, limiting its utility. My solution, on the other hand, utilized three variables, ultimately proving more versatile. Maybe that one ought to be in the schoolbooks.

The second issue stemmed from a need for a deeper grasp of multiplication concepts. One day, I pondered a question: "If I knew the result of raising x to the nth power, how could I find the results of (x+1) and (x-1) to the same power without having to do the long math?" Surprisingly, a systematic approach emerged, leading to a formula. This problem was solved before my time, so academic credit goes to a mathematician whose name eludes me. In a book on seminal mathematical breakthroughs, I stumbled upon his work during my first year at university. On one of the pages lay the framework I had independently conceived. Moreover, this understanding of multiplication's intricacies proved invaluable in aiding software engineers in optimizing code for specific mathematical tasks in binary and assembler languages. This contribution warranted its place in the annals of mathematical history. Reflecting on Mr. Lacy's influence on my journey, I realize it's another testament to what young minds can achieve with encouragement.

Do truly original thoughts exist? In his renowned "shoulders of giants" quote, Isaac Newton suggests they may not. My chance to discover long-published formulas that I reproduced in a vacuum seemed to epitomize the closest I've come to originality. It's as if the universe conspires to reward noble or creative endeavors. In essence, stumbling upon those formulas in those two books was destined to happen.

From my junior high school days, I recognize the above events as pivotal, representing my initial moments of resonating validation. These accomplishments, buoyed by the support and encouragement of two influential teachers, played a crucial role in bolstering my confidence and shaping the course of my unique university journey.

Transitioning from junior high to high school marked a significant shift. Despite my earlier successes, high school felt like a pause in the story. After bidding farewell to competitive running post-junior high, a decision I now consider the worst mistake of my life, I ventured into other pursuits. In my senior year, I was a point guard on the basketball team (briefly, until I played myself out of the starting role before the season even began) and played the number two board in the provincial chess championships. While I dabbled in various sports, my talent was never sufficient to go beyond high school and compete, except in distance running. Yet, I quit—the only absolute failure there is in life. The weight of expectation I placed upon myself to excel became overwhelming, and the thought of persisting on that path became agonizing. I acknowledge full accountability for that choice made in my adolescence, though I can't help but speculate on alternate outcomes had my family offered more encouragement. Ironically, the sole race my father witnessed was when I clinched the provincial title.

During my high school years, various memories stand out, providing glimpses into my character and mindset.

At 17, I was at a party hosted by my neighbor, Peter, while his parents were away. Despite the prevalent smoking, drinking, and marijuana, which I didn't condone, I faced a moment of peer pressure when an intoxicated lad insisted I join in. Understanding who I was, Peter intervened, saying to the other kid, "Man, that's Greg. If he doesn't want to drink, he won't drink. Leave him alone." This resolve against peer pressure often left me spending Saturday nights alone while my peers reveled in socializing. My friends eventually stopped inviting me out (the legal drinking age was only 19 in Nova Scotia) because they knew what my answer would be.

Another instance etched in memory comes from a high school rugby game. Despite my diminutive stature compared to my peers, I confronted a physically formidable opponent, Martin Greenough, charging forward with the ball. While one of my teammates meekly stepped aside for fear of being hurt, I launched myself at him to impede his progress. Though likely sustaining a mild concussion, I emerged knowing I had given my all. I refused to back down—a trait that persisted (stubbornly) into adulthood.

I gleaned valuable insights from the remarkable athletes and coaches whose stories I immersed myself in. They emphasized a fundamental principle: to distinguish oneself, one must undertake endeavors that others cannot or will not pursue. While my high school years didn't yield many standout moments, one unusual experience is worth noting. I learned to play chess from my best friend, whose father was a chess player. Although I never benefited from the instruction given by chess masters, I had an immediate affinity for the game because of its profound challenge. One of the ultimate tests in the game is to compete blindfolded. I played my friend twice when blindfolded and achieved virtually identical results. I could play even up for almost 50 combined moves before he gained an advantage. When that occurred, I resigned, knowing the game was fundamentally over. Despite being unable to win, I learned about my abilities and limitations. This has always been a theme in my life.

As it seems fitting, I've saved discussing my social development during my youth for last. Typically, we begin to explore socially during our teenage years as our desires become more apparent. However, this exploration didn't happen during my youth due to social insecurities and fear. One distressing example of this is my experience with prom night. Lacking confidence, it took me a couple of days to gather the courage to ask a girl to the event after learning she wanted to go with me. Unfortunately, as you may have anticipated, I was turned down. This unexpected rejection was devastating. So not only did I miss out on my high school graduation ceremony, as mentioned earlier, but I also missed out on the prom.

Jumping ahead for a moment, as it's related, when I was 24 and still living in Toronto, I decided my life had to change lest I wind up unmarried and childless, the latter being the fate of my siblings. Our emotionally detached upbringing had far-reaching consequences. After moving back to Halifax, I recall the day when a work colleague asked if I wanted two tickets to see Macbeth that night. Sure. But I had no date. So, I went into the streets and walked into a women's clothing store. I approached the first pretty woman I saw and told her the story. She declined but said that one of her colleagues might be interested. She was a beautiful college gal, and I had a date that night. Generally, I jump in head first to solve problems. For dating, it just took a while to wake up. I think it was Reverend Ike who talked about the power of a made-up mind.

While social awkwardness plagued my youth, my voracious reading instilled a profound sense of purpose and determination. I embraced servant leadership principles while harboring unwavering confidence in my capabilities to excel. The next chapter of my life would put that confidence to the ultimate test.

University—"A young man in a hurry."

In my formative years, my parents' lack of encouragement regarding my abilities or achievements was a challenge I had to overcome. To compensate, I turned to competition, craving feedback and validation. Long-distance running became my outlet, offering me a sense of accomplishment. However, upon leaving the sport, I faced a void in my life during university. Unlike in grade school, I knew my performance in university would significantly impact my future. Therefore, I was determined to graduate with a distinguished record of accomplishments that would capture attention, ensuring that my resume would be on top.

In the weeks and months before my high school graduation, my focus had already shifted towards envisioning my university journey. Thanks to previous experience, I was filled with confidence in my ability to navigate this new chapter. Equally vital was my meticulously crafted plan. The day after bidding farewell to high school in late June, I embarked on a 60-mile journey to Acadia University in Nova Scotia. It was the institution of my choice, and I was eager to introduce myself.

That day marked a pivotal moment for me as I engaged in a productive conversation with Richard Hunt, the American head basketball coach at the school. I sought and successfully secured an offer to become the team manager for the upcoming season. Upon my arrival at Acadia in September to pursue computer science studies, I embarked on a proactive endeavor. I contacted approximately 60 prominent universities in the United States, soliciting copies of their latest football and basketball brochures. To my delight, the majority of these schools responded. However, in Canada, university sports lack the prominence enjoyed by their American counterparts, and Acadia never produced an athletic team brochure. I was determined to create the first-ever brochure in the school's history, driven by a passion for sports and the potential for significant financial gain.

Despite my initial pursuit of computer science, my interest in the field waned within the first month of classes. Following my first year, my father arranged a remarkable summer job for me in the computer department of a telephone company. I dedicated myself to the work for three weeks, diligently saving every penny. However, my father was furious when I informed him of my decision to quit. He admonished me, expressing his disappointment, and declared, "If this is the kind of decision you're going to make with your life, I'm through. I will not pay for any more of your education. You are on your own." I didn't need another penny from him for my education. Instead, I turned to entrepreneurship, selling advertising space for the sports brochure I conceived that was published in the fall. This venture marked one of the most significant achievements of my life, attracting considerable attention, including recognition from notable figures like the university president, Dr. J.M.R. Beveridge, who knew me personally. Through this experience, I emerged as one of the campus's student leaders, something on which I would later capitalize.

During my time at university, my primary dedication lay with my business endeavors, which I deemed more significant than any diploma. In today's credential-focused climate, such a perspective might seem anachronistic. To me, practical skills trump theoretical knowledge; it's about "what can you do" rather than "what have you studied." While I appreciated intellectual pursuits, my academic interests gradually shifted towards disciplines like history, economics, philosophy, sociology, and psychology, which captivated me more than my high school interests in mathematics and physics. This shift was not arbitrary. It was a result of my experiences and self-reflection. I realized my passion lay in these disciplines, and pursuing them would be more fulfilling and beneficial for my personal growth. Regrettably, my performance in these subjects didn't match my enthusiasm, leading to uninspired grades. In my third year, I attempted to immerse myself in math courses, only to realize within a week that it was a misguided decision—the passion was absent. Given my business achievement, I struggled to envision a future in a technical field.

After dropping out of school about two weeks into my third year to ponder my future, I decided to leave my home province, a pivotal decision. Transitioning to the University of Western Ontario in London, Ontario, I dedicated myself to earning a Bachelor's degree in Economics, which I successfully achieved in 1980. I actively contributed to creating three annual Acadia sports brochures during my academic journey. Upon my arrival at UWO, I orchestrated the production and dissemination of the final brochure by enlisting local students from Acadia to manage logistics in my stead.

During those years, amidst various comments about me, one stood out: a written remark from Gilbert Chapman, the American athletic director at Acadia University. He wrote, "Greg is a young man in a hurry." This comment left me wondering about its implications. On the one hand, it suggested a young man who could make things happen. On the other hand, it hinted at a young man who would eventually encounter a challenge that would compel him to learn some hard lessons. The latter came to pass, although it was still a few years away.

One memory stands out as remarkably prescient when reflecting on my university days.

On September 6, 1975, just as my university journey began, I watched Season 6, Episode 1 of the television show *All in the Family*. In that episode, Gloria shares her pregnancy news with her husband, Michael, anticipating his reaction. His response, predictably, is one of anger, questioning the wisdom of bringing a child into a troubled world. The episode concluded with a poignant thought from Alistair Cooke, urging us not to let crises overshadow life's simple joys. It read:

> *In the best of times, our days are numbered anyway. So, it would be a crime against nature for any generation to take the world crisis so solemnly that it puts off enjoying those things for which we were designed in the first place: the opportunity to do good work, to enjoy friends, to fall in love, to hit a ball, and to bounce a baby.*

While most viewers grasped the sagacity of Norman Lear and Alistair Cooke, I found myself contemplating another perspective. Motivated by Michael's concerns about overpopulation and other societal troubles, I wondered, "Why bring a child into the world when there are already so many without families?" That day marked the first time the idea of adoption crossed my mind.

Adult in Canada—"The IQ test results came back. Greg, you are NOT bright!"

During my final semester at the University of Western Ontario, I seized the opportunity to interview for two positions facilitated by the recruitment office. The initial interview was with a leading global bank, followed by a meeting with a multinational insurance corporation. Boring! During a stroll home with my classmate, David Lloyd, I confided in him about uncertainty regarding my career path within the business community. Given my reluctance towards traditional corporate trajectories, David, a native of Toronto and familiar with its financial landscape, proposed, "Greg, I think you would be great at investment banking. You should look into it." Inspired by his suggestion, I embarked on exploring this avenue.

After delving into the industry, I uncovered three pivotal insights:

- Its intellectual challenges were profoundly enticing.
- The potential remuneration, even for new bankers, could be remarkably substantial.
- Rather than conforming to a traditional corporate structure, it thrived as a dynamic meritocracy.

Sink or swim—was there a better-suited environment for me? However, the real challenge lay in execution. For:

- I was not going to graduate with a business degree.
- Investment banks did not actively recruit social science graduates. They were recruiting at UWO's elite Ivey School of Business.
- I lacked influential connections.

The odds seemed daunting. Yet my research identified nine prominent firms with a global presence. I enthusiastically pursued each, reaching out to domestic and foreign offices. Accompanying my inquiries was the Acadia University sports brochure showcasing my picture alongside images of the university president and athletic director on the opening page. Remarkably, five of the firms responded, leading to interviews. Of those five, Richardson Securities, Pitfield Mackay Ross, and Midland Doherty extended follow-ups. Conversely, McLeod Young Wier and Wood Gundy declined. During the Wood Gundy interview, the managing director bluntly asked, "Do you want to know why I called you in for an interview? My head office forced me to meet with you." Although disheartened by the attitude, it validated that my resume made its way to the top of the pile on someone's desk at Wood Gundy.

Arnold Shykofsky entered my life for merely 90 minutes, spread over three meetings. Despite the brevity, his impact remains indelible. Initially trained as an architect, Arnold completed one of North America's most rigorous programs at McGill University in Montreal. However, he made a midlife pivot into investment banking, ascending to the role of Vice President at Richardson Securities. At Richardsons, I first encountered Arnold amidst a nationwide recruitment process involving rigorous evaluations, including Myers–Briggs and IQ testing, a standard industry practice.

When I received the call to visit Arnold's office, anticipation enveloped me; I believed I was on the brink of securing my inaugural job offer. Yet, our interaction took an unexpected turn. Arnold's opening statement cut straight to the point: "The IQ test results came back. Greg, you are NOT bright!" What!? His blunt assessment stunned me. However, Arnold quickly clarified by juxtaposing my results with those of other candidates from around the country who had undergone the same testing. Arnold, apparently, had a whimsical way of communicating. After elucidating, he finished with, "... and that's why I am offering you a job today." After getting their test results back, the other two firms followed suit and promptly extended offers. The vision I had for my university career had come to fruition.

In our society, the emphasis often falls on drawing attention to ourselves. However, my perspective shifted after delving into biographies. During that pivotal encounter with Arnold, I received feedback on my abilities that differed vastly from what I had heard from my parents. Even now, forty-five years later, I vividly recall that moment and the precise words he spoke. This lasting impact stems from the fundamental human need for validation. My unnoteworthy academic record in university left me uncertain about specific capabilities. After that explicit conversation with Arnold, I have never doubted myself again.

In 2021, amidst the COVID-19 lockdown, I embarked on a quest to reconnect with Arnold, only to learn of his passing in 2018. Undeterred, I reached out to his son, Jonathan, residing in Toronto, and a delightful 40-minute conversation ensued. Despite my limited interaction with his father, I felt compelled to express Arnold's profound influence on my life. Ultimately, in 1980, I accepted the job offer from Midland Doherty.

My professional journey began in September after I passed the Canadian Securities Exam. Throughout a comprehensive six-month training program, I gained exposure to various facets of the investment industry, including commodity futures markets. Post-training, I ventured into bond arbitrage on the trading desk in Toronto. In the summer of 1981, I received an offer from Pitfield Mackay Ross, prompting my return to Nova Scotia. Reflecting on that decision, I'm still uncertain of its impetus, though I suspect a sense of social isolation in Toronto played a role. I resolved to change that aspect of my life upon my arrival in Halifax. Settling into an apartment and delving into the dating scene marked a significant turning point in my life, as I finally embraced newfound social confidence at 24.

However, fate often has its own plans. I had moved away from Nova Scotia for a reason; I craved the opportunity to forge my path and sought the excitement of doing so in a bustling metropolis. While Nova Scotia holds undeniable charm, I knew it wasn't the perfect match for me. Craving something different, I delved into research in the spring of 1982 (long before the advent of the internet) about The Chicago Board of Trade (CBOT), the hub for commodity futures trading. With dreams of philanthropy fueling my ambition, I, as a "young man in a hurry," saw trading futures in Chicago as the fastest track to realizing my vision. Success in this pursuit, I believed, would empower me to pursue my true life's passion. Looking back, I can't help but see the naivety in my ambition, but that ambition, as is often the case, led me to take the leap.

That summer, I made a pivotal decision and entered John Edgecombe's office to tender my resignation. He offered his best wishes, and I boarded an airplane bound for Chicago with unwavering aspirations of becoming a floor trader. The night before the flight, I was filled with dissonance and other powerful emotions, tears streaming down my face as I spoke with my parents. I could not comprehend the forces compelling me to continuously isolate myself. Oh, I understood intellectually—ambition. However, left-brained comprehension fails to satisfy the right brain's need for harmony. Nonetheless, there was no turning back, and the bridges were burned. This was the path to my destiny, and I was committed to it, no matter the challenges.

After arriving in Chicago and seeking directions from a woman named Shauntel, who would eventually become my wife, I descended to the basement floor of the CBOT, where the administrative office resided. The room was spacious and occupied by only one other individual besides the staff. Approaching the window, I inquired about membership in the exchange, and the clerk promptly handed me all the necessary forms. Just as I was about to leave, a distinguished gentleman behind me interjected, "Excuse me, I couldn't help but overhear your conversation. Please, take my business card. Reach out when you return from Canada." Despite my thorough research before resigning, I'd overlooked a critical detail; securing a sponsor who had known me for at least two years was essential to obtaining a seat on the exchange. However, there was one exception to this rule; if an officer of a trading firm acted as your sponsor. Oops! Fate intervened when the gentleman who had handed me his card was none other than Henry (Hank) Shatkin, the president of Shatkin Trading, the world's largest commodity trade clearing firm. He would later become my sponsor for membership.

Upon returning to Nova Scotia, I embarked on the quest to secure financial support from potential business partners for my exchange seat. This endeavor spanned several months. Upon my return to Chicago, I reached out to Shauntel, my sole acquaintance besides Hank Shatkin in the city. I mentioned earlier how "a young man in a hurry" inevitably will meet a challenge that will extract a price when he is forced to learn a life lesson. I was about to learn mine—a lesson that placed my most cherished dream, to impact the lives of others, in a 37-year-long limbo. Only through grace did that dream never perish.

Adult in the USA—"But what separated Greg from everyone else was..."

A year into my trading journey, I found myself at rock bottom, having lost everything. During this tumultuous time, Shauntel and I decided to take our relationship to the next level, tying the knot in August 1984. Inspired by a passage from a hockey biography, I confronted my moral obligations head-on rather than running away from them. So, filled with a deep sense of responsibility, I embarked on a journey to Nova Scotia to meet my five investors face-to-face, offering sincere apologies for my failure. In a surprising turn of events, each investor encouraged me to stay strong and seek new opportunities. Upon returning to Chicago, I wasted no time securing a job to help support us financially. However, life had more challenges in store. Shauntel's business faced difficulties, and we found ourselves drowning in six-figure debts. At 27, transitioning from being a successful arbitrageur at a global investment bank in Toronto to working for the minimum wage in a Chicago store was a harsh reality check. I entered the first phase of my American journey, facing life's formidable tests head-on.

Over the next four and a half years, I faced numerous challenges. I dedicated myself to supporting Shauntel in her business ventures and we bought our first computer from Radio Shack. Driven by my passion for technology, I immersed myself in learning DOS and exploring various software platforms. I held multiple dead-end jobs but used my growing computer skills to land more lucrative freelance assignments. Despite the slow process of rebuilding my life, my ultimate goals still seemed far away. But I was determined to keep pushing forward.

During a freelance project at Jacobs Engineering, I met Mike Tamburo, who would later become my business partner. On March 9, 1989, we launched a software company catering to a diverse clientele. Initially, it was a part-time venture, but more lucrative opportunities arose as we honed our software engineering skills. By 1996, we transitioned to full-time operation, and one of our clients, Abbott Laboratories, engaged me for on-site work. One of those projects turned into a long-term commitment. This paved the way for an exciting full-time role offered in September 1997. Mike bought my stake in the company we founded, marking an unexpected transition into a corporate career in the pharmaceutical industry at 40.

On my 39th birthday, May 1, 1996, I found myself at a pivotal moment despite my consulting gig at Abbott. This particular day marked the nadir of my existence. Living in downtown Chicago and commuting daily by train to Abbott's North Chicago campus,

I experienced a moment of clarity amidst the bustling routine. As I stepped off the train and approached the shuttle bus, the azure sky above served as a backdrop for reflection. I acknowledged the complexities of my life with a mix of gratitude for what I had and solemnity in recognizing the suffocating weight of debt on aspirations and morale. At that very moment, 8:30 am, I made a solemn vow never to descend to such depths again. That day, I engaged in a profound dialogue with a higher power.

Two of my lifelong dreams were to experience fatherhood and share the world's wonders with my children. However, on that particular day, I faced the cruel reality that neither of these dreams would come true. Both Shauntel and I agreed that bringing a child into our lives wouldn't be responsible, given her financial struggles. At 39, becoming a parent felt like an impossible feat. As I gazed up, I silently prayed for understanding from the universe, wondering why this cherished dream seemed out of reach. With a heavy heart, I whispered, "I give her up to You." Somehow, I had always imagined myself as the father of a little girl.

For nearly 18 months, I upheld a daily practice of gratitude by saying "Thank You," witnessing gradual improvements in our lives, though Shauntel's business continued to struggle. While we relied on a single income, it was sufficient. Then, in March 2000, Shauntel introduced me to adopting from China, assuring me that age was no barrier and that local support was available. Intrigued, I eagerly listened.

On February 25, 2002, fate smiled upon me, and I welcomed a baby girl from Guangzhou, China, into my life. Amongst 12 other hopeful parents, I experienced a whirlwind of emotions. One woman whimpered as she received her child. When it was our turn, as the eighth and final family, I couldn't help but steal a glance through the open door. In her nanny's arms was Tang Si Wen, my daughter. Overwhelmed by the experience, tears streamed down my face uncontrollably.

Each person in that room had walked a unique path filled with challenges. For me, it meant spiritually releasing my daughter before I could physically hold her. The intensity of that moment stayed with me for years, making it nearly a decade before I could speak of it without tears. Just two months shy of my 45th birthday, I embarked on the next phase of my life as a father.

During the adoption process, I received a generous eight-week leave from work. After returning home, we embarked on a journey to Nova Scotia to visit my parents. Despite the entire adoption process lasting 22 months, because of what was at stake and echoing the "pearls before swine" sentiment in Matthew 7:6, I had only confided in two individuals about my plans before our departure to China. One was my boss, who needed to provide a character reference for me, and the other was my eldest sister, who shared the same responsibility. My parents remained unaware until the moment we surprised them at their doorstep.

The adoption of my only child is the most extraordinary story of my life. In it, I intimately learned the meaning of two words. The first is grace. In becoming a father as I did, I experienced a transcendent grace that only the Infinite One can bestow. In traversing the depths of despair following my 39th birthday, and emerging such that I can hug my 23-year-old daughter and tell her how much I love her, I know gratitude.

I shared with Shauntel that beyond reconnecting with family and close friends, there was another person I felt compelled to see: Charles Weatherby, the most influential teacher in my life. Fortunately, he resided just a five-minute walk from my parents' house. Upon visiting, Charles greeted me warmly, and I was equally thrilled to meet him and his wife. As we reminisced, Charles turned to my wife and said, "Let me tell you about Greg." It was a momentous occasion, as I finally had the opportunity to understand how this pivotal figure viewed me. He opened with, "Among the countless student-athletes I've taught over the years, Greg ranked among the top five." Considering he had likely taught between 4,000 and 5,000 boys, this placed me in the elite percentile. He continued, "But what set Greg apart from everyone else was his attitude." It was profound to realize that this educator, who knew me better than any other and consistently emphasized the significance of attitude, regarded me as the benchmark for others. This remains the most memorable compliment I've ever received.

My career flourished. In 2008, when Hospira, the Abbott spin-off where I was employed, announced significant layoffs due to outsourcing jobs to India, I was among the fortunate few to secure a position in another department. Remaining in R&D until my retirement in 2021 from Pfizer, which acquired Hospira in 2015, I navigated the shifting tides of the pharmaceutical industry.

During a casual meeting with a former boss over a beer post-retirement, an intriguing anecdote surfaced about my journey within the company. Apparently, during my candidacy for a promotion, the management team had engaging discussions about my unconventional background. Despite lacking formal scientific education, I managed to carve out a niche in the competitive field of Big Pharma. While traditional corporate structures often prioritize paper qualifications, my unwavering attitude and approach were attributed to my success. In conveying this message about attitude, Dave was echoing Charles Weatherby.

Reflecting on broader contexts, such as the 2024 Congressional hearings on campus antisemitism, where highly credentialed university presidents were publicly discredited, it becomes evident that qualifications on paper don't always guarantee credibility or success. If I have succeeded in anything, it was because of my attitude. If I have overcome setbacks, it was that attitude that sustained me.

In 2008, Shauntel and I parted ways, but we chose to handle our divorce with grace. We shared a belief that harboring bitterness poisons one's own life. Our daughter, Jennifer, benefited from our cooperative approach, splitting her time equally between us, though she spent more time with me in her younger years. As Jennifer grew, so did the balance of her time with her mother. Shauntel also generously allowed me 17 days annually to travel abroad with Jennifer, resulting in her exploring 22 countries by age 17.

My long-awaited dream of fatherhood had finally materialized, and with it, the prospect of sharing the world's wonders with my child. However, another aspiration remained unfulfilled, deferred at 27 when I detonated myself, resulting from an ambition to effect changes beyond my immediate reach. Would it ever be within my grasp?

Retirement and Reflection—"The dream endured."

In Dan McAdams's interview questionnaire, one query stands out:

> Looking back over your entire life story with all its chapters, scenes, and challenges and extending back into the past and ahead into the future, do you discern a central theme, message, or idea that runs throughout the story? What is the major theme in your life story?

While I titled this chapter of my life "Retirement and Reflection," the retirement part is only partially correct. True, I no longer pay the bills by actively working Monday through Friday, but on the day I retired from Pfizer, the dream I lost at age 27 was reborn. That ambitious vision was about my relationship with the world. When I reflect, as McAdams urges us to, I see life's gamut. Achievements, setbacks, one enormous failure (remember, the only failure is in quitting on yourself), joy, disappointment, love, loss, and hope that Bill Randall was right when he wrote in the Foreword, "...Leeson has set off a ripple effect of positivity the impact of which he will never fully know," are all manifested.

But there are questions, too. Like everyone, I suspect, I wonder about what might have been. How would my life have evolved had I been born into a warm and encouraging family? Would I have been less inclined to push myself to accomplish things that seemingly led to isolating activities? Would I not have descended into "...living his own world," as Mrs. Dolan implied? Would life have been easier in some way?

But then there are these musings. Had my mother not left me alone that day at age six when I was crying for her, I may never have developed the extreme independence of thought that led me to a world of possibilities. Had that imprint not happened, I likely would have been more concerned about pleasing others and what their thoughts about me were rather than carving out my destiny regardless of how people like my father perceived me when he said, in a stark lack of faith in my abilities, that I would be "...on your own." I reflect on the numerous biographies I read as a child that taught me how to think. I reflect on the two great teachers I had who believed in me and what I accomplished for them with the encouragement they provided. I reflect on my best friend's words when I was 27: "...nothing you do in your life will ever surprise me." As David Brooks might say, very few people see you to that extent.

So, I have concluded that one's destiny is what it will be. The what-ifs were never meant to happen. We don't live in the movie *Back to the Future*. My ultimate philosophical epiphany that we are all servants has shaped my life narrative and inspired me to share my story with you today. Perhaps, like in the 66 mini-stories, there is something relatable for you.

Had I succeeded in trading on the commodity market floor, my goal would have been to establish a foundation that positively impacted the lives of others. While that never came to fruition, its essence remained alive inside me. To realize that ambition, I embarked on four transformative journeys after retiring from Pfizer on October 4, 2021. These journeys, starting on May 1, 2022, and lasting over 13 months, were not about me but about connecting with individuals eager to share their life stories. By writing a book and delivering speeches, I aim to counterbalance the prevailing winds of cancel culture and vitriol that dominate today's landscape. I strive to embody the creed that *lives impact lives* and help people comprehend the profound interconnectedness we all share.

At my 2015 high school reunion, where I had the honor of serving as the Master of Ceremonies, I shared a story that encapsulates the power of personal narratives. It was the story of a gentleman who entered my professional life in 1997 and, unbeknownst to him, played a pivotal role in my journey to becoming an adoptive father. Many years later, I enlisted the help of a mutual friend to locate him, arranged a lunch meeting, and introduced him to my daughter, whom he had never met. This story is a powerful reminder of the influence our narratives can have on others. I encouraged my classmates attending that reunion, and now you, to do likewise. Not by text message. Not by email. Not by phone call. Not by video call. Do it, if possible, in person with those who have impacted your life.

As of this book's publication in 2024, I am still uncertain about the reach of my vision. Will the media listen to my story? Will I secure more speaking engagements? Will my book find its audience? These questions linger, but they do not deter me. I am committed to fully immersing myself in this dream despite doubts I had about my writing abilities when I started this project. This journey has taught me that anything can happen when the two rules for living I had framed and presented to my daughter in 2022 as a Christmas present are followed.

1. *For anything you do, have no fear.*
2. *For anything you do, there is no substitute for preparation.*

APPENDIX C

JOURNEY MAPS

"All he needed was a wheel in his hand and four on the road."

Jack Kerouac
(Author's note: Amen, Jack!)

THE EASTERN JOURNEY – 6,521 MILES

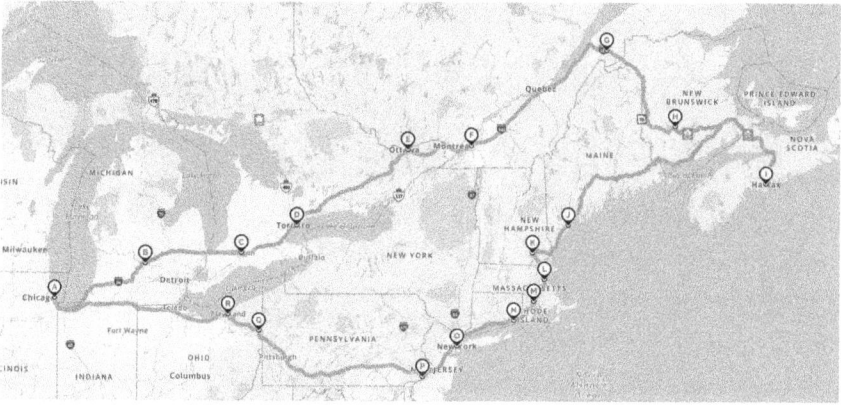

Map from MapQuest.com

A - Chicago, IL	K - Manchester, NH
B - Lansing, MI	L - Boston, MA
C - London, ON	M - Providence, RI
D Toronto, ON	N – New London, CT
E - Ottawa, ON	O - New York, NY
F - Montreal, PQ	P - Philadelphia, PA
G - Saint Louis-du-Ha! Ha!, PQ	Bridgewater, NS
H - Fredericton, NB	Q - Youngstown, OH
I - Halifax, NS	R - Cleveland, OH
J - Portland, ME	A - Home

Not shown on the map is tiny Bridgewater, NS, which I visited after flying to Halifax from Philadelphia. On that trip, I aimed to take part in a golf tournament with former high school buddies and give a speech. Saint Louis-du-Ha! Ha! (yes, that's the correct spelling) and Youngstown were one-night stops.

THE WESTERN JOURNEY – 8,274 MILES

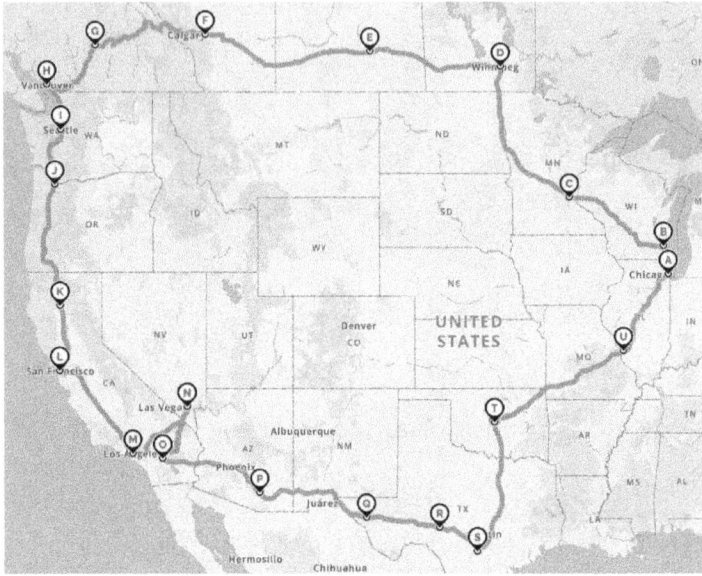

Map from MapQuest.com

A - Home	L - San Francisco, CA
B - Milwaukee, WI	M - Los Angeles, CA
C - Minneapolis, MN	N - Las Vegas, NV
D - Winnipeg, MB	O - Palm Springs, CA
E - Regina, SK	P - Tucson, AZ
F - Calgary, AB	Q - Van Horn, TX
G - Kamloops, BC	R - Sonora, TX
H - Vancouver, BC	S - San Antonio, TX
I - Seattle, WA	T - Oklahoma City, OK
J - Portland, OR	U - Saint Louis, MO
K - Redding, CA	A - Home

Kamloops, Redding, Van Horn, and Sonora were one-night stops.

THE SOUTHERN JOURNEY – 5,178 MILES

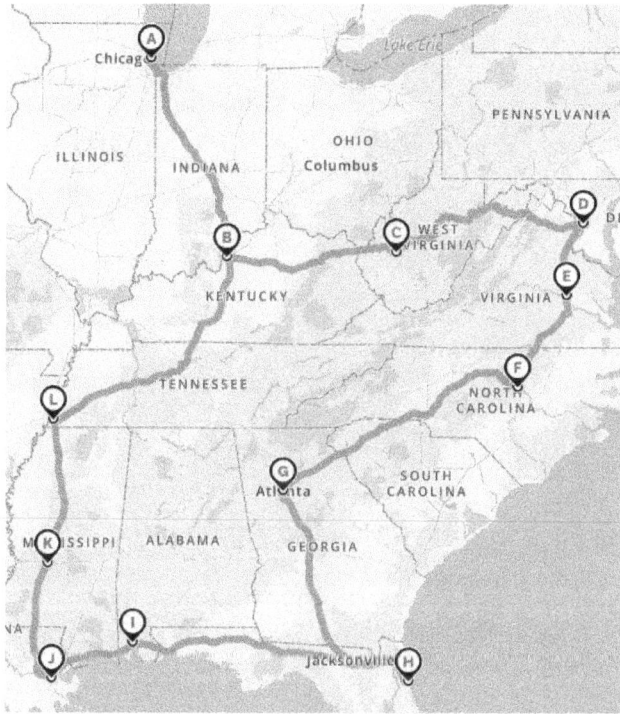

Map from MapQuest.com

A - Home	H - Saint Augustine, FL
B - Louisville, KY	I - Mobile, AL
C - Charleston, WV	J - New Orleans, LA
D - Washington, DC	K - Jackson, MS
E - Richmond, VA	L - Memphis, TN
F - Raleigh, NC	B - Louisville, KY
G - Atlanta, GA	A - Home

My second Louisville visit was for two nights to have dinner with an interviewee I met earlier.

THE GREAT PLAINS JOURNEY – 6,430 MILES

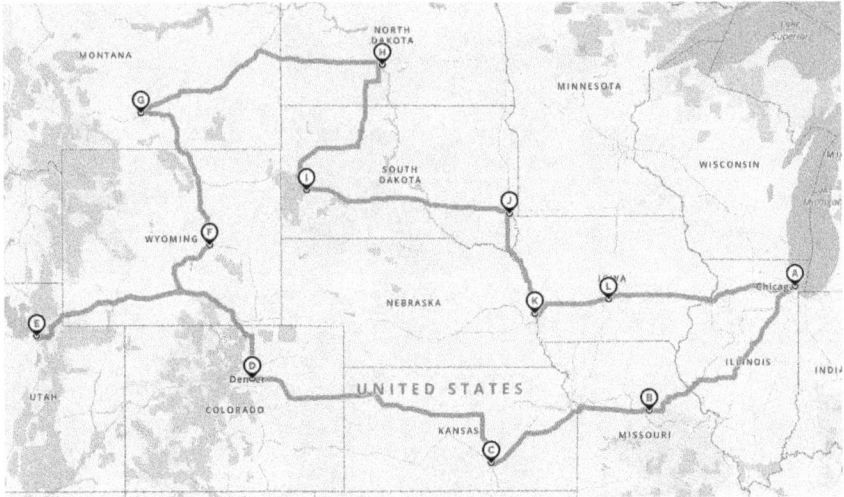

Map from MapQuest.com

A - Home	H - Bismarck, ND
B - Columbia, MO	I - Rapid City, SD
C - Wichita, KS	J - Sioux Falls, SD
D - Denver, CO	K - Omaha, NE
E - Salt Lake City, UT	L - Des Moines, IA
F - Casper, WY	A - Home
G - Billings, MT	

Columbia was a one-night stop to stay in a tiny Airbnb tree house. Rapid City was a one-night stop to see Mount Rushmore.

REFERENCES

"If I have seen further, it is by standing on the shoulders of giants."

Isaac Newton

Brooks, D. (2023). *How to Know a Person*. New York: Penguin Random House.

Covey, S. R. (2004 – reprint). *The 7 Habits of Highly Effective People*. New York: Simon & Schuster.

Dalio, R. (2021). *The Changing World Order*. New York: Simon & Schuster.

Feiler, B. (2021). *Life Is in the Transitions*. New York: Penguin Random House.

Friedman, G. (2020). *The Storm Before the Calm*. New York: Penguin Random House.

Half-Moon, W. L. (1982). *Blue Highways*. Boston: Little, Brown and Company.

Howe, N. (2023). *The Fourth Turning Is Here*. New York: Simon & Schuster.

Howe/Strauss. (1997). *The Fourth Turning*. New York: Penguin Random House.

Kerouac, J. (1957). *On the Road*. New York: Viking Press.

Longfellow, H. W. (1847). *Evangeline*. Boston: William D. Ticknor & Company.

McAdams, D. (1996 – reprint). *the stories we live by*. New York: The Guilford Press.

Steinbeck, J. (2017 – reprint). *Travels With Charley in Search of America*. New York: Penguin Random House.

Terkel, S. (1970). *Working*. New York: The New Press.

Turchin, P. (2023). *End Times*. New York: Penguin Random House.

INDEX

Symbols

Lynnette Grey Bull xii, 81

M

Madison Avenue 156
Mafia Don 139
MAGA 26, 30
Maharishi International University 118
Maharishi Mahesh Yogi 118
Mahatma Gandhi xi
Maine 173, 174
Mako Sica 188
Manchester iv, 71, 72, 122, 123, 175, 241
Manchester Historic Association 72
Manhattan 129, 175
Manitoba 96, 139, 177
Marine Le Pen 11
Maritime province 79
Maritimer 66, 80
Marshall University 75, 183
Martin Greenough 223
Martin Luther King 25, 33, 163
Mary Lou Casey viii
Mary Shelley 215
Massachusetts 123, 156, 175
Massachusetts General Hospital 175
Master of Ceremonies 1, 239
Mathew McConaughey 183
Mathscaper 106
Matteo Salvini 11
Matthew 7:6 235
Mayo Clinic 217
McCarthyism 5
McGill University 67, 87, 88, 212, 229
McLeod Young Wier 229
Mecca xiv, 61
Medical Assistance in Dying 142
Melbourne 154
Memphis 177, 186, 243

Merrill Lynch 156
Merritt 165
Métis 177
Me Too 37
Mexican-American War 14
Mexico 33, 80, 180, 185, 208, 218
Miami 19
Michael Bloomberg 140
Michael Corleone 144
Michigan 9, 91, 122, 129
Microsoft Word 2
Middle East 9, 105
Middleton 141
Midland Doherty 229, 230
Mike James 182
Mike Tamburo 233
Mikhail Gorbachev 140
Millennial 5
Milwaukee 162, 177, 242
mini-biographies xiii, 57, 193
Minirth Meier Clinic 70
Minneapolis 9, 168, 177, 242
Mississippi vi, xiii, 23, 58, 117, 162, 164, 184, 186, 195
Mississippi Civil Rights Museum 162, 164, 186
Missouri 182
Mobile 185, 243
Montana 58, 67, 69, 82, 127, 195
Montego Bay 159
Montreal 66, 67, 78, 87, 138, 159, 174, 182, 212, 217, 229, 241
Montreal Canadiens 217
Montreal General Hospital 67
Montreal Olympics 182
Moose Jaw 177, 178
Morehouse College iii, iv, 18, 46, 47, 53
Mormon 69, 187

www.ingramcontent.com/pod-product-compliance
Lightning Source LLC
Chambersburg PA
CBHW030837300326
41935CB00037B/465